TOWARD GREEN ECONOMY:
OPPORTUNITIES AND OBSTACLES
FOR WESTERN BALKAN COUNTRIES

TOWARD GREEN ECONOMY: OPPORTUNITIES AND OBSTACLES FOR WESTERN BALKAN COUNTRIES

M.Radovic-Markovic, Z.Nikitovic
and D. Jovancevic

Rev. date: 05/19/2015

CONTENTS

FOREWORD

Concept of green economy is not a new one, but it was really brought to the focus when the world economic crisis escalated after 2008. The explanation can be found in the fact that many scientists and creators of economic policy saw the way out of the crisis in the development of green economy. Moreover, we can see the emerging consensus among scientists and creators of economic policy in the fact that the green economy should be given the priority with forming the strategy of sustainable economic growth. We find the explanation in the fact that the green economy represents an important support to economic growth, investments and competitiveness. Therefore, it is considered to be an important alternative in attaining the general wellbeing of the humans, which is seen in the decrease of the risk while preserving the environment and using alternative energy sources. Atmospheric gases, especially carbon dioxide, create the greenhouse effect which influences the climate changes. They are already generating the extreme weather conditions, including powerful hurricanes and floods which have recently affected the Western Balkans. Furthermore, switching to lower level of carbon dioxide emission will bring many benefits to our environment and create new opportunities for growth of competitiveness, as well as economic growth. Also, green economy opens new areas of work and generates new jobs. It is extremely significant for the Western Balkan countries, which are experiencing the growth of poverty and high unemployment rate (26.8 % in the second quarter of 2013)[1] in the Region.

Having this in mind, I designed this book with the intention not only to point out to the extent to which the Western Balkan countries have accepted the concept of green growth, but also to see what results

---

[1]   Radovic-Markovic, M. (2014). Youth unemployment in Montenegro, Round table, Faculty of Economy in Podgorica and Association of Economists of Montenegro, 28. May 2014.

are achieved in respect of implementation of this concept with the goal of overcoming the economic and financial crisis and creating the conditions for sustainable growth of this Region. Besides this, my intention was to emphasise the political, economic and legal limitations that are blocking faster development of green economy, as well as the possibilities of their overcoming,

This monograph has a very broad topic range, with the goal of comprising the most important aspects and considerations of these issues. As the end result of theoretical and research considerations of the author, in approximately twenty chapters, one gets a clear insight in how the Region has progressed in respect of making the most important sectors "green".

Mirjana Radovic-Markovic
7th July, 2014.

I. THE GROWTH OF GREEN ECONOMY AS A PREREQUISITE FOR SUSTAINABLE AND BALANCED ECONOMIC DEVELOPMENT

TOWARDS SUSTAINABILITY IN THE "GREEN ECONOMY"-THEORETICAL OVERVIEW[2]

Mirjana Radovic-Markovic[3]

"The world must quickly design strategies that will allow nations to move from their present, often destructive, processes of growth and development to sustainable development paths. (Ecimovic, et.al. 2013)

INTRODUCTION

The paper analyses the concept of "sustainable growth" in the context of "green economy". The concept is a recent one, emerging in literature since 2008. The new concept of economic development has emerged in recent years as necessary in the conditions of the economic crisis, when the prevailing model of economic growth failed to meet the increasing demand for consumption of limited resources and also as a result of a limited capacity of the ecosystem. Since this is a genuinely new approach to economic development, it is not surprising that there is not enough literature in this area yet. Consequently, there is no unique and generally accepted definition of green economy nor of the strategy of sustainable

[2]   This chapter is created as part of the project OI 179015 and 47009 II, funded by the Ministry of Education, Science and Technology of the Republic of Serbia.

[3]   Full University Professor and Academician, Institute of Economic Sciences and Faculty of Business Economics, Belgrade, Serbia, mradovic@gmail.com

growth. This is reflected in the variety of economic policies concerning the green growth pursued by certain countries, ranging from those that deem it a priority goal to those that do not focus upon it at all. In answer to the lack of an integrated approach to these issues, the Green Growth Knowledge Platform (World Bank, 2012) was adopted. It is meant to serve as a starting point for research and understanding to what extent the new concept of sustainable growth within green economy has come into effect. In addition to the assessment of the results achieved, it is also to determine the guidelines for further development of the green growth concept. Shortly upon its adoption, the Platform was promoted at the United Nations Summit, in mid-2012 (UNCSD 2012). Despite the efforts made by the international community to promote a new approach to economic development, the extent to which it will come into effect will depend on the governments of certain countries whose responsibility is to create conditions for sustainable growth on the path to a green economy.Namely, the transition to a green economy will vary considerably from one nation to another, as it depends on the specifics of each country's natural and human capital and on its relative level of development (UNEP, 2011).

The first part of this chapter offers a short overview of the definitions of sustainable growth and green economy. This review of literature is to help understand the new concept of economic growth, but also its importance and what it is expected to be achieved through it. The subject of the following segment will be the review of how sustainability, equity and private sector in the "green economy" have been developed.

EXPLORING THE DEFINITION OF SUSTAINABLE DEVELOPMENT AND GREEN GROWTH

The concept of economic growth which also meets environmental objectives is not new (Jacobs, 2012). However, this concept has attracted attention in scientific circles and opened new possibilities for a way out of the economic crisis after 2008. Namely, on the one hand, the economic crisis and the inefficiency of economies of many countries and, on the other hand, increased environmental risk as well as the growth of social inequality, have made a considerableimpact on the prevailing economic paradigm.

There is no universally agreed definition of "Sustainable Development" and "Green Economy". Besides, it is widely known that "sustainable development is development that meets the needs of the present without compromising the ability of future generations to meet their own needs" (Ecimovic, etal., 2013). Sustainable development emphasizes a holistic, equitable and far-sighted approach to decision-making at all levels (UN, 2011). It is based on the integration of social, economic and environmental objectives (Figure1).

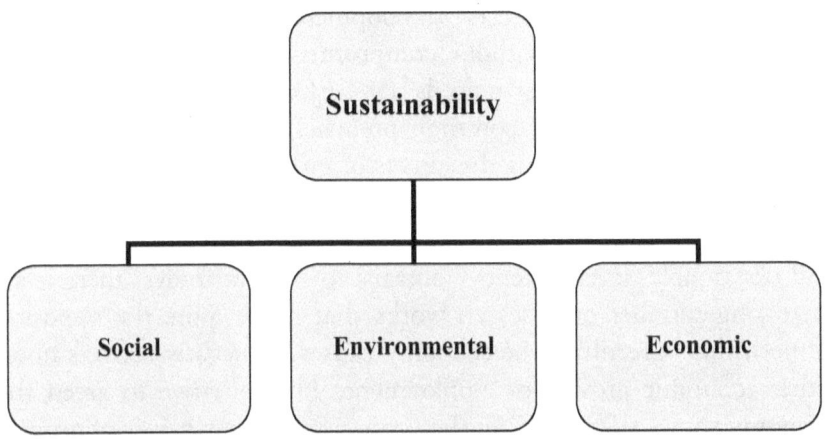

Figure 1. The three pillars of sustainability
Source:Author

The Green Economy can be defined as an economy where economic prosperity goes hand-in-hand with ecological sustainability (Sam Min, 2011). According to a number of experts, the green economy is the clean energy economy, consisting primarily of four sectors: renewable energy, green building and energy efficiency technology, energy-efficient infrastructure and transportation and recycling and waste-to-energy (Gordon and Hays, 2008; Cheerla, 2009; Maharaj et. al., 2012). The United Nations Environment Programme defined green economy as "one that results in improved human well-being and social equity, while significantly reducing environmental risks and ecological scarcities."(UNEP, 2011).

THE TRANSITION TO THE "GREEN ECONOMY" AND SUSTAINABILITY

Different schools of thought on sustainability and green economy have emerged. Among the first studies that dealt with the issues of sustainable development and green economy is one by Pearce (Pearce et. al., 1989). It has been followed by a large number of studies that are predominantly based on the Report of the World Commission on Environment and Development. The Report describes the notion of sustainable development as "development which meets the needs of current generations without compromising the ability of future generations to meet their own needs" (WCED, 1987). Many researchers in this area started from common premises, however, they came to strongly disagree as regards the effects of greening the economy upon economic growth. Accordingly, there are opinions in literature that a compromise has to be reached between environmental protection and sustainable development. Contrary to such attitudes, there is an increasing number od research works that prove quite the opposite, namely, that "greening" the economy causes no negative effects upon either economic growth or employment. The initiative to green the economy shows that greening the economy is a new driver of growth that generates new jobs and contributes to poverty reduction. In accordance with the above, there is a growning number of propositions to create new conditions that would enable a gradual transition to green economy (UNEP, 2011). A number of experts, however, maintain that such conditions can be created only in highly developed countries; this will remain unattainable to the developing countries. In terms of adapting to climate change, economists maintain that richer countries will find it easier to act preventively due to having financial assets at their disposal, which will not be the case with poor countries. The latter will have difficulties in adapting, especially as regards the measures directly related to the latest technologies'."They have not enough money to invest in the environment" (Martinez-Alier, 1995). This statement is supported by the opinion that there are many people in this world who are so poor that thinking about a more ecological and sustainable way of living is a luxury they cannot afford (Gehrke,2012). Contrary to this perception, numerous examples of greening transitions can be found in the developing world (APGF, 2010). In other words, practice has challenged this myth showing that greening the economy is not a luxury but a necessity. "A green economy recognizes that the goal of sustainable development is improving the quality of human life within the constraints of the environment, which include combating global climate change, energy insecurity, and ecological scarcity" (APGF, 2010). Furthermore, it has been shown that it is necessary that economic research should be linked with the research in the fields of ecology and environmental protection in order to anticipate and mitigate the effects of climate change, soil degradation, greenhouse gas emissions and anything that is a threat to the future and survival of the global population. Namely, it is widely known that damages caused by natural disasters are numerous and can be manifested in various ways, inducing consequences for both the population and the states. They can primarily be manifested in the deterioration of soil structure (lower soil productivity) and exposure to new pests and plant and animal diseases. Consequently, we are faced with new challenges to plant and animal genetics and management (Radovic-Markovic and Grozdanic, 2013). Hence the issue of defining the potential short-term and long-term effects of climate change calls for permanent monitoring and analysis of these changes, which is to serve as basis for assessment of both the risk and the intensity of damage caused by natural disasters. Despite the fact that the research on the effects of climate change is already extensive, some aspects have to a great extent been the topic of mainly scientific analysis, while others have been paid less attention to (Radovic-Markovic and Grozdanic, 2013). In the first place, numerous issues and aspects of climate change effects have been analysed in a one-sided manner. Namely, although climate changes are global in terms of their causes and consequences, it is evident that they do not affect everybody in the same way and that they differ among them, a problem analysed in the papers of numerous scientists (Curry, Weaver and Wiebe; Boykoff).

THE SUSTAINABLE DEVELOPMENT AND THE SUSTAINABLE FUTURE OF HUMANKIND

Ecological environment undergoes an accelerated change influenced by the population boom, the growth of megapolises and the change in the behaviour of the global population, which is all reflected in climate change.

In line with this, the world trend of urbanisation increasingly makes this problem more severe. "More than a half of the world population already lives in cities, with a tendency of further growth in the number of the world population of 3.1 billion people by 2050. By 2025, eight cities will have more than 20 million inhabitants, while 22 cities will have more than 10 million inhabitants each" (Loubières, 2010). However, in spite of a rapid global urbanization, the rural population of developing regions continues to grow (APGF, 2010).

Consequently, climate change alters the ecological contents. It is in this context that a need for a different and new approach towards available natural resources and human environment emerges. "The Age of globalization is asking for new – requisitely holistic – human eco centred - approaches and behaviour" (Ecimovic, et.al.,2014). According to Ecimovic, "…a new approach is needed for a redirection of scientific work towards the needed knowledge and values capable of saving the nature, science, and the environment including the climate change system – for mankind to survive" (Ecimovic, et al., 2012). Literature knows only few of such approaches, despite certain recorded attempts. Hence the scientist Ecimovic and a group of international experts were the first to draw attention to and highlight the importance of interrelation between mankind and the natural environment (Figure2).

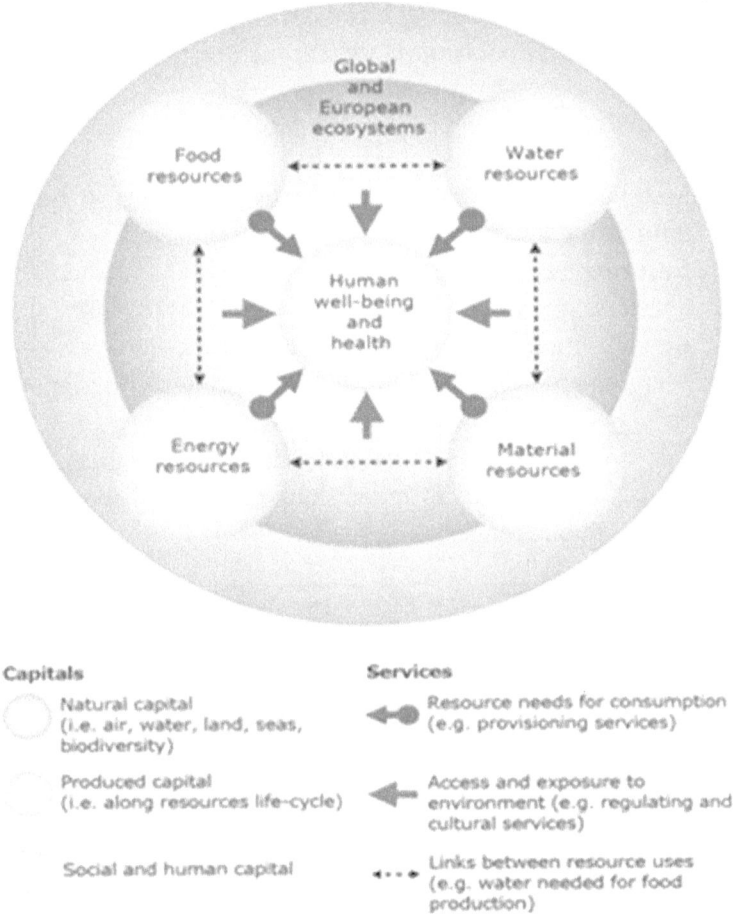

Figure 2. Link between natural and material resources
and their impact upon human well-being and health

Source: http://www.eea.europa.eu/themes/agriculture/greening-
agricultural-policy/copy_of_Figure2GreeningtheCAP.jpg

"The sustainable development and the sustainable future of humankind
as harmonious and complementary coexistence of the global community
of humankind and the nature are among the not-mentioned contents"
(Ecimovic, et.al.,2014). In this context, balancing human demand for
land and food with the need to protect the world's natural resources is
a global challenge.

Critical objectives for environment and development policies that follow from concept of sustainable development include (Ecimovic,2013):

1. Reviving growth;
2. Changing the quality of growth;
3. Meeting the essential needs for jobs, food, energy, water, and sanitation;
4. Ensuring a sustainable level of population;
5. Conserving and enhancing the resource base;
6. Reorienting technology and managing risk; and
7. Merging environment and economics in decision making".

In line with the concept of sustainable development, the green economy policies should be designed to reflect long-term social, economic and environmental public interests (Figure3).

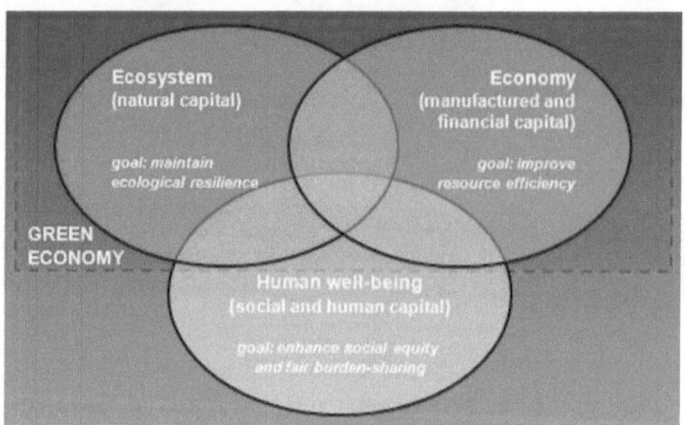

Figure 3. Green economy and human well-being

Source: http://geoengineering2012.files.
wordpress.com/2012/04/diagram.jpg

GREEN GROWTH AND PRIVATE SECTOR

*"Innovation and entrepreneurship will be at the heart of
the passionate progress needed to take the green economy
from dream toward reality" (Barrell, 2010).*

Climate change poses not only a direct threat to individuals and communities, but also threatens the private sector, a key contributor to job creation, economic growth and poverty reduction. The creation of green jobs which can deliver environmental benefits as well as pathways to economic empowerment is of key importance. According to some research, it is expected that over 400 million people will join the workforce within the next decade and green jobs creation is thus seen as an opportunity to address this challenge as countries transition to green economies (UNDP, 2013).

Literature distinguishes between direct and indirect climate risks to the private sector (Coppock and Stephanie, 2004). According to a study conducted by the PWC (2010), the climate change will predominantly make an impact on agriculture, infrastructure and tourism (DCED, 2014).

The value of damages caused by adverse weather conditions rises simultaneously with the global warming process. The total economic expenditures caused by natural disasters have risen 5.3 times in the past years in comparison with the 1960s, while insurance-covered damages have become 9.6 times larger, primarily due to floods and storms, that is, disasters caused by weather extremes (Njegomir and Markovic, 2009). In accordance with these statistical data, climate change is considered to be a major threat in terms of risks and damage, and consequently may be of major importance for the insurance industry in the years to come (Radovic-Markovic and Grozdanic, 2013)."Insurance will become more expensive and access to capital may be reduced. Market demand will also change as customers respond to climate change" (DCED, 2014).

There is a perception that social entrepreneurship is a good solution to the management of climate change. These socially oriented enterprises have attempted to address social problems such as community development and environmental protection, among others. Examples include: crisis, pollution problems, clean drinking water, empowerment of women, human rights; educational opportunities, gender equality (Radovic-Markovic,2010). According to our opinion, the global examples of social entrepreneurship show that it is possible to simultaneously successfully run a business and manage climate change. In this context, it is necessary that social economy enterprises and their role in tackling climate change should be promoted.

TOWARDS EQUITY IN THE "GREEN ECONOMY"

Green economics seeks to include the perspectives of those who are marginalized within the present economic structure — primarily women and the poor of the world—as well as take seriously the needs of the planet itself (Cato, 2009). Namely, since women constitute the majority of the world's poor and are comparatively more dependent on scarce natural resources, it is they in particular who suffer from these effects and the repercussions of climate change (DCED, 2012). In addition, the literature on the topic offers few articles that investigate the effects of climate change viewed from the gender perspective (Radovic-Markovic and Grozdanic,2013). This perspective cannot be ruled out given that women all around the world are largely subject to adverse effects of natural disasters. "Women and the poor in the developing countries are most exposed to climate change. They are especially sensitive to the degradation of the ecosystem and to natural disasters since they are more dependent on agriculture and their socio-economic status is lower in comparison with men" (Radovic-Markovic, 2010). Climate change affects the production of women farmers in transition countries as the women most often work in agriculture and food production and are considerably less engaged in non-agricultural activities. For example, African women farmers produce up to 90% of the continent's food, although women own only about 1% of the land (Radovi -Markovi , 2010a). The agricultural extension services have been one way in which innovative practices are disseminated in rural areas, but there are often problems with sustainability and variability in local adoption (Walker, 1990). Namely, women are less adapted to changes than men due to a lot of obstacles. Successful adaptation depends on factors such as local institutional arrangements, availability of finance resources, information exchange, instruments to collect data and technological change (Radovic-Markovic, 2010). We also point out that women in rural areas lack the knowledge on the environment disasters. In other words, their skills and knowledge do not correspond with the skills needed in the emerging green economy, which constitutes another obstacle. There is also a lack of information and instruments to collect data, lack of financial resources to combat climate changes and women are not engaged enough in developing social strategies on climate change risks. In this context, "...investments are required in human capital, including green-related knowledge, management and technical skills to ensure a smooth transition to a more sustainable pathway" (NGLS, 2009).

CONCLUSION

Exposure to natural disasters will in the near future have important bearing on the public policies in the fields of health, biodiversity, as well as of important economic sectors: water resources, agriculture, forestry, energy supply and tourism. It will also affect the growth of costs incurred by these natural disasters. In this context, in order that the costs of natural disasters and climate change induced ecological, economic, social and geopolitical risks should be reduced, it is necessary that preventive steps should be taken, economists maintain (Radovic-Markovic and Grozdanic, 2013).

Many data suggest that transitioning to a green economy has sound economic and social justification. Greening the economy refers to "the process of reconfiguring businesses and infrastructure to deliver better returns on natural, human and economic capital investments, while at the same time reducing greenhouse gas emissions, extracting and using less natural resources, creating less waste and reducing social disparities"(Maclean, Akoh and Egede-Nissen, 2011). Namely, in a green economy, growth in income and employment is driven by public and private investments that reduce carbon emissions and pollution, enhance energy and resource efficiency, and prevent the loss of biodiversity and ecosystem services (UNEP, 2011). In line with this, the concept of "green economy" does not replace sustainable development. Quite the opposite, these two have to be closely linked. It means that the sustainable development should suppport environmental sustainability, economic growth, and social equity among peoples. However, the time distance from the promotion of this concept is rather short, nevertheless, there is already evidence of obstructions to it by certain interest groups who do not support the vision of this new economy.

In the end, it can be concluded that the literature on green growth and environmental management is of a general character in its nature. In addition, more research is needed on how disasters and climate changes impact the social structure and gender.

REFERENCES

1. APGF (2010). Towards a Green Economy: Pathways to Sustainable Development and Poverty Eradication. Accessed April 12,2014. http://www.asiapacificgreens.org/towards-green-economy-pathways-sustainable-development-and-poverty-eradication

2. Barrell, A.(2010). Entrepreneurship in the Green Economy, Cambridge University. On the Internet : http://www.eauc.org.uk/entrepreneurship in the green economy

3. Boykoff, J. (2011). Why the insurance industry gets climate change?, The Guardian. On the Internet : http://www.guardian.co.uk/commentisfree/cifamerica/2011/jun/28/climate-change-climate-change-scepticism

4. Coppock, R., Stephanie, J.(2004)." References ." Direct and Indirect Human Contributions to Terrestrial Carbon Fluxes: A Workshop Summary. Washington, DC: The National Academies Press, 2004 .

5. Cato, M.S. (2009). Green Economics: an introduction to theory, policy and practice London: Earthscan.

6. Cheerla, A.K.(2009).The New, Green Economy, The George Washington university. Accessed April 21,2014. http://www.managedecisions.com/blog/wp-content/uploads/2009/04/thenewgreeneconomy_cheerla_mbad260.pdf

7. Chichilnisky, G., & Heal, G. M. (1993). Global Environmental Risks. Journal of Economic Perspectives, 7(4), 64-86.

8. Curry, C.,Weaver,A.and Wiebe,E.(2012).Determiningthe "Impact"of"Climate"Change"on"Insurance"Risk" and "theGlobal Community",Solterra Solutions Ltd,Canada .

9. DCED,(2012). Women's participation in green growth – a potential fully realised? On the Internet: http://www.enterprise-development.org/page/greengrowth

10. DeLacy, T., Wong, E., Jiang, M., Dominey-Howes, D., and Harrison, D. (2010), Policy analysis for enhancing the resilience of Pacific Islands tourism sector against impacts of climate change, the third International Conference on Sustainable Tourism, Crete, Greece.

11. Ecimovic,T. etal.,(2014)."C&ISR – The Individual Social Responsibility and Harmony with the Nature".Working paper. www.institut-climatechange.si

12. Ecimovic,T.etal.,(2013)."Philosophy of the Sustainable Development and the Sustainable Future of Humankind – the Survival of Humanity, Zg. Medosi, Korte, Slovenia, April 2013.

13. Ecimovic,T. etal.,(2012). "The Sustainable Future of Humankind – V, the Action Plan", Zg. Medosi, Korte, Slovenia and Penang Malaysia, December 2012.

14. Economy(Apollo Alliance and Green for All, 2008). Accessed April 10,2014 http://www.apolloalliance.org/downloads/greencollarjobs.pdf

15. Gehrke,M. (2012).Africa expert: 'Sustainable living is a luxury'. Accessed April 21,2014. http://www.dw.de/africa-expert-sustainable-living-is-a-luxury/a-16418370

16. Gordon,K. and Hays,J. (2008). Green-Collar Jobs in America's Cities: Building Pathways out of Poverty and Careers in the Clean Energy

17. Harris,M. and Roach,B.(2009). Global Development And Environment Institute, Tufts University.

18. Jacobs,M. (2012). Green Growth: Economic Theory and Political Discourse, Centre for Climate Change Economics and Policy Working Paper No. 108. Accessed April 16,2014. http://www.lse.ac.uk/GranthamInstitute/publications/WorkingPapers/Papers/90-99/WP92-green-growth-economic-theory-political-discourse.pdf

19. Loubières,L.(2010). Insurers and Climate Change: Taking Risk Management to the Next Level, Sustainalytics- A global leader in sustainability analysis.

20. Maclean,D., Akoh,B. and Egede-Nissen,B.(2011). ICTs, sustainability and the green economy, International Institute for Sustainable Development (IISD).www.iisd.org

21. Martlnez-Alier,J. (1995) . The environment as a luxury good or "too poor to be green"?, Ecological Economics, No. 13,1995,pp. 1-10. Accessed April 23,2014. https://is.muni.cz/el/1423/jaro2013/HEN581/um/Martinez-Alier_Ecological_economics.pdf

22. NGLS (2009). Towards a Green Economy: Pathways to Sustainable Development and Poverty Eradication . On the Internet: http://www.un-ngls.org/spip.php?page=article_s&id_article=3615

23. Njegomir,V. and Markovic,D.(2009). Klimatske promene i njihov uticaj na osiguranje i reosiguranje, ŠKOLA BIZNISA.

24. Pearce et al. (1989). Blueprint for a green economy, Earthscan Publications, London.

25. PWC (2010) . The true value of water:Best practices for managing water risks and opportunities. On the Internet:http://www.pwc. com/en GX/gx/sustainability/publications/assets/pwc-the-value-of-water.pdf

26. Radovic-Markovic,M. and Grozdanic,R.(2013).Risks and damages in the conditions of globalization and climate change, in Product specifics on the markets of insurance and reinsurance (ed., Ko ovi , Jovanovic-Gavrilovic, Radovi -Markovi), Belgrade: University of Belgrade, Faculty of Economics, Publishing Centre, Serbia,460 pp.

27. Radovic-Markovic,M.(2010).Female and Social Entrepreneurship in Tackling Climate Change,Said Business School,Oxford,June 2010.

28. Radovic Markovic, M. (2010 a). Rural entrepreneurship and sustainable economic development in Serbia. Agricultural Economy, 57 (No. SB/SI-2: 1-656), 583-589. Institute of Agricultural Economics,Belgrade, Serbia.

29. Sam Min,K.(2011). A Measurement Strategy for Green Economy in Korea, UNESCAP. Accessed April 10,2014.http://www.unescap. org/sites/default/files/session7-Rep-Korea.pdf

30. Walker, S.T. (1990). Innovative agricultural extension for women: A case study in Cameroon, Volume 1. The World Bank, Policy Research Working Paper, WPS 403. Retrieved from http:// wwwwds. worldbank.org/external/default/WDSContentServer/ IW3P/IB/1990/06/01/000009265_3960929095527/Rendered/ PDF/multi_page.pdf

31. World Bank. (2012). Green Growth Knowledge Platform.Accessed April 14,2014. http://www.greengrowthknowledge.org/Pages/ GGKPHome.aspx.

32. UNCSD (United Nations Conference on Sustainable Development) (2012). Accessed April 14,2014. http://www.uncsd2012.org/rio20/

33. UNDP,(2013).Green Jobs for Women and Youth: What Can Local Governments Do? On the Internet: http://www.undp. org/content/undp/en/home/librarypage/poverty-reduction/ participatory_localdevelopment/green-jobs-for-women-and-youth--what-can-local-governaments-do-/

34. UNEP,(2011). Towards a Green Economy:Pathways to Sustainable Development and Poverty Eradication. Nairobi: United Nations Environment Programme.

INTERACTION BETWEEN ENVIRONMENT AND ECONOMIC GROWTH

Marko Malovic[4]

"Growth for the sake of growth is the ideology of a cancer cell"-E. Abbey-

"Why shouldn't the productivity of most natural resources rise more or less steadily through time, like the productivity of labor?"-Robert Solow-

INTRODUCTION

In order to keep up even the present (already crisis stricken) trend of economic growth, by 2050 mankind would have to consume three times the quantity of biomass, mineral and fossil fuels as well as ores *per annum* than it consumes today, with proverbially drastic gap between consumption of developed vs. developing, resource-abundant vs. resource-constrained economies, along with global consequences for the environment and bio-economic constellation in which we are to leave our posterity. In contrast, relevant UN institutions have been warning for years that under current demographic developments (10 billion people by 2050) and rising economic welfare in key parts of the emerging world additional progression in annual and *per capita* consumption of non-renewable or slowly and hardly renewable natural resources simply doesn't represent a viable option any longer. Finally, for small open economies in transition, Gordian knot of simultaneous tackling environment protection, balanced regional growth, poverty reduction, favourable birth rate, attractiveness for foreign investors and snappy rural development, definitely becomes ever more tightened and entangled than ever before. Over the last 60 years world economy has lost around 20% of top notcharable land, fifth of its rain forests and

---

[4]   Institute of Economic Sciences, Belgrade, Serbia marko.malovic@ien.bg.ac.rs

thousands of plant- and wild-life species, while CO_2 emissions together with other human agents have pierced the ozone layer and caused the greenhouse effect[Haider Zaidi, 2008]. Nevertheless, Grossman and Krueger (1995) in their seminal paper from the end of XX century were the first to realize that continuous or even accelerating economic growth does not result (at least not inevitably) in *pro rata* pollution increase and worsening environment quality. As a matter of fact, experiments of an array of researchers thereafter confirmed a concave parabolic shape of relationship between pollution cum resource depletion (on ordinate) and economic growth i.e. income (on X axis), relationship which for its resemblance with Kuznets's (1955) findings[5] in respect to income inequality trajectory in developing economies was dubbed Environmental Kuznets Curve (EKC).

This paper reviews theoretical paradigms and empirical investigation of topsy-turvy relationship between environmental policies (or lack thereof) and economy's growth efforts. By utilizing EKC, Green Solow and alike frameworks we reexamine the environmental triangle of varying 1)activity scale, 2)output composition in terms of cleanliness or outsourcing and 3)production/abatement technology advances for growth dynamics in a small open economy. After introducing the problem of internalization distribution of externalities, this research briefly reflects on theoretical insights a propos EKC and variations of its empirical verification, only to move on to specific ingredients of environmentally sustainable growth path, including international trade and globalization impact, as well as ecological standards imposed by aspiring EU accession. First of all, the paper deals with prerequisites and determinants of inverted U-shaped curvature of EKC, followed by instruments at disposal of economic policy makers to that end, notwithstanding foreseeable investment induced by politeconomic and ecological trends in Western Balkans.

---

[5]   By the way, latest empirical research did not confirm famous Kuznets (1955) conclusions that growth initially causes income inequality to spike only to even it out in more mature stages of growth. Actually, growth doesn't create income inequality, policies do (Milanovic, 2011).

The rest of the paper is organized as features: Section 2 reviews theory and policy ofenvironmental externalities and determinants of concavity of EKC relationship. Section 3 deals with origins of green growth for small open economy (emphasizing ways to reach negative slope of EKC more quickly and enhance its concavity), with special attention paid to impact of environmental policies on international trade flows, globalization of investment and plant location. Section 4 goes on to conclude what lies ahead for small open economies of W. Balkans in terms of interaction between environment and their economic growth, followed by bibliographical register at the very end.

EXTERNALITIES, GROWTH AND EKC RELATIONSHIP

Goods and services based on technologies which pollute more and relentlessly deplete resources, as a rule of thumb, are much cheaper from ecologically responsible technologies. Price theory and ever increasing scarcity of pristine natural resources have recently incentivized and instructed policy makers to internalize the costs of depleting and degrading environment so as to make environmentally greenest goods simultaneously the most attractive for consumers (Chouinard-Ellison-Ridgeway, 2011). For example, CO_2 emissions and air pollution are a textbook primer of ecological externality in an extensive growth process. Externality is intentional economic activity or collateral by-product of individual economic activity which imposes involuntary costs (or benefits) on society, even though its consequences aren't at all or aren't fully reflected in market prices (Varian, 1999). This causes individual decision makers to burn more fossil fuel and/or consume more CO_2 emitting goods and services, than should be optimal from the social perspective. In theory, carbon price -calibrated so that polluter pays above the market price for entire burden emissions impose on society (and future generations)- would result in private producers polluting only if their private revenue exceeds the social costs of respective emission. Similarly, economic efficiency principle requires that marginal social benefits from abatement must equal marginal costs of abatement efforts (Nordhaus-Samuelson, 2001). Unfortunately, irrevocable damage caused by economic growth to the environment stems not only from (until recently or indeed still) tolerating gargantuan negative externalities, but also from (not long ago objective) lack of knowledge and technologies needed for adequate pricing of ecological benefits/costs neglected by the market. Precisely because many of the benefits (long-term health corollaries, well-functioning eco-system) are not (or not properly) factored in by the market, private polluters engage in environmentally conscious production technology and/or abatement only up to the point E_1 of intersection between private marginal benefits of green growth and its marginal cost. However, effective and efficient engagement is represented by intersection between social marginal benefits of environmentally conscious production/abatement and marginal cost curve at E_2 as evident from Picture 1.

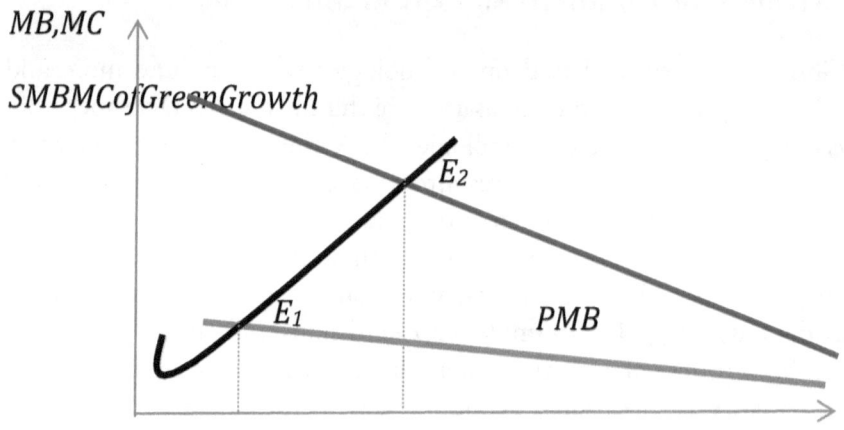

Pollution prevented and/or removed

Figure 1. Environmental externalities and market inefficiency *Source:* Nordhaus and Samuleson (2001)

Several quantitative undertakings from the late 1990s applied neoclassical utility theory to assign the value of world eco-systems and natural capital at about 30 trillion US$. Thus, ecological economist ended up fully embracing both method and slogan of welfare economics that protecting the environment is the matter of getting the prices right (Sagoff, 2012). Be that as it may, what if one polluter finds it relatively inexpensive to reduce emissions of say CO_2, whereas the other finds it very dear: should they both be obliged to decrease pollution by the same physical amount, proportional amount or some other measure (Varian, 1999)? Whichever we go for, marginal cost of pollutants must be equalized across producers, be that through direct government regulation, emission fees, or tradable pollution vouchers (Nordhaus-Samuelson, 2001). These efforts are expectedly riddled with free-riding impediments not only within the country, but even more in international terms, which is probably the major culprit for non-existence of EKC concavity effect when it comes to carbon-emissions and greenhouse gas emissions phenomena (Frankel, 2003). Somewhat ironically, there is in fact ample reason to believe that, thus far, cost benefit analysis hasn't significantly affected either rulemaking or regulation in practice (Sagoff, 2012).

Now, why then the environment may still appear as a bottle-neck to growth and just how it may contribute to it after all? Firstly, growth may be stalled or completely halted either by physical exhaustion or economic exhaustion of natural resources (Sachs-Warner, 1995). One speaks of economic shortage when holders of resources contemplate whether marginal profit of selling a unit of scarce resource today plus the interest from proceeds outweighs or not marginal profit of keeping it for future (postponed) sales. In such a setting, marginal product of other inputs compared with marginal product of severely depleted environmental contribution required is next to negligible, as demonstrated by Hallegatte and *alia* (2012) under the standard CES production function pretext:

$$Y=A[aO^{1-(1/\varphi)}+(1-a)E^{1-(1/\varphi)}]^{\varphi/(\varphi-1)} \tag{1}$$

$$O'/E' = \frac{a}{1-a}(\frac{E}{O})^{1\varphi} \tag{2}$$

Temporarily disabled environment due to natural disasters like 2014 flooding in Balkans could be a special case of thus formalized limitation. On the other hand, when it comes to environment as explicit or implicit contributor to sustainable economic activity, potential allies of green growth can be dissected by totally differentiating Cobb-Douglas production function with respect to environmental policy, featuring technical progress and environment formally introduced among the usual factors:

$$dY/d\Pi_E = \psi'f + \psi(f_A A' + f_K K' + f_L L' + f_E E') \qquad (3)$$

where ψ denotes efficiency parameter encompassing supply producing organization as well as demand-led stimuli. Therefore, the last term captures direct contribution of environment as a factor to economic growth, while former terms denote different collateral benefits (Hallegatte *et alia*, 2012). The first term quantifies impact of energy efficiency and additive and/or multiplicative effect of environmental stimulus (conundrum still being whether green economy raises only the level or also the growth rate of overall economic activity). The second term depicts impact of environmental policy on technological break-through or, quite to the contrary, on impeding and crowding out productivity-increasing patents. The third term measures opportunity cost (in otherwise wasted or lost capital) of avoided natural disasters brought about by global warming, climate change etc., Balkans once again protruding as the most striking recent example. Lastly, but not least, labor force and intellectual capital preservation and enhancement makes the causal estimates of the environmental pollution to human health. Moreover, Neidell and Zivin (2013) go an extra mile in developing quasi-experimental techniques to pinpoint evidence beyond traditional health outcomes of neglected environment ranging from quality of posterity and future labor supply, measures of cognition and human capital formation to productivity and well-being of employees.

However, often detected invertly U-shaped concavity of growth/income and environment relationship has fused many different theoretical hypotheses (and hence differing approaches to its empirical verification) in respect to determinants, dynamics and modalities for achieving aforementioned ecological internalization. EKC is, no doubt, essentially empirical phenomenon, nonetheless, econometrics deployed to examine this theoretical paradigm over the last 20 years suffers from dozen of methodological shortcomings (Malovic, 2014). Namely, its empirical verification specifications typically exhibited sample sensitivity, stark discrepancies between cross-country and country-specific evidence, heteroscedasticity in panel regressions, omitted variable biasness, autocorrelation in residues etc. (Copeland-Taylor, 2003), (Stern, 2003).

By all means, identified econometric weaknesses and often unsatisfactory/ not robust enough empirical specification merely reflect(ed) disarray of theoretical ideas regarding determinants of and preconditions for concavity of EKC. The most frequent explanations underscored threshold effects in terms of critical mass of knowledge, income or investment minimum having been reached in order for environmentally sustainable production and/or abatement technologies to be feasibly deployed. That is why environment preservation and restoration effects come about only with a time lag, i.e. after growth has already materialized (IBRD, 1992). Other explications accentuated distributional aberrations and income inequality which by definition time leaps behind acquired GDP, e.g. Kuznetz (1955), Lopez (1994). Thus, in early stages of industrialization environment degradation is ruthless but tiny, since low wages set imperative of fulfilling basic individual and social needs and eco-systems are largely intact. Pristine clean eco-systems in early phases of economic growth are being treated as abundant and assumed resource or viewed as unaffordable and dispensable luxury. What's more, Fisher-Kowalski, Swilling *et alia* (2011, p.19) picking up on earlier work by Wilkinson and Holdren revived hypothesis on divergent (rather than unison) interaction of environment degradation and scale of economic activity when decomposed into household level (where one identifies a drop in polluting as prolonged negative EKC slope), macro&societal level as well as corporate&industrial (stylized parabolic EKC relationship) and finally world economy or global level (where pollution is still rising). Therefore, certain explanations of EKC have concentrated upon production structure metamorphosis in postindustrial societies in favor of environmentally much more responsive services sector. At last, several novel studies underline the importance of disproportionately falling costs (and increasing returns) of abatement as the cause for decreasing costs of environmental control in spite of robust economic growth (Brock-Taylor, 2004), (Hallegatte *et alia*, 2012). Bradford, Schlieckert and Shore (2000), while econometrically estimating fixed effects of pollution-growth relationship, as well as Stern (2003), *inter alia*, corroborate that EKC U-shaped relationship exists for many yet by no means for all pollutants and all aspects of environmental degradation. Dasgupta *et alia* (2002) warn that traditional toxins and pollutants could be successfully suppressed and by-passed along the upward-sloping *per capita* growth trajectory, but that they are often superseded and supplemented by others which monotonically rise with intensifying economic activity. However, data show that even a propos conventional EKC relationships, decreasing environmental degradation and retiring dirty technologies does not immediately reduce emissions! To the contrary, today we know that for many harmful substances decrease in intensity of emission per unit of output increases pollution total over number of years before income- and/or technology-driven inflection point kicks in [Brock-Taylor, 2010].[6] In addition, relatively tiny costs/investment in abatement in comparison with impressive results in terms of reducing pollution could not possibly overstate the crucial significance of environmentally conscious technical progress yet not in production, but in post-festum reparation and rehabilitation of environment. Andreoni and Levinson (1998) followed by Brock and Taylor (2004) offer theoretical explication of empirically identified concavity in income (i.e. economic growth) hike and environment degradation interaction, by means of mathematically elegant formalization of link between consumption of given goods/service and enhancement of potential for eliminating their environmentally undesirable by-products. Environmental quality is being seen as a stock resource that depreciates over time unless maintained by investment in environment, above all in clean-up technologies. Both papers basically do so through straight-forward insertion of technical progress and environmental policy in Solow-like or Cobb-Douglas production functions. Baseline Solow's framework, for instance, defines output growth as a positive function of production factors engaged:

$$Y=f(A, K, L); \; dY/dA>0, dY/dK>0, dY/dL>0 \qquad (4)$$

---

6   For example, emissions per unit of output of SO2, CO and unstable organic compounds have been falling at almost constant percentage rate of emition per dolar of output over 60 years now, although inflection points and negative slope of EKC came about much more recently and with considerable time lag compared to environmentally concious technical progress or introduction of green regulation [Ibidem].

apart from technical progress and productivity boost, growth is driven by population increase, participation rate and education penetration, as well as by capital investment, net of capital depreciation:

$$dK/dt=I-\delta K \tag{5}$$

Andreoni and Levinson (1998) insist on close quarters technological link between the two factors of representative consumer's utility:

$$U=U(C, E) \tag{6}$$

$$Y=C+I \tag{7}$$

Green Solow model introduces net aggregate pollution as a difference between gross environment degradation (fΩ, where Ω denotes pollution created per unit of output) and pollution abated [Brock-Taylor, 2010]:

$$E_{net}=f\Omega-\Omega A(f_A,f)=fe(\theta) \tag{8}$$

$$fe(\theta)=\Omega[1-A(1,\theta)] \tag{9}$$

$$\theta=f_A/f \tag{10}$$

Having in mind that output is actually decomposed not only into current consumption and investment in further production but also in investment in abatement technologies as in equation *(11)*,

$$Y=C+I_Q+I_A \tag{11}$$

environmentally sustainable Solow modelslightly modifies its basic notation as follows:

$$y=f(k)(1-\theta) \tag{12}$$

$$dk/dt=sf(k)(1-\theta)-(\delta+n+g)k \tag{13}$$

$$E_{net}=f(k)e(\theta) \tag{14}$$

$$d\Omega/dt=-g^A\Omega \tag{15}$$

Small letter variables denote output, capital and net emissions normalized by *IBL,* where *B* earmarks environmental boundary for pollution after which there could be no life on earth [*Ibidem*]. In other words, green version of Solow's model endogenizes technical progress in abatement in such a fashion that falling pollution levels can go hand in hand with rising income for as long as continuous reductions in emissions per unit of output could be achieved and bullet-proof environmental protection technologies are asymptotically conceivable. Thereby, economic agent haven't been forced into giving up too much and progressively more consumption for each and every incremental improvement in quality of environment (Andreoni-Levinson, 1998), (Brock-Taylor, 2004). Environmentally sustainable growth from Solow's model perspective requires some advancement in production technologies to enable *per capita* income growth and technical progress in abatement to exceed the one in production technologies in order to account for population expansion. Nonetheless, exact trajectories of pollutant stocks, extreme values and magnitude of*per capita* income at inflection point tend to be sizably different from country to country (Brock-Taylor, 2010).

ORIGINS OF GREEN GROWTH AND IMPACT OF ENVIRONMENT ON TRADE, GLOBAL INVESTMENT AND PLANT LOCATION

Since in the open economy setting GDP doesn't get spent on consumption and investment only, but is also determined by interplay between country's exports and imports, legitimate question to be posed is whether origins of green growth change as compared with autarky case and what may be the impact of environment (and environmental policies) on international trade, global investment and plant location? Despite its empirical ambiguity, EKC literature raised pertinent questions about how growth and trade affect the environment, as well as tipped the iceberg of whether often convincingly positive effect of rising income on environmental quality shapes environmental policies that affect economic growth and even more impressively rising international trade in return. Notwithstanding the importance of income-environment relationship, trade may alter environmental outcomes through variety of other channels: the most obvious being that trade could encourage relocation of polluting industries from countries with strict environmental policy to those with less stringent ecological standards (Copeland-Taylor, 2003). There are three paramount consequences of such an eventuality. The first is that developing countries cannot replicate growth strategies of OECD countries because there are no reserve countries left with technological capabilities yet even lower environmental bars (Frankel, 2003). The second is that developing countries are expected to be reluctant about tightening of environmental regulations due to concerns over thus deteriorating international competitiveness, while the third asks whether national environmental policies ought to be constrained by international trade law in order to prevent them being abused as guises for the new trade protectionism (Copeland-Taylor, 2003).

True enough, international trade and globalization trends do offer alternative abatement mechanism- import the good from overseas when higher pollution taxes make it prohibitively expensive for domestic production, thereby making pollution demand more elastic. However, globalization and trade typically also pave the way for technology transfer, labor and capital mobility which may save some production factors and reallocate them to a better use (*Ibidem*). Hence, globalization and trade could end up economizing with natural resources and aiding with dissemination and advancement of abatement technologies. Moreover, empirical evidence suggests that, even though tightening of environmental regulation does at the margin affect trade flows and plant location decisions, reduction of environmental tariff and non-tariff barriers does not decisively influence pollution-intensive trade and investment flows (Brock-Taylor, 2004). Namely, many other equally prominent factors are at play, aggregated by the term revealed relative advantages, that should be taken into account. Besides, some environment-related trade barriers provide only fiscal revenue, others inspire transportation and logistical activities[7] that round-trip them, whereas yet others create nothing but red-tape and trading costs (Copeland-Taylor, 2003).

---

[7]   Domestic and/or foreign…

From a strategic perspective, environmental policy amidst the battle for sustainable economic growth rests upon three kinds of values: *1)* individual preferences (with or without opportunity cost filters) which policymakers cannot tackle directly, *2)* public/social/national values which indirectly modify individuals and *3)* ever more apparent value of a physically functional eco-system (Haider Zaidi, 2008). On operational (tactical) level, concavity of EKC i.e. decoupling of growth dynamics from progressive pollution could be achieved via *1)* straight-forward channeling of accumulation from further production I_Q to abatement activity I_A *2)* altering the GDP structure at the expense of dirty industries literally and/or by means of outsourcing or *3)* delivering and capitalizing on technical progress, either through *3a)* economizing on inputs and fostering environmentally responsible production or *3b)* cost-cutting and efficiency-enhancing equipment utilized and procedures followed under abatement efforts (Brock-Taylor, 2004). In the short run, of course, quicker and optimal concavity of EKC is greatly dependent on more generous financial funds, which in times of crisis, especially in underdeveloped transition economies usually aren't available.

DISCUSSION

Ecological legacy of Western Balkans confirms seminal prediction that in an environmentally unregulated markets there appears to be too little abatement and too much pollution. Nevertheless, as a discipline that just a decade or two earlier had insisted the market was embedded in the nature, environmental economics had finally begun to embed the nature into the market (Sagoff, 2012). Be that as it may, the multidisciplinary field still copes with loads of unknowns about sustainable growth and corollaries of economic (and natural resource exploitation) activity on the environment. Prevention of one type of pollution often gives birth to another, interdependence of eco-systems and our civilization, the world economy and biodiversity, makes them so obscurely intertwined that, for instance, disappearance of bees from the face of the earth would endanger the very human existence only 4 years later. More broadly, seemingly stellar cases, ecological role models so to speak - e.g. deep sea fishing of cod in Norwegian territorial waters versus GMO spawning pools for fish breeding in captivity- often times hide environmentally devastating flipside - actually, Norwegian cod has been processed in China with huge CO_2 emitting imprint (Jovanovic, 2013). Hence, 'environmentally conscious' outsourcing from developing world for beneficiaries in the OECD countries has nevertheless been increasing the global warming and other aspects of environmental degradation of the planet (Malovic, 2014).

As for developing countries themselves, plethora of measures and policies lie ahead, *inter alia*, internalization (and exact price determination) of particularly negative environmental externalities, abolishment of ecologically harmful subsidies, strengthening of environmental standards and stricter honoring of property rights (Yandle-Vijayaghavan-Bhattarai, 2002). However, it isn't seldom that internalization of environmental damage gets partially or totally wedged into consumer price index, a practice which represents a brute violation of polluter pays principle cherished by the EU. Even when polluter indeed covers for or prevents environmental degradation, for tiny local firms in small open economies aforementioned internalization signifies incredible, often indigestible expenditure on which subsequently free-ride all other enterprises that use environmentally responsible product as an input down the manufacturing or value chain.

Therefore, lack of technological supremacy and financial gap between the short and the long run will be fundamental obstacles in administering the optimal dosage and sequence of ecological reforms in small open developing economies. Having in mind that EU candidate countries to that end have recourse to next to no grants whatsoever - instead, directions of European Commission and acquis communotaire are being implemented backed up by pretty expensive international loans (Jovanovic, 2013) - it becomes patently obvious that prematurely raised environmental standards may, depending on the case at point, either boost or seriously decelerate economic growth rate of underdeveloped, crisis stricken transition countries (Fullerton-Kim, 2006).

In conclusion, as pointed out by Malovic (2014), since EU environmental standards along accession process of candidate countries are bound to impose certain norms (and expenditures) well before their reaching growth levels which could independently support and develop sustainably green economy, it is to be expected for small open economies of W. Balkans (in comparison with OECD members) that there and then sustainable growth trend might slow down or even flatten its trajectory, while pollution level and natural resource exploitation are likely to reach inflection point slightly faster - yet with extremely slow and protracted progress in abatement.

Inflection determinants of the Environmental Kuznets Curve, where and when it applies, as well as internal mechanics of the Green Solow Model, have given us both the pitch and the rules of the ecologically sustainable growth game. Moreover, the game is afoot already. Although being far from favorites, and struggling with less players than the field requires, small developing countries nevertheless need to tip the balance to the best of their ability. And the fine balance of winning, as always, stretches along the conflicting benefit of protecting one's own goal and simultaneous imperative to score. We all know how short is the long run in environmental terms nowadays, yet, from equally unforgiving economics viewpoint, when underdeveloped, in order to even reach the long run, one has to grow. In an attempt to strike a dynamic consistency between the two, developing countries might need to rely not only on knowledge and resources available, but also on that one last evolutionary factor we abstained from putting in either the EKC trajectory or the Green Solow production function, namely the lady luck.

Nota Bene: This paper is a part of research projects: 179015 (Challenges and prospects of structural changes in Serbia: Strategic directions for economic development and harmonization with EU requirements) and 47009 (European integrations and social and economic changes in Serbian economy on the way to the EU), financed by the Ministry of Education, Science and Technological Development of the Republic of Serbia. The usual disclaimer applies.

REFERENCES

1. Andreoni, J.-Levinson, A. (1998), "The Simple Analytics of Environmental Kuznets Curve", NBER Working Paper 6739, Cambridge, MA.

2. Bradford, D.-Schlieckert, R.-Shore, S. (2000), "The Environmental Kuznets Curve: Exploring a fresh specification", NBER Working Paper 8001, Cambridge, MA, November.

3. Brock, W.-Taylor, M. S. (2004), "Economic Growth and the Environment: A Review of Theory and Empirics", NBER Working Paper 10854, Cambridge, MA, October.

4. Brock, W.-Taylor, M. S. (2010), "The Green Solow Model", Journal of Economic Growth, Springer, vol. 15(2), pages 127-153, June.

5. Chouinard, Y.-Ellison, J.-Ridgeway, R. (2011), "The Big Idea: The Sustainable Economy", Harvard Business Review, October, mimeo.

6. Copeland, B.-Taylor, M. S. (2003), "Trade, Growth and the Environment", NBER Working Paper 9823, Cambridge, MA, July.

7. Dasgupta, S.-Laplante, B.-Wang, H.-Wheeler, D. (2002), "Confronting the Environmental Kuznets Curve", Journal of Economic Perspectives Vol. 16, pp. 147-168.

8. Fischer-Kowalski, M.-Swilling, M. et alia (2011), "Decoupling Natural Resource Use and Environmental Impacts from Economic Growth", UNEP, United Nations, Geneve.

9. Frankel, J. (2003), "The Environment and Globalization", NBER Working Paper 10090, Cambridge, MA, November.

10. Fullerton, D.- Kim, S.-R. (2008), "Environmental Investment and Policy with Distortionary Taxes and Endogenous Growth," Journal of Environmental Economics and Management, Elsevier, vol. 56(2), pages 141-154, September.

11. Grossman, G.-Krueger, A. (1995), "Economic Growth and the Environment", The Quarterly Journal of Economics, MIT Press, vol. 110(2), pages 353-77, May.

12. Haider Zaidi, M. (2008), "Economics of Environmental Sustainability", University of Engineering and Technology, Lahore, December 30th, mimeo.

13. Halegatte, S.-Heal, G.-Fay, M-Treguer, D. (2012), "From Growth to Green Growth- A Framework", NBER Working Paper 17841, Cambridge, MA, February.

14. IBRD (1992), "World Development Report: Development and the Environment", Oxford University Press, New York.

15. Jones, L. -Manueli, R. (1995), "A Positive Model of Growth and Pollution Controls", NBER Working Paper 5205, Cambridge, MA, August.

16. Jovanovic, M. (2013), "The Economics of European Integration", 2nd Edition, Edward Elgar Publishing Ltd., Cheltenham UK &Northampton USA, Ch. 14.

17. Kuznets, S. (1955), "Economic Growth and Income Inequality", American Economic Review 49, pp.1-28.

18. Lopez, R. (1994), "The environment as a Factor of Production: the Effects of Economic Growth and Trade Liberalization", Journal of Environmental Economics and Management, Vol. 27, pp. 163-184.

19. Malovic, M. (2014), "Održivi rast i životna sredina: Šta smo nau ili i šta nas eka?", Ecologica, No.74, Year XXI, June, forthcoming.

20. Milanovic, B. (2011), "The Haves and the Have-Nots: A brief idiosyncratic History of global Inequality", Basic Books. N. York.

21. Neidell, M.-Zivin, J. (2013), "Environment, Health and Human Capital", NBER Working Paper 18935, Cambridge, MA, April.

22. Nordhaus, W.-Samuelson, P. (2001), "Economics", 17th Edition, McGraw-Hill&Irwin, New York, Ch.18 .

23. Sachs, J.-Warner, A. (1995), "Natural Resource Abundance and Economic Growth", NBER Working Paper 5398, Cambrudge, MA.

24. Sagoff, M. (2012), "The Rise and Fall of Ecological Economics- A Cautionary Tale", Breakthrough Institute Journal, Winter Issue, *mimeo.*

25. Stern, D. (2003), "The Rise and Fall of the Environmental Kuznets Curve", Renselaer Working Paper #0302, Renselaer Politechinc Institute, October.

26. Varian, H. (1999), "Intermediate Microeconomics- a modern approach", 5th Edition, Norton Publishers, New York, Ch. 32.

27. Yandle, B.- Vijayaghavan, M.-Bhattarai, M. (2002), "The Environmental Kuznets Curve: A Primer", PERC Research Study No. 1, May.

ENVIRONMENT VS. ECONOMIC GROWTH DEBATE[8]

Bojana Radovanović[9]

Mihajlo Djukić[10]

INTRODUCTION

During the two decades after the World War Two, the world economy recorded the unprecedented economic growth. This period is known as *the postwar economic boom*, *the long boom*, and *the Golden Age of Capitalism*. In this period, the European countries recorded the average real gross national product (GDP) growth of almost 5% each year during the 1950s and 1960s (Temin, 2002). However, during the 1960s the implications of such growth, particularly on environment, have been questioned. This is known as the "growth-versus-environment debate" (de Bruyn, 2000). This debate has been examining the relationship between economic growth and environmental quality, and it is still open. The main issue within this debate is whether the economic growth threatens the environment, or whether it actually has positive effect on environmental quality.

In his summary of different approaches within the "growth-versus-environment debate", de Bruynclassifies them into four different perspectives (Ibid). Firstly, there are "radical supporters" of economic

---

[8] This paper is a part of research projects: 47009 (European integrations and social and economic changes in Serbian economy on the way to the EU) and 179015 (Challenges and prospects of structural changes in Serbia: Strategic directions for economic development and harmonization with EU requirements).

[9] Research Associate, Institute of Economic Sciences, Belgrade, Serbia, bojana.radovanovic@ien.bg.ac.rs

[10] Research Associate, Institute of Economic Sciences, Belgrade, Serbia, mihajlo.djukic@ien.bg.ac.rs

growth, postulating a direct positive relationship between economic growth and environmental quality. This is a free market approach, where the environmental quality is seen as a luxury good. The supporters of this approach argue that economic growth influences technological innovations and changes in lifestyles that improve environmental quality. Thus, the economic growth should be stimulated and the governmental intervention through environmental policy reduced. According to this view, the environmental problems can be alleviated through market mechanisms. Secondly, there are "conditional supporters", who also assume a positive link between economic growth and environmental quality, but on different grounds. According to this perspective economic growth can have negative environmental effects. However, it at the same time raises the funds from which environmental policies can be financed. Thus, the economic growth is considered as a prerequisite for environmental policy. In other words, the environmental policy is necessary for the environmental protection, but it cannot be financed without the economic growth. Thus, the economic growth should be stimulated while simultaneously implementing environmental policies. Thirdly, there are the "weak antagonists" who take a more sceptical perspective on the desirability of economic growth. According to this approach, economic growth results in a higher physical output which in turn causes deterioration of the environment. Although environmental policies can alleviate the environmental degradation, reduction of the growth in certain industries is also required, as the supporters of this view argue. Finally, the "strong antagonists" state that in the long run economic growth is always harmful to the environment. Although environmental policies may have a positive effect on environmental quality it is only in the short run. No substantial improvements in environmental quality can be made without getting off the growth path. The policy recommendation is therefore to reduce economic growth. In short, the views on the relationship between the economic growth and the environment are controversial, which will be further elaborated in this paper.

When looking at the relationship between environment and economic growth, we should have in mind two roles that nature plays in the economic process. On the one hand, nature gives resources necessary for the economic activities. On the other, it absorbs the waste and undesirable by-products (Brock & Taylor, 2005). In this paper, we will discuss the relationship between the economic growth and environment concerning natural resource extraction on the one hand, and pollution on the other.

Importance of this paper comes from the fact that Serbia still does not have a coherent policy for the resource management and pollution control. In the process of the EU integrations, Serbia has always been torn between two issues. In one hand, process of EU integration is followed by adoption of numerous laws and relatively strict rules in the field of resource management and pollution. This will also be a subject of the future negotiation processes, particularly within the Chapter 27 on "Environment". Based on the estimation of the National Environmental Approximation Strategy for the Republic of Serbia, Serbia will need more than 10.6 billion EUR in order to adjust its environmental policy with the EU, including adoption and implementation of the appropriate legislative (National Environmental Approximation Strategy, 2011). On the other hand, relatively modest economic growth achieved in the past may induce different stakeholders, mainly political elites and business lobbies, to use every available instrument to achieve short term growth and profit instead of the investment in environmental protection. Since our approach is mainly theoretical and descriptive, the contribution of this paper is primarily to inform scientific community and policy makers about the current knowledge on the relationship between the economic growth and environment, concerning natural resource extraction on the one hand, and pollution on the other. This knowledge is particularly importantin the process of developing an adequate environmental policy. It is also important to support critical thinking in these areas since the environmental policy is a subject of continuous examination even in the developed EU countries that are permanently looking for the better and cheaper environmental solutions and new sources of economic growth.

NATURAL RESOURCES AND ECONOMIC GROWTH

In this section we would like to shed some light on the issues regarding the relationship between natural resources and economic growth.

Natural resources have been considered as a vitally important for various reasons. They were, they are, and unfortunately will be probably one of the main reasons for the arm conflicts around the world. Why are the natural resources of such a big importance for the nations? Is the scarcity of natural resources real threat for the economic growth? The relationship between the natural resources and economic growth can be analysed from two perspectives. Firstly, there is a problem of potential limit of natural resources andthe unsustainable economic growth which is based on the exploitation of non-renewable natural resources. Exploitation of resources in that sense may have negative effects on economic growth in the future. Secondly, there is the question of the relationship between the abundance of the natural resources and economic growth. The question is whether the abundance in natural resources is a necessary precondition for the country's economic growth. What are the countries' growth experiences when it comes to natural wealth or sudden discovery of natural resources? Both issues will be analysed in this section.

To begin with, the natural resources are part of the total wealth of the national economy. In the economic activities, they are considered as a specific form of the capital from which many other forms of capital are made. Natural resources might be renewable and non-renewable. Classification is based on their potential for regeneration. Non-renewable resources are of special importance since their ability to regenerate is limitedor even impossible. In developing countries natural resources, especiallynon-renewable, are the basis of income creation. Goods produced from non-renewable resources such as oil and minerals are important export products with a very large share of employment, while fishery and forestry are crucial economic sectors. Natural resources are usually of dramatic importance when it comes to the poor people, presenting important source of food, building materials and income. Approximately 26% of wealth of low income countries is natural capital comparing to the 13% in middle income and 2% in OECD countries (OECD 2008).

However, the growth which is based on non-renewable resources is short term oriented and could jeopardize future growth potentials. Firstly, as explained by Beckerman we could approach limits of the world resources (Beckerman, 1992). Meadows et al. argued that if the prevailing annual rates of consumption (of several key minerals) were to be maintained, these reserves would soon be exhausted(Meadows, 1972). As a consequence, natural resource management is recognized as an important part of development strategies of countries and international organisations. Adverse management of natural resources has deteriorating effects on the long term development potentials. Examples for such a policy could be found in Kirgizstan where shortage of water and consequently energy took place(Fumagalli, 2008). The lost opportunities that poor natural resource management leads to results in a poor decision-making that values higher current growth over the long-term economic development (OECD, 2011).

The exploitation of natural resources may decrease the abilities of future generation to create an additional value, which is the core issue of all concepts of sustainable economic development. This concept refers to the responsible exploitation of natural resources. Concept of sustainable growth was initially presented by *BrundtlandComission* as an economic growth which meets the needs of the present without compromising the ability of future generations to meet their own needs (Brundtland,1987). The central issue of the report is on proposing long-term environmental strategy in order to achieve sustainable development by 2000. Long term strategy for sustainable development assumes achievement of responsible economic growth in the social but also in the environmental context. In the moment when Brundtland agenda appeared, political and economic conditions were quite different than today. Nowadays, the scarce resources exploitation is not the dominant issue in the debate on sustainable development, but the human intervention that might jeopardize future development. It is a special responsibility of rich countries to reduce negative environmental effects showing the model of development which might be applied in the future. However, there are arguments that the availability of natural resources does not constrain economic growth since there are certain economic feedback mechanisms on resource scarcity, such as rise in the price of the resource that is becoming scarce or replacement of the resource by its substitutes (Beckerman, 1992)

Now we will turn to the question of whether the abundance of natural resources is a precondition of economic growth. Economic development is broader concept than economic growth. Growth as the only one factor of development is required but does not represent the only condition for the improvement of the national economy performances. There is no doubt that growth is essential in order to eliminate poverty and improve living standards. Without significant rise of both production quantity and productivity it is quite impossible to spend more on many different important activities. However, while frequently criticised as narrow and inadequate, failing to include all important aspects of economic development, it is still one of the mostly used measures of economic progress. What are the real factors affecting economic growth and what is the role of natural resources? First, as a relatively complex term, economic growth is affected by many factors. There are economic but also the other factors influencing growth such as political, social, psychological, religious, and many others. Economic factors are technological development, human capital, natural resources, capital formation, population growth, etc. Natural resources are one of certainly very important factors to achieve growth.

The exploitation of natural resources as an instrument to achieve economic growth has been particularly analysed in the context of developing countries. Sachs and Warner performed OLS regression for the period 1970-1990 showing that countries that were specialized in natural resources experienced lower average rate of GDP growth (Sachs & Warner, 2001). This is known in the literature as the *resource curse* - situation when countries with great abundance in natural resource wealth tend to grow more slowly than resource-poor countries. Scarcity of natural resources in their model is captured by four different measures: a) the ratio of natural resource exports to GDP, b) the share of natural resource exports in total exports, c) the ratio of mineral production to total GNP, d) and per capita agricultural land extent (Ibid). Moreover, Manzano and Rigobon (2008) proved slightly negative correlation between export of primary products and economic growth. In their study, the negative correlation is not very strong, but excludes any possibility of favourable impact of natural wealth on growth (Manzano & Rigobon, 2001). It was rather hard to precisely explain empirically traced hypotheses that the resource-abundant countries faced stagnation in economic growth since the early 1970s. Leite and Weidmann (1999) argued that due to the rent seeking behaviour resource abundant countries experienced higher level of corruption (Leite & Weidmann, 2001). There are many different experiences. The Although petroleum industry in Nigeria is the largest industry and main generator of GDP, this country had the same GDP in 2001 as forty years ago. Moreover, oil nations such as Venezuela, Iran or Kuwait recorded very disappointing growth results in the period 1965-1998 (Larsen, 2005). On the other hand, Norway escaped curse of natural wealth. Hansen argued that Norway did not face resource cursedue to the proper management which should have twofold objective. Norway is the real example that the discovery of natural resources may be blessing. What really matters are the institutional conditions under which resource management takes place rather than orientation of natural wealth.

To conclude, natural resources are considered as an important factor for economic growth. However, the empirical analyses on the relationship between the abundance in natural resources and economic growth are inconclusive. While there are scholars who argue that the countries with ample of natural resources experience the resource curse, there are also contra-arguments, that abundance of resources do not put a curse on countries' economic development. Moreover, since the natural resources are scarce, the argument goes, and since we are approaching the limits of available resources, economic growth of the conventional kind is not sustainable. However, there are arguments that the availability of natural resources does not constrain economic growth since there are certain economic feedback mechanisms on resource scarcity, such as rise in the price of the resource that is becoming scarce or replacement of the resource by its substitutes. In short, the discussion on the relationship between the economic growth and natural resources stays open.

POLLUTION AND ECONOMIC GROWTH

Nature absorbs the waste and undesirable by-products of the economic activities. The economic activities are seen as the main pollutants of the environment. English Oxford Dictionary defines pollution as the presence in or introduction into the environment of a substance which has harmful or poisonous effects. In this section, we will analyse the relationship between the economic growth and environment concerning pollution. This link has received much attention lately. There is a growing literature on the relationship between per capita income and pollution. Both scholars and general public are more and more concerned over "air quality, global warming, and the emissions of industrial production" (Brock and Taylor, 2005: 2).

The most influential literature on the link between the economic growth and pollution is known as the Environmental Kuznets Curve (EKC) literature (Ibid). Environmental Kuznets Curve, or the inverse U-shaped curve, depicts the tendency that the environment worsens at the lower levels of income (GDP per capita) and then improves on higher levels of income (GDP per capita)[11]. In other words, as the argument goes, while industrialisation and modernisation may result in pollution, they are necessary for the economic development and once a county reaches certain level of economic development, the pollution starts to fall. Different factors influence this downturn of the pollution, such as: a) positive income elasticities for environmental quality, b) changes in the composition of production and consumption, c) increasing levels of education and environmental awareness, and d) more open political systems (Selden & Song, 1994: 147). Moreover, structural change in the economy and more effective regulation are also important sources of change in pollution.

It can be noticed that the environment is improving in developed countries. It is noticeable that the level of emissions for regulated pollutants is falling, and also that the quality of air in cities is rising (Brock and Taylor, 2005). The quality of their environments has been improved in the U.S. and other advanced industrial countries over the last 30 years. Moreover, cities are cleaner than in the past, emissions of health-threatening toxics are reduced, and in some cases the changes in environmental quality are quite dramatic (Ibid). However, there is also

---

[11]   In his famous paper form 1955, analysing available data, Simon Kuznets noticed that the income inequality in a country rises with the increase of GDP per capita up to a certain point of economic growth, when it starts to fall (Kuznets, 1955). This is known as Kuznets Curve.

much controversy over the relationship between the economic growth and pollution. In this section, we will give an overview of the empirical literature concerning the evidence of the EKC related to air pollution and water pollution.

To begin with, we will present the analyses of the relationship between the air pollution and economic growth. In their empirical analyses, Grossman and Krueger (1993) and Seldon and Song (1994) have searched for systematic relationships between the air pollution and economic growth, by regressing cross-country measures of ambient air quality on various levels of GDP per capita. Grossman and Krueger, using a cross-country panel data on urban air pollution levels, particularly atmospheric concentration of suspended particulate matter (SPM) and sulphur dioxide (SO_2), analysed at which levels of GDP per capita the atmospheric concentration of suspended particulate matter (SPM) and sulphur dioxide (SO_2) become decreasing functions of income. According to their estimates the turning points for these pollutants are under 5000 US dollars of per capita GDP (Seldon& Song, 1994).

In order to test the EKC hypothesis, Selden and Song analysed data for four air pollutants: suspended particulate matter (SPM), sulphur dioxide (SO_2), oxides of nitrogen (NO_x) and carbon monoxide (CO). Using these four air pollutants, they find substantial support for the EKC hypothesis. However, they find higher turning points than it has previously been estimated by Grossman and Kruger. In other words, Selden and Song predict that aggregate emissions of these four pollutants will eventually turn down as the level of GDP per capita increases. Their estimated turning points are $10391. However, they forecast an increase in global emissions in the foreseeable future. They predict that the emissions will not return to current levels before the end of this century "unless concerned actions are taken that move us away from the historical emissions-GDP relations" (Ibid 161). This is because large parts of the world's population still have to reach the levels of economic development, in other words, the turning points for emissions, the authors argue.

Moreover, Shafik and Bandyopadhyay's study showed that local air pollutant concentrations conformed to the EKC hypothesis with turning points between $3000 and $4000 (Stern, 2003). In short, these studies, which have been influential in the literature on the relationship between the air pollution and economic growth, indicate that on certain level of economic growth the air pollution decreases. However, the datasets used in these studies are dominated by, or consist solely of, emissions from OECD countries. However, when the more representative samples are used, the findings show a monotonic relation between sulfur emissions and income, as well as between carbon dioxide and income (Stern, 2003).

Now, we will turn to the relationship between the water pollutiona and economic growth. Hettige, Mani and Wheeler analysed international data to test Kuznets relationship between industrial water pollution and economic development (Hettige, Mani & Wheeler, 1997). They measure the effect of income growth on three proximate determinants of water pollution: a) the share of manufacturing in total output; b) the sectoral composition of manufacturing; c) and the intensity (per unit of output) of industrial pollution at the end-of-pipe. They find that the manufacturing share of output follows a Kuznets-type trajectory, but the other two determinants do not. Sectoral composition gets 'cleaner' through middle-income status and then stabilizes. At the end-of pipe, pollution intensity declines strongly with income. The authors attribute part of this to stricter regulation as income increases, and part to pollution-labour complementarity in production (Ibid). When they combine the three relationships, they do not find a Kuznets curve. In fact, total industrial water pollution rises rapidly through middle-income status and remains approximately constant thereafter. In Shafik and Bandyopadhyay's study, the lack of clean water and lack of urban sanitation were found to decline uniformly with increasing income, and over time, while river quality tended to worsen with increasing income (Stern, 2003).

To sum up, there is certain evidence, Grossman and Krueger (1993) and Seldon and Song (1994), that when certain level of economic growth is reached, the air pollution starts to decrease. There is also some econometric proves that the lack of clean water and lack of urban sanitation are found to decline uniformly with increasing income, however, total industrial water pollution rises rapidly through middle-income status and remains approximately constant thereafter. Thus, the relationship between the air pollution and economic growth seems much more straightforward than the one between the economic growth and water pollution. However, some authors argue that the econometric evidence put forward in support of the EKC is not as reliable and robustas previously thought. For example, the choice of model used to describe the relationship between income and pollution has a significant impact on the results of the analysis (Stern, 2004). Moreover, the most indicators of environmental degradation are monotonically rising in income though the "income elasticity" is less than one and is not a simple function of income alone (Ibid). Furthermore, the time related effects reduce environmental impacts in countries at all levels of income. However, in rapidly growing middle income countries the scale effect, which increases pollution and other degradation, overwhelms the time effect, while in wealthy countries, growth is slower, and pollution reduction efforts can overcome the scale effect, which is the origin of the apparent EKC effect (Ibid).

In addition, alimited set of pollutants are analysed when looked at the relationship between the environment and economic growth (Everttet al. 2010). Therefore, the conclusions reached by these analyses are not applicableto all types of environmental damage. When the relationship between the aggregate measure of the pressure human beingsplace on the environment - Ecological Footprint and the economic growth is analysed no evidence of an EKCwas found (Ibid). Also, the Environmental Kuznets relationship appears strongest for pollutants withsignificant local impacts, while for carbon and other greenhouse gases, wherethe impacts are global and diffuse, emissions have continued to rise with increases in incomeper capita even in the richest countries (Ibid).

While the EKC literature has been the predominant in the environment-economic growth debate, there are other theories that analyse this relationship. The limits theorylooks at the possibility of breaching environmental thresholds before the economy reaches the EKC turning point. This theory, suggest that solely focussing on economic growth to deliver environmental outcomes could be counter-productive (Ibid). The new toxics view is another theory that questions the existence of turning points, and considers the possibility that environmental damage continues to increase as economies grow, where emissions of existing pollutants are decreasing with further economic growth, but the new pollutants increase. Moreover, international competition initially leads to increasing environmental damage, up to the point when developed countries start reducing their environmental impact but also outsource polluting activities to poorer countries. The net effect is, in the best case scenario, a non-improving situation. This model is known as 'race to the bottom' (Ibid).

To conclude, while there is some evidence that pollution decreases at certain level of economic growth, in certain countries and for certain local pollutants, it cannot be generalised to all types of pollution and across allcountries and income levels. In other words, there is no enough evidence to support the Environmental Kuznets relationship.

ENVIRONMENT, ECONOMIC GROWTH AND THE INSTITUTIONS

The dominant view in the so called mainstream literature on economic development is that institutions are the most important determinants of economic development (Chang, 2011). The debate on the role of institutions in economic development has become one of the central issues explaining differences in economic development since the late 1990s, when the World Bank and the International Monetary Fund "started to impose many 'governance related conditionalities', which required that the borrowing country adopts 'better' institutions that improve 'governance'" (Ibid, 473). 'Better institutions', called the Global Standard Institutions (GSIs), are those that are supposed to maximise market freedom and protect private property rights most strongly (Ibid). Moreover, the Organization for Economic Cooperation and Development (OECD), the G7, the World Economic Forum, and many other think-tanks and policy forums have been arguing that developing countries should adopt such institutions (Ibid). Theyare also seen, by the aforementioned organisations, to be the most efficient in creating the responsible environment policy under which sustainable economic growth is possible.

There are several specific measures regarding the environmental policy proposed by the OECD document - *Natural Resources and Pro-Poor Growth* (2008):

- Market-based measures– measures adopted to adjust pricing mechanism. They are usually aimed to reflect real prices of goods and services. This is also related to the issue of internalization of costs of natural resources extraction which is considered to be a very powerful incentive.
- Regulation measures – often used to support or replace market measures. They are supposed to ensure economic actors are protected and not systematically disturbed by other actors including the government.
- Co-operation and information – used to support the private property management in a sustainable and efficient way.

Moreover, in order to escape resource curse, developing countries are advised to follow certain policy rules systematized by OECD within a document *The Economic Significance of Natural Resources: Key Points for Reformers in Eastern Europe, Caucasus and Central Asia* (OECD, 2011). Some of them are as follows:

- Facilitating the development of property rights and markets;
- Removing subsidies that hamper sustainable resource use;
- Reducing resource degradation and enhancing the provision of environmental services;
- Improving the management of publicly owned natural resources.
- Reducing pollution by natural-resource-based industries;
- Dealing with information shortfalls; and
- Addressing distributive implications of natural resource management policies (OECD, 2011).

Those organisations see government action as necessary to support adopted market mechanisms, especially in the area of strengthening competition, attracting foreign direct investments, energy efficiency improvement, stimulate measures for private sector, etc. (Towards Green Growth, OECD 2011).

However, having in mind the complex and inconclusive relationship between environment and economic growth, insisting on market freedoms and property rights and particularly proposing a set of same measures to each and every country is rather simplistic. There is and there should be an always present and still open dilemma on whether more market or government instruments are necessary to apply in order to create proper regulatory framework to address the complex relationship between the environment and economic growth. Although experiences of other countries and theoretical and empirical knowledge on the relationship between the economic growth and environment should be taken into consideration, each country should be able to create an environmental policy which suits it the best, depending on the level of development, values, specific political goals and the characteristics of the economy.

CONCLUSION

In this paper, we have analysed the interaction between the environment and economic growth from theoretical and empirical perspective. When looking at the relationship between environment and economic growth, we should have in mind two roles that nature plays in the economic processes. On the one hand, nature gives resources necessary for the economic activities. On the other, it absorbs the waste and undesirable by-products.

Natural resources are considered as an important factor for economic growth. However, the empirical analyses on the relationship between the abundance in natural resources and economic growth are inconclusive. While there are scholars who argue that the countries with ample of natural resources experience the resource curse, there are also contra-arguments, that abundance of resources do not put a curse on countries' economic development. Moreover, since the natural resources are scarce, the argument goes, and since we are approaching the limits of available resources, economic growth of the conventional kind is not sustainable. However, there are arguments that the availability of natural resources does not constrain economic growth since there are certain economic feedback mechanisms on resource scarcity, such as rise in the price of the resource that is becoming scarce or replacement of the resource by its substitutes.

As for the relationship between the pollution and economic growth, the arguments presented in this paper show that while there is some evidence that pollution decreases at certain level of economic growth in certain countries and for certain local pollutants – that there is the environmental Kuznets relationship, it cannot be generalised to all types of pollution and across allcountries and income levels. This however may have different implications for environmental policy. While the "radical supporters" of economic growth may see in the EKC the encouragement to foster economic growth and avoid environmental regulations – particularly in developed countries that have gone past the turning point. They argue that the early implementation of tight environmental regulations could actually harm growth, and cause increased environmental damage in the long run (Evertt et al. 2010). However, the empirical evidence can also lead to the conclusion which is closer to the antagonists' view, where economic growth is seen as a threat to environment, and where environmental policies together with the giving up of growth in "dirty" sectors are recommended.

In short, as it is presented in this paper, the relationship between the environment and economic growth is controversial. Thus, each country should be able to create an environmental policy which suits it the best, depending on the level of development, values, specific political goals and the characteristics of the economy.

REFERENCES

1. Brundtland, Gro Harlem (1987), Report of the World Commission on environment and development: "Our common future, "United Nations, 1987.

2. Beckerman, W. (1992). Economic growth and the environment: Whose growth? whose environment? *World Development*, *20*(4), 481–496. doi:10.1016/0305-750X(92)90038-W

3. Brock W. & Taylor S. (2005). Economic Growth and the Environment: A Review of theory and empirics in "Handbook of Economic Growth" Ed. P. Aghion and S. Durlauf, 1750-1819, Elsevier.

4. Chang, Ha-Joon. (2011). "Institutions and Economic Development: Theory, Policy and History", Journal of Institutional Economics (2011), 7: 4, 473–498.

5. de Bruyn S. (2000). "Economic Growth and the Environment An Empirical Analysis" Springer Science+Business Media Dordrecht

6. Grossman G. M. and A. B. Krueger, (1995), "Economic Growth and the Environment", The QuarterlyJournal of Economics, MIT Press, vol. 110(2), pages 353-77,

7. Hettige H., Mani M. & Wheeler D. (1997). "Industrial Pollution in Economic Development: Kuznets Revisited" Policy Research Working Paper Series, Development Research Group, World Bank

8. Fumagalli, M. (2008). The "Food Energy Water" Nexus in Central Asia : Regional Implications of and the International Response to the Crises in Tajikistan The "Food-Energy-Water" Nexus in Central Asia : Regional Implications of and the International Response to the Cris.

9. Everett T., Ishwaran M., Ansaloni G.P. and Rubin A. (2010). "Economic Growth and the Environment" Defra Evidence and Analysis Series

10. Kuznets S. (1955). "Economic growth and income inequality," American Economic Review, 49. 1-28.

11. Larsen, E. R. (2005). Are rich countries immune to the resource curse? Evidence from Norway's management of its oil riches. Resources Policy, 30(2), 75–86. doi:10.1016/j.resourpol.2004.12.001

12. Leite, C. A., & Weidmann, J. (2001). Does Mother Nature Corrupt? Natural Resources, Corruption, and Economic Growth. SSRN Electronic Journal. doi:10.2139/ssrn.259928

13. Manzano, O., & Rigobon, R. (2001). Resource Curse or Debt Overhang? Retrieved from http://www.nber.org/papers/w8390

14. Meadows, et al. (1972). EBSCOhost | 38313461 | Limits to Growth: Tools for theTransition to Sustainability. Retrieved May 16, 2014

15. National Environmental Approximation Strategy,(2011), Official Journal of the Republic of Serbia, No. 80/11 of 28 October 2011,

16. OECD Report, (2011), Economic Significance of Natural Resources - Key Points for Reformers in Eastern Europe, Caucasus and Central Asia.

17. OECD Report, (2008), Natural Resources and Pro-Poor Growth.

18. OECD Report, (2011), Towards Green Growth, The OECD Green Growth Strategy: A lens for examining growth

19. Sachs, J. D., & Warner, A. M. (2001). The curse of natural resources. *European Economic Review*, *45*(4-6), 827–838. doi:10.1016/ S0014-2921(01)00125-8

20. Temin P. (2002). "The Golden Age of European growthreconsidered" *European Review of Economic History*, 6, 3-22.

21. Selden S. & Song M. (1994). "Environmental Quality and Development: Is There a Kuznets Curve for Air Pollution Emissions?" *Journal of Environmental Economics and Management*Volume 27, Issue 2, September 1994, Pages 147–162.

22. Stern D. (2003). "The Environmental Kuznets Curve" International Society for Ecological Economics, Internet Encyclopaedia of Ecological Economics.

23. Stern D., (2004), "The Rise and Fall of the Environmental Kuznets Curve." World Development, Elsevier, 32(8), 1419-1439.

24. Strange, T. & Bayley A. (2008), Sustainable Development, Linking Economy, Society, Environment, OECD Insights.

ENVIRONMENTAL SUSTAINABILITY AS A COMPONENT SUSTAINABLE COMPETITIVENESS

Vladimir Knezevic[12]

Dragan Ivkovic[13]

INTRODUCTION

More than three decades in economic theory, the term of sustainable development has appeared. This approach is especially developed since the 80s of the last century, and is widely accepted by most reputable institutions that are involved in the monitoring of the global economy. And in the report on Global competitiveness in the world 2011-2012. this matter is handled for the first time by the World Economic Forum. Specifically, it isGCI (Global Competitiveness Index), which is regularly treated to the annual reports of this forum since 2005.year, does not reflect the long-term perspective of competitiveness, but only measure the current performance of each national economy.

This is the main reason why the index of sustainable competitiveness is defined (SCI), as well as outlining the methodology for its measurement and monitoring. This index includes factors that determine competitiveness in the long run, even if some of them are not integrated in the GCI. The general concept of competitiveness is preliminarily defined "... as the set of institutions, policies and factors that determine the level of productivity of a country, while ensuring the ability of future generations to meet their own needs." (Schwab 2011, p.54)

[12] Assistant Professor, Faculty of Business Economics and Entrepreneurship, Belgrade, Serbia, vknezevic40@yahoo.com

[13] Assistant Professor, Faculty of Business Economics and Entrepreneurship, Belgrade, Serbia, dragan.ict@gmail.com

Sustainable competitiveness concept includes all the factors contained in GCI which have long-term impact on competitiveness, as well as some new ones, concerning the environment, demography and society. Sustainable competitiveness according to this approach relates to the time horizon of the next twenty years. Here we have as many as 17 pillars of sustainable (or long term) competitiveness, which, by its nature, is divided into 5 even groups. (We recall that the already known and mentioned GCI is based on 12 pillars which are grouped into three sections.)

In any case, the interesting concept of long-term competitiveness index was not operationally useful in 2011, but in this Report its development actually began. Then it was noted that there are a whole set of issues that affect this aspect of the competition, but it has not resolved the question of their quantification in a satisfactory manner, and in particular:

1. Frequency of political conflict and mass violence;
2. Imbalances in the financial market crisis with potential;
3. The frequency of natural disasters;
4. Violation of the environment and use of resources;
5. Food security;
6. The spread of diseases that are not contagious;
7. Protection of workers.

THEORETICAL BASIS

In the next Global Competitiveness Report 2012-2013 of the world, the World Economic Forum has continued to work on further development of indicators and effectively established a new concept of sustainable competitiveness. The basic idea in designing the SCI is to show the relationship between economic development, environmental management and social sustainability. (Figure 1) is therefore led to a kind of redefinition of the very concept of sustainable competitiveness that now, according to the World Economic Forum, means "... set of institutions, policies and factors that make up the nation to remain productive in the long run while ensuring social and environmental sustainability"(Schwab 2012, p.52-53).

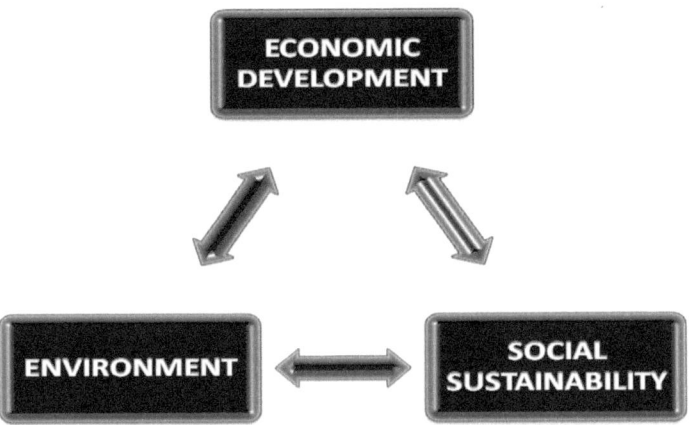

Figure 1. The philosophy of SCI

Source: Authors

This means that in the long-term competitiveness is considered as a kind of correction of GCI indicators relating to the management of environmental and social sustainability. It is thought that environmental sustainability is: "... the institutions, policies and factors that ensure the effective management of resources to ensure the prosperity of present and future generations." (Schwab 2012, p.52) On the other hand, social sustainability is: "... institutions and policy factors that allow all members of society to live in the best possible health, participation in politics, security, and to maximize their potential to contribute to and use of economic prosperity for the country in which they live." (Schwab 2012, p.52)

The subject of our interest is influence of environmental sustainability at the competitiveness of the national economy. This is theoretically a new approach to studying the relationship between ecology and economy. It departs from the traditional approach by which the environment, basically, represents for the economy a certain level of growth since the non-renewable resources are exploited and further narrows the possibility of pollution caused by industry (Schwab 2013, p.56) In fact, in practice, we examine events and trends that give us the right to conclude that the environment does not have to be a limiting factor in the growth of the global economy. It is more of a lower level of economic development, but as a national economy away from the stage, the growing awareness of the need for environmental sustainability, forming the political will in this regard, there is technological progress and economic structure ... Therefore, it is unrealistic to expect poor countries pressed urgent need to solve their difficult problems have as their objective the maintenance policy environment as a contribution to sustainable competitiveness in the coming decades. In this aspect, global cooperation and kind assistance of developed economies is necessary.

In theoretical terms, we could say that environmental sustainability and long-term competitiveness of the national economy has three primary connections as follows:

1. Efficiency in the use of natural resources with reliability;
2. Improved health;
3. Biodiversity for innovation.

Efficient use of natural resources involves extremely rational use of non-renewable and renewable only within their regenerative capacity in a reasonable time. This means that in terms of the sustainability of the environment necessary to reconcile economic rationality in the present with the needs of future generations of natural resources. This is also the case in further iteration and reducing environmental pollution. In this regard to provide sustainable competitiveness, it is necessary to engage all individuals and public and private institutions. The basis for each activity in this direction is primarily regulated the ownership of all economic resources.

Health of the nation is one of the main factors of competitiveness in the short and the long term. Specificity of sustainable competitiveness is that it is environmental sustainability factor affecting the long-term health of the population. This problem is particularly acute in developing countries, where it first developmental steps may be even intensified (Pacific Basin). In the world's leading economies (the U.S.) is a widespread awareness of the impact of environmental quality on national productivity, and conducted a number of analyzes aimed at determining the quantitative relationship between productivity in the national economy and the performance of different natural environments. We could conclude that in the long run, investment in environment sustainability indirectly means investing in people's health, and the main economic resource of which ultimately depends on the sustainable competitiveness.

Biodiversity in the shortest terms is the diversity of flora and fauna in the ecosystem. It is very important to the survival of the people in a particular territory. Thus, degradation of the environment in a particular country threatens the long-term productivity and worsening living conditions and work by reducing certain natural populations, and even their complete disappearance. These causes a threat to the raw material base for future economic development and even the survival of mankind have adverse effects on agricultural production. This problem is particularly acute in developing countries. For the future of the economy, the most important innovation, a reduction in the diversity of plant and animal life, and reduces the space for innovation and technological advancement, we now feel the most advanced and tomorrow it may limit competitiveness of other countries.

From all this it follows that the sustainability of the environment, as one of the two elements of sustainable competitiveness has special significance for developing countries as the most direct way threatens the long-term productivity in industries that are highly significant in their economic structure, such as agriculture, fisheries, forestry and tourism.

In addition, the improvement of the environment in another way contributes to the improvement of sustainable competitiveness, and to the reduction and mitigation of natural disasters, especially droughts, floods, destructive winds ... Thus it is made the protection of all economic resources from destruction, including most important - people.

It is an undeniable link between environmental sustainability and sustainable competitiveness, which, recall, has a time horizon of two decades. However, it remains questionable how environmental sustainability has an impact on current business productivity. There are indications that give this effect, at least at a high level of development, positive. (Schwab 2013, p.58)

ELEMENTS OF ENVIRONMENTAL SUSTAINABILITY

Of course, this developed approach to sustainable competitiveness implies a different methodology. We are here limited only to set of indicators to measure the sustainability of the environment (Figure 2), and then we will analyze them in detail.

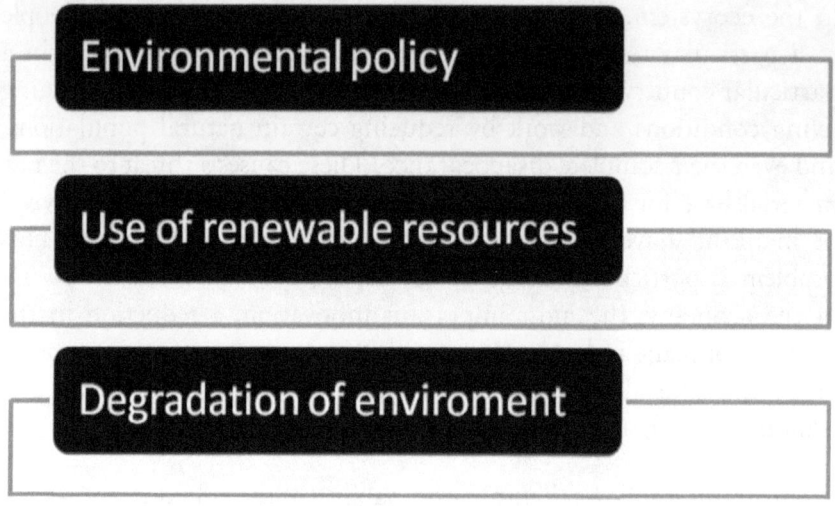

Figure 2. Environmental sustainability

Source: Authors

Each of these groups, however, still consists of three indicators separately evaluated.

Thus, the policy environment is monitored and evaluated through:

- environmental regulations (rigor and application);
- number of ratified international treaties on the protection of the environment, and
- protection of the biosphere on Earth.

So, the first indicator shows how much of the territory of a country is environmentally protected, and how these regulations are complied with. This actually shows how a country is dedicated to the preservation of its natural resources. Another indicator that shows exactly how many of the twenty-five international treaties in the field of a State has ratified, says in effect on the willingness of countries to international engagement and cooperation in the conservation and enhancement of the environment which is extremely important since it is almost impossible to do so only on national level. This is closely connected with the protection of the biosphere on Earth, which is practically inseparable, so this whole group of indicators actually assesses the political will of a country to engage in environmental protection.

Using renewable resources includes:

- intensity of irrigation in agriculture;
- exploitation of forests, and
- over-harvesting of fish.

As you can see, this group of factors deals with rationality, the use of natural resources, and their commercial exploitation. Foremost is the use of water for agricultural irrigation, which also represents an important element in ensuring food of the population. As for the ecological balance and the impact on the climate, harvesting for commercial purposes is even more important. The data for this indicator is very hard to come by, since the satellite record needed to monitor changes in the size of the territory covered by forests, but must undertake efforts in that direction, considering the great importance of this indicator. Similarly, the amount of harvested fish, which is economically very important today, but there is a great danger that uncontrolled conger threaten the survival of future generations.

Under the harm to the environment means:

- level of air pollution;
- intensity of carbon dioxide emissions, and
- quality of the environment.

The first group of indicators measures the political will to sustain the environment, another measures economic exploitation of the most important elements related to environmental sustainability, and the third group measures the specific level already achieved its degradation. This aspect is the most direct way connected with the violation of human health, and is therefore the first indicator related to the concentration of airborne particles harmful to health. It is certain that the damage to health of the population today, in the long run jeopardize not only the competition, but perhaps even survival. Therefore, the daily measurement of this phenomenon highlights the growing number of countries. In this connection, the parameter of carbon dioxide in addition to the health component has multiple meanings: represents a measure of energy efficiency, but also the negative impact of climate change that threaten the entire planet. Therefore, the issue of carbon emissions is to be solved on the global level.

THE IMPORTANCE OF ENVIRONMENTAL SUSTAINABILITY

The methodology of already known and standardized Global Competitiveness Index (GCI) is extended in this way, using the pillar of sustainable environment, which is the subject of our special interest, and social pillars of sustainability, in order to achieve a complex measure of sustainable competitiveness, which is the sustainable competitiveness index (SCI). The SCI is the average value of two custom GCI: correction using social sustainability and adjustments based on environmental sustainability. In doing so, it assumes that both approaches are equally affect the correction. This shows us the concept (Figure 3) to social sustainability and sustainable environment adjusted current competitiveness of the national economy, and help to assess the competitiveness of a particular national economy in the future, in the next 20 years, which is expressed through the SCI.

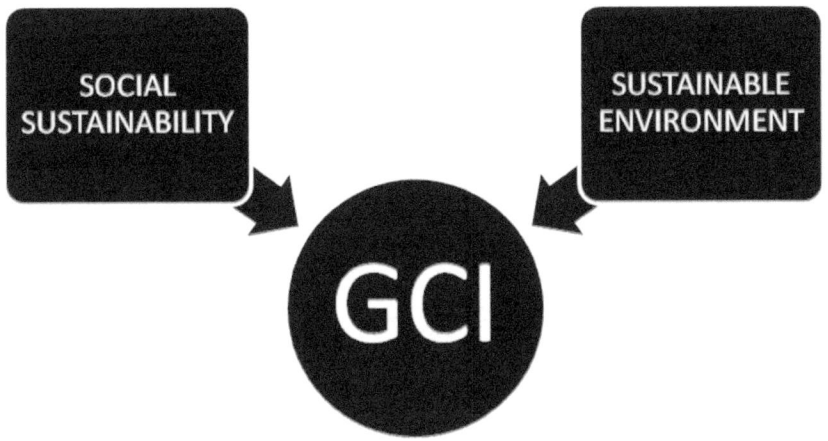

Figure 3. Formation of SCI

Source: Authors

Also, all of the mentioned indicators of environmental sustainability, a total of nine, which are described above, are of equal influence. For each national economy is measured from grade 0 to 7. This is the end of all quantified after mathematical operations (Schwab 2012, p.64-65), and the overall sustainability of the environment for the concrete industry, as a kind of corrective coefficient, whose value can range from 0.8 to 1.2.

At the end of the GCI is multiplied by the appropriate coefficient (0.8 to 1.2) in accordance with the value of the two new pillars of sustainable competitiveness (social viability and sustainability of the environment). These two resulting valuesare added together and divided by two. In this way, finally, in total, raised, or lowered, a basic value of the Global Competitiveness Index to a maximum of 20%.

Pilot study was carried out in 79 countries, according to the available data for 2012.or for 121 countries in 2013. Even the superficial look at this data tells us that the availability of data for the evaluation of sustainable competitiveness for far lower than that required for a standard calculation for the Global Competitiveness Index, given that the country coverage is lower. However, it is also noted the significant progress in this respect in a relatively short period of time. However, it is still very difficult to draw conclusions about the movement of sustainable competitiveness of individual countries, and further analyze the impact of environmental sustainability on this indicator in individual economies. This is because of short period of only two years, and about a relatively modest number of countries included in both of these reports.

We will take this opportunity to keep the results of the Western Balkan countries in which we illustrate the foregoing restrictions. In both World Economic Forum reports concerning sustainable competitiveness do not include all countries in the Western Balkans and to have that reminder, Croatia, Serbia, Bosnia and Herzegovina, Montenegro, Macedonia and Albania. Coverage of the region by measuring the sustainable competitiveness is partial, as observed in the first report includes data for only three countries, and only in the following are all represented.

According to the Report on Competition in the world, the countries of the Western Balkans are forward-exposed methodology observed the following assessment of environmental sustainability.

Table 1. Environmental sustainability in the Western Balkans

State	Mark	Impact on GCI	SCI
Croatia	4,39	Sparingly positive	4,24
Montenegro	4,13	Neutral	4,13
Macedonia	3,83	Sparingly negative	3,91
Serbia	3,74	Neutral	3,60
Albania	3,72	Neutral	3,76
B i H	3,44	Sparingly negative	3,55

Source: The Global Competitiveness Report 2013-2014

When considering environmental sustainability in the countries of the Western Balkans as a component of sustainable competitiveness it should be reminded that all these countries are relatively low ranked according to the value of the Global Competitiveness Index. In the same year in which the related data in the table the best placed country is Montenegro in 67 place, and even the weakest Serbia in 101 place out of 148 surveyed countries. Also it should be noted that in all cases the evaluations of environmental sustainability is weaker (score range is from 1 to 7) than the value of GCI, except in Croatia (GCI = 4.20)

From the table we also see that only in the case of Croatia environmental sustainability factor positively affects the long-term competitiveness, while in other countries of the Western Balkans the effect is generally neutral, while in Macedonia and Bosnia and Herzegovina is negative. It is also indicative that in the majority of countries in the areas of sustainable competitiveness weaker than current except in the case of Croatia and Albania. Thus, we may conclude that in general the Western Balkans constitute uncompetitive economy with poor prospects, and therefore all should make efforts to improve the environment that can fix the long term in this unsatisfactory situation.

THE CASE OF SERBIA

It is known that Serbia has an unsatisfactory competitiveness of the national economy that is getting worse in recent years. Since our country is ranked in both previous reports dealing with the sustainable competitiveness of the forward-exposed methodology, let's look at the results in the following table.

Table 2. Environmental sustainability in Serbia

Report	Mark	Influence	SCI
2012-13	3,71	Neutral	3.59
2013-14	3,74	Neutral	3,60

Source: The Global Competitiveness report 2012-13, 2013-14

The presented data do not give reason for optimism even in the long run. The first impression is that the sustainability of the environment and the overall index of sustainable competitiveness in our country the last two years is in stagnation. This is not to be satisfied with because the stagnation is rather low (recall that the assessment of the scale of 1 to 7). If we add to this the low and decreasing rank according to GCI in the specified period (95th and 101st place), we conclude that the neutral effect of environmental sustainability in the long-term competitiveness of the Serbian economy is certainly not acceptable. It is obvious that there is room for improvement.

CONCLUSION

In this paper, we give a brief overview of environmental sustainability as a component of 50% in the index of sustainable competitiveness of the methodology of the World Economic Forum. We have highlighted which elements constitute competitiveness, how they are quantitatively and qualitatively important, and how they influence the assessment of long-term competitiveness of the national economy. In particular, we look at the results of the Western Balkans, which were presented in last year's report on Global Competitiveness of the World economic to the forum since before they were all included in this analysis, but only half of them. Serbia additionally receives attention because of its results are in both so far published reports that deal with environmental sustainability as an element of sustainable competitiveness.

This paper is intended as a first step to indicate the importance of sustainable competitiveness as a relatively new idea in economic theory. In fact, there is a risk that due to current economic problems, long-term perspective is forgotten. On the other hand, we wanted to highlight economic aspects of environmental sustainability. Everybody is familiar with the importance of preserving and improving the environment from various aspects, which are by nature long-term themes, but the World Economic Forum makes the first shows how sustainability is an important environment for the sustainable competitiveness of the national economy. This is important for all the countries of the Western Balkans, and especially for our country.

REFERENCES

1. Alain, M., & Jean-Michel. (Eds.). (2007). Democrasy, freedom and Coercion, Cheltenham, UK: Edward Elgar Publishing Limited

2. Behrad, S. (2013) Performance Measures for Social Entrepeneur Institucions: Case of Iranian National Commission for UNESCO, International Review, br. 1-2

3. Bošnjak M. (2005) Konkurentnost i razvoj kao poluge evropske perspektive Srbije, Economic Annals No. 166, July-September

4. Chris J. Nutall (2003) Busines, Cambridge University Press, Cambridge, UK

5. Francois, L., & Howard, S. (Eds.). (2005). Antitrust, patents and copyright. Cheltenham, UK: Edward Elgar Publishing Limited

6. Friedman M. (1997) Kapitalizam i sloboda, Global Print, Novi Sad

7. Ghanbar, M., Mohsen, A. & Vahid, M. (2012). Impact of social capital on the identification and exploitation of entrepeneurial opportunities. International Review, 5-18

8. Hamel, G. i Prahald, C.K. (1994) Competing for the future, Harvard Business School Press, Boston

9. Kneževi , V. (2012) Contribution of entrepreneurship education competetiveness of the economy as a measure of its success in Radovic-Markovic, M. (Eds.), Education, Beograd: Faculty of Business Economics and Entrepreneurship, pp.219-240.

10. Kotlica S. i Cvetkovi N. (2007) Nova ekonomija u svetu koji se menja, Megatrend univerzitet, Beograd

11. Michelle, C., & Nieves Perez, S. (Eds.). (2010). European Union politics-thirdedition, New York: Oxford university press.

12. Mihajlovi , B., Parauši , V., i Simonovi , Z. (2007) Analiza faktora poslovnog ambijenta Srbije u završnoj fazi ekonomske tranzicije, Institut za ekonomiku poljoprivrede, Beograd

13. Schwab, K. (Eds.). (2010). The global competitiveness report 2010-2011 Geneva: World economic forum. Preuzeto sa: http://www.weforum.org/reports

14. Schwab, K. (Eds.). (2011). The global competitiveness report 2011-2012 Geneva: World economic forum. Preuzeto sa: http://www.weforum.org/reports

15. Schwab, K. (Eds.). (2012). The global competitiveness report 2012-2013 Geneva: World economic forum. Preuzeto sa: http://www.weforum.org/reports

16. Schwab, K. (Eds.). (2013). The global competitiveness report 2013-2014 Geneva: World economic forum. Preuzeto sa: http://www.weforum.org/reports

OPPORTUNITIES AND OBSTACLES FOR COMPOSTING SOLID WASTE: THE CASE OF SMALL SIZE MUNICIPALITY IN SERBIA[14]

Ivan Stosic[15]

Zvonko Brnjas[16]

INTRODUCTION

The Green Economy could be a possible answer to the great challenges which the world is facing in the current time of economic and financial crisis. It could be an answer not only for large developed economies, but also for small underdeveloped, poor performing societies and economies similar to that of Serbia. Actually, applying the concept of the Green Economy may happen to be the only chance for these countries to recover and catch up with the developed world.

The Green Economy is about connecting two key issues related to the economy and social development: creation of benefits for the people in general and at the same time providing socially balanced development. In this way Green Economy is becoming key pillar of the sustainable development of the economy and society as a whole. In this sense Green Economy comprise all human activities aiming at production

---

[14] This paper is a part of research project: 179015 - Challenges and prospects of structural changes in Serbia: Strategic directions for economic development and harmonization with EU requirements financed by the Ministry of Education and Science of the Republic of Serbia

[15] Institute of Economic Sciences, Belgrade, Serbia, ivan.stosic@ien.bg.ac.rs, stosic80@ptt.rs

[16] Belgrade Banking Academy, Belgrade, Serbia, zvonko.brnjas@bba.edu.rs

of goods and providing of services which result in preservation and improved quality of the environment. More specifically, Green Economy includes all businesses which contribute to preservation of eco-systems, biodiversity, increased energy efficiency and decreased waste creation and pollution of all kinds.

Sustainable waste management complements the Green Economy concept especially given the pivotal role of the waste sector in creating a low carbon, circular economy where the generation of waste and harmful substances is minimized, the use of reutilized, recycled or recovered materials is maximized, and disposed waste minimized; where all these processes are managed to avoid damage to the environment and human health (*Sustainable Solid Waste Management & the Green Economy, 2013*).

METHODOLOGY

This paper is dealing with a very specific segment of the Green Economy – the process of composting which, having in mind the Serbian natural resources and importance of agriculture for its economy – could be important piece in developing Green Economy.

The aim of this paper is to study opportunities for and obstacles to solid waste composting based on empirical evaluation of the possibilities for establishing a centralized composting facility in a small municipality in Serbia and its viable functioning. The approach reported in this paper could be applied to "a pre-feasibility first cut comparison" in a decision-making framework for enhancing solid waste management though the Western Balkan countries.

For the purpose of research in this study, the scientific literature has been systematically and logically studied as well as selected external secondary data taken from "multi-country" comparative empirical examinations and a case study examining the potential for production and placement of compost in the market produced in a small Serbian municipality.

COMPOSTING

Composting is a biological process, in which the organic matter is biodegraded by microorganisms under controlled conditions of temperature, moisture content, oxygen, PH and the retention time that can be initiated by mixing biodegradable organic matter with bulking agents to enhance the porosity of the mixture. This method has a lot of qualitative benefits such as: reducing the amount of municipal solid waste, transportation cost of carrying municipal solid waste to land fill, emissions and leachate of landfill, increasing life span of landfill and reducing land use.

Composting has a long history in many parts of Europe. Originally it was used in the form of simple processes on a small scale for farm and back yard composting. In the last two decades, composting has received renewed and widened interest as a means of addressing current waste management challenges, in particular for reducing the amount of wastes going to landfills. The production of compost is also seen as an opportunity for providing a material that can be used as an organic fertilizer or as a component in growing media or soil improver.

The main driving force to enhance composting in European Union (EU) has been given by policy - *The European Landfill Directive EC, 1999*, and biodegradable waste disposal ban. Today, modern waste treatment programs in most countries of EU cannot be imagined without source separation and composting, either at individual, local or regional level, to treat part of this organic fraction, namely garden and park waste (green waste), kitchen waste, and also agricultural and biodegradable industrial waste.

Serbia has also introduced a regulation (*Decree on Waste Disposal of Landfills, 2010*) which anticipates the establishment of a controlled biodegradable waste disposal system and reduction of biodegradable waste disposal at landfills at least by 50% by 2020. This has enabled Serbia to take into consideration the feasibility and cost effectiveness of various composting methods.

CASE-STUDY PRESENTATION

Starting from the possibilities of collecting certain types of organic solid waste from the municipality area, as well as the local marketing potentials, the viability of establishing central composting facility has been analyzed in the case of small municipality D. in Serbia.

Existing Utility Solid Waste Management System

Faced with problems in solid waste management the D. municipality in Serbia began considering its options and the cost effectiveness of building a composting facility in its territory.

This is a relatively small municipality. Namely, D. municipality occupies 481 square kmand has population of 11,748 people, where 6,968 of them live in the urban area, and 3,147 in suburban villages and 1,623 in other villages. The density is 24 people per 1 square km. The density of population in the municipality varies from one extreme to another. The population mostly lives in the urban area and in several suburban places.

Local Public Utility Company (PUC) is responsible to collect, transport and dispose solid waste from the urban area and from the area of five suburban local communities. Local PUC covers a territory of around 295 hectares. Waste collection covers around 9,000 inhabitants, or over 2,500 households. In addition to the household waste, the PC collects commercial waste, primarily, from local stores, office buildings, banks, hotels, restaurants, gas stations, etc. The said buildings dispose of their waste in containers made to hold household waste.

Currently solid waste in D. municipality is collected by means of standard metal containers and plastic bins. Over 300 metal containers are used and over 1,500 standard plastic bins (green and blue) – green bins are used for utility waste and blue ones are used for secondary raw material disposal. Containers in the urban area are emptied daily while bins scattered around suburban local communities are emptied once a week.

Around 5,407 tons of utility waste was disposed to the local landfill during 2010. By analyzing the morphological composition of the waste it has been found that biodegradable waste (food remains, waste collected from public areas, wood, paper, etc.), suitable for anaerobic or aerobic degradation, accounts for a significant share in the structure of the waste.

Table 1. Utility waste amount and structure on
the D. municipality landfill in 2010

Waste Type	Amount (kg/ per day)	Structure in %
Organic Matter	215	19.6
Paper	172	15.7
Textile	81.5	7.4
Metal	10	0.9
Plastic	152	13.9
Rubber	13	1.2
Glass	16	1.5
Construction Waste	59	5.4
Wood	50	4.5
Waste Collected from Public Areas	138	12.6
Other	191	17.5
Total	1,097.5	100.0

With the aim of reducing the amount of waste disposed at the local landfill, and in order to protect and improve the environment and create conditions which would enable reduction of the utility fee, the local authorities of D. municipality decided to organize solid waste recycling by composting.

PLANNED COMPOSTING FACILITY IN D. MUNICIPALITY, SERBIA

Composting, generally, may be organized in several ways. One concept implies building a central composting facility to serve a particular area (municipality), while the other concept involves composting of garden waste in individual households at home. D. municipality opted for a centralized composting facility.

Depending on the waste collection system the centralized composting facility may: compost utility waste and garden waste or have those two separated. In that respect, waste collection may be organized in such way to include only garden waste, or only utility waste or both of them together. In the case of D. municipality central composting facility it is recommendable to collect garden waste separately from other organic household waste.

A composting process in a central facility serving a particular area (municipality) is basically composed of the following elements: receiving and sorting waste, waste grinding, composting in a closed system, outdoor stabilization of the compost – lined up piles, waste sieving and waste storage. The basic process diagram is shown below (*Feasibility Study for Building Composting Facility, 2011*):

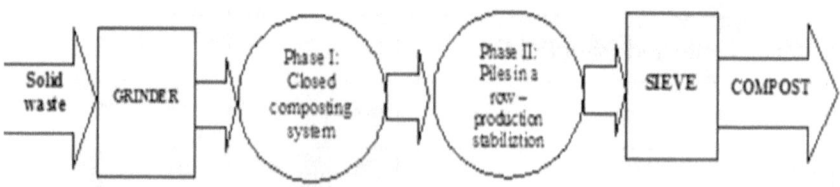

Figure 1. Diagram of the composting process in D. municipality

According to the conceptual design of the composting facility in D. municipality, Serbia, waste would be received in an indoor space-hangar, where the waste would be directly unloaded from trucks. The hangar should have an appropriate concrete base and be roofed with an appropriate steel structure. The anticipated area of the facility is 100 square m, and its height 5 m. Waste would be disposed for a week before the appropriate amount which can be composted is collected.

Once the waste is unloaded from trucks workers will manually separate waste which is not suitable for composting: all types of plastic, textile waste, metal waste, etc. Waste that can be composted is of organic origin (food waste), garden waste (green waste) and wood. However, in order for garden waste composting to be feasible a separate waste collection system needs to be put in place.

Once sorted out, the waste needs to be crushed. This operation helps mixing the waste and obtaining waste particles of appropriate size which are easy to degrade. Considering that the project is made for small amounts of waste (up to 5.4 tons a day), a HFG I type composting grinder should be installed in the hangar used for waste collection.

Utility waste should be composted in a closed system (in-vessel composting box) in order to control the composting process at the beginning in terms of the amount of moisture and oxygen and to provide optimal temperature that would allow destroying pathogens and weed seeds. Here, two options were taken into consideration:

Option A –This option included consideration of mixing utility waste and waste collected from public areas (garden waste) and wood for obtaining an optimal composition in terms of ratio of carbon and nitrogen. The content of moisture would be regulated by adding water until 60% of water is achieved. The amounts of waste that could be composted within Option A (which suggested mixing organic waste with wood and waste collected from public areas – green waste) in D. municipality are as follows:

Table 2. Amounts of waste for composting – Option A

Waste Type	Mass t/y	Mass kg/day	C/N
Organic Matter	1,059,230.07	2,902.00	15.6
Wood	246,332.57	674.88	200.0
Waste Collected from Public Areas	679,877.90	1,862.68	22.8
Total	3,185,440.55	5,439.56	40.94

Option B –This Option only considered mixing utility waste with wood while green waste would be composted in separate space. The amounts of waste that could be composted within Option B (suggesting mixing organic waste with wood and separate composting of waste collected from public areas) in D. municipality are as follows:

Table 3. Amounts of waste for composting – Option B

Waste Type	Mass t/y	Mass kg/day	C/N
Organic Matter	1,059,230.07	2,902,00	15.6
Wood	246,332.57	674.88	200.0
Total	2,205,562.64	3,576.88	50.39

An in-vessel reactor or a closed composting system implies the use of closed "containers", with appropriate air nozzles. The process includes filling containers with waste of appropriate composition (waste is collected for a week) and granulation (after grinding) and leaving it inside to get composted within seven days. During this period, air is blown inside to secure a sufficient amount of oxygen and aerobic conditions. After a week the waste would be transferred into another container where composting would be continued and the first container would be filled with new waste.

The system is presented with two identical containers which enable additional mixing of waste during composting. This process provides temperature above 55°C which is sufficient to destroy pathogens which may be present due to the composition of the waste, subject to composting. In order to make sure that the waste continues its stabilization, the presence of pathogens should be checked after 14 days.

It is anticipated not to use any additional air blowing systems but to form a pile that would allow natural ventilation. In order to achieve this, piles need to be not more than 3 m high and 12-15 m long. Since the compost needs to be additionally mixed during the maturing process, sufficient space needs to be secured to allow composting several piles at once.

Composting lasts for 9 weeks (63 days) in total, or 2 weeks in an in-vessel composting system and 7 weeks of stabilization and maturing. The anticipated time for composting green waste is 120 days. Keeping the waste in one place should last for 15 days. Once the stabilization and maturing of compost is done, it needs to be sieved in order to obtain granules of the size required by the market. Larger particles (fractions) may be used as inert material for covering waste on landfills. Compost should be kept in a closed space – a hangar, which would be of the same or similar construction as the space used for waste disposal and grinding.

Compost production is from a technological and technical standpoint a relatively simple process which does not require any special high technology. The total investments into fixed assets, or rather the construction of a hangar for waste disposal and a hangar for compost storage and the accompanying infrastructure, that is a concrete pad, equipment - a composting grinder, a loader, a composting system and a sieve are as follows:

Table 4. Investments into fixed assets for a waste composting facility

	Cost Items	Investments in €
I	*Fixed Assets*	*283,000*
1.	Building	20,000
1.1.	Hangar for Waste Disposal	10,000
1.2.	Hangar for Waste Storage	10,000
2.	Concrete Pad (400 m²)	33,000
3.	Equipment	230,000
3.1.	Composting Grinder Type HFG I	20,000
3.2.	Loader	35,000
3.3.	Composting System (2 pieces)	150,000
3.4.	Sieve	25,000

The working capital is planned at the lowest level of 5% of the total revenues. The assumed average turnover ratio is 20.

The proposed funding for the structure includes two main sources of finance: a) local, municipal revenues which would be used to fund the construction of structures and infrastructure and for working capital. This accounts for around 60 thousand €, that is, around 20% of the total investment; b) equipment would be procured thanks to domestic and foreign donations. In total this is 230 thousand €, or, around 80% of the total investment.

VARIOUS COMPOST USES

The use of municipal solid waste compost in agriculture has many benefits to soil, crops, and the environment. If the fermentation is correctly managed, pathogens are killed during the heat period. Compost can reduce the incidence of variant plant diseases. Some researchers have shown that applying compost may efficiently prevent some plant diseases (*Hoitink, et. al., 1997*). Bacteria attached to the roots are able to secrete antibiotics which improve a plant's resistance to illness. Based on that, pesticides may be eliminated or considerably reduced from plant production.

Composting helps to optimize nutrient management and the land application of compost may contribute to combating soil organic matter decline and soil erosion (*Van Camp et al, 2004*). Compost land application completes a circle whereby nutrients and organic matter which have been removed in the harvested produce are replaced (*Diener et al, 1993*). The recycling of compost to land is considered as a way of maintaining or restoring the quality of soils, mainly because of the fertilizing or improving properties of the organic matter contained in them.

Furthermore, it may contribute to carbon sequestration and may partially replace peat and fertilizers (*Smith et al, 2001*). Compost application to agricultural land needs to be carried out in a manner that ensures sustainable development. Management systems have to be developed to enable to maximize agronomics benefit, whilst ensuring the protection of environmental quality. The main determinant for efficient agronomics use is nitrogen availability, high nitrogen utilization in agriculture from mineral fertilizers is well established and understood, whereas increasing the nitrogen use efficiency of organic fertilizers requires further investigation (*Amlinger et al, 2003*).

Compost is considered a multifunctional soil improver. It is therefore used in agriculture and horticulture as well as to produce topsoil for landscaping or land restoration. The application of compost usually improves the physical, biological and chemical properties of soil. Repeated application of compost leads to an increase in soil organic matter, it often helps to reduce erosion, it increases water retention capacity and pH buffer capacity, and it improves the physical structure of soil (aggregate stability, density, pore size). Composts may also improve the biological activity of the soil.

Compost is often considered an organic fertilizer, although the fertilizer function of compost (supply of nutrients) is, in many cases, less pronounced than the general soil improvement function. Furthermore, compost is used as component of growing media particularly in hobby applications (potting soil), and in professional applications (greenhouses, container cultures).

According to the *"Compost production and use in the EU"* study, compost's basic purposes in the EU are as follows:

- Agriculture, with average share of 50%, where this percentage is showing a growing tendency; for these purposes predominantly fresh compost is used
- Landscaping – soil conditioning - with 20% share
- Production of some intermediate products and potting soil – with an average 20% share in the EU
- Retail sale with average 20% share (potting soil)

EU countries pay a lot of attention to regular control of compost production and use. Germany and Austria have established clear standards of use: for organic food production, for food production and for non-food purposes. On the other hand, some EU countries still haven't set them - Romania, Bulgaria, Latvia, etc. (*Barth, 2010*).

TRENDS IN COMPOST PRODUCTION AND USE IN THE EU

In EU27 compost use is relatively high and rising. It is estimated (due to incomplete or insufficiently reliable data) that in 2008 compost use was around 12-13 million tons (*Biodegradable waste subject to biological treatment, 2012*).

Of the total amount of compost produced in the EU green compost (peels from fruit and vegetables, cut flowers or waste from mowed grass, branches, etc.) accounted for around 43% or around 5.7 million tons, bio-waste compost (obtained by recycling selected organic waste collected from households) was around 36% or around 4.8 million tons, while the consumption of compost obtained by recycling non-selected utility waste – brown compost was around 1.4 million tons or around 10.3%, and compost obtained by recycling of sewer material around 1.4 million tons.

Generally, in 2010 demand in the EU exceeded supply. Namely, the potential of the EU27 market in terms of compost demand is considerably higher and its absorption possibilities are estimated at as many as around 40 million tons a year. Due to insufficient supply in some countries compost is used only for organic production, processing and soil mixtures and gardening.

COMPOST PRICES

The prices of compost considerably vary depending on its quality, packaging and brand. Simultaneously, depending on specific market circumstances prices vary significantly from one EU country to another.

Basically, different uses of compost cost differently. In the EU, the average price for compost used in agriculture is around 5-6.5 €/t, but in some EU countries producers manage to place it at a price of 14-15 €/t. Average prices of compost intended for organic agricultural production are around 15 €/t (in some EU countries they are considerably higher – around 40 €/t) (*Barth, 2010*).

Compost produced by the recognized producers and packed in smaller commercial packages (recognizable brands) has the highest price tags, its prices range between 160 €/t and 300 €/t. On the other hand, the lowest priced compost (of poorer quality) is that used for soil re-cultivation and covering and in the EU its price is on average 0.6 € /t (*Barth, 2010*).

TRENDS IN COMPOST PRODUCTION AND USE IN SERBIA

Compost production in Serbia has not been developed yet. According to the available data, with the exception of some smaller pilot facilities, no business is handling compost production for fertilizing purposes of for soil conditioning. Also, as opposed to the situation in many EU countries, local composting at homes and/or contracted composting by interested individuals have also been poorly developed (only compost production for mushroom growing the situation is somewhat developed in Serbia).

Due to relatively low price which cannot "bear" costs of long distance transport, compost has not been subject to foreign trade. This is confirmed by the data provided by the Serbian Statistics Office about trends in the Serbian foreign trade of fertilizers originating from animals or plants. The data show that around 125-250 tons of this type of fertilizers is imported annually in Serbia.

POTENTIAL FOR THE COMPOST USE IN SERBIA

Potential for the compost use in Serbia is not insignificant. This has been concluded from the analysis of the basic determinants of demand for compost. The basic determinants of demand for compost in the domestic market are as follows: the level and structure of vegetable and fruit production in Serbia, tendencies in organic agricultural production, the level of development of flower growing and gardening as well as the tendency regarding the use of some types of fertilizers and compost.

The level and structure of vegetables and fruit production in Serbia – InEU27 around 3% of the total arable land needs to be treated with various types of compost. The largest part of that pertains to vegetable and fruit production. By analogy, compost may be used in Serbia for vegetable and fruit production.

Vegetable and fruit production in Serbia has been relatively developed and requires significant amounts of various fertilizers, despite of numerous problems and large oscillations in annual yields. In 2007-2013, the level of vegetable and fruit production in Serbia, according to the Serbian Statistics Office was as follows: potato 800-900 thousand tones, tomato 150-200 thousand tones, peas 35-42 thousand tones, cabbage 280-330 thousand tones, onion 116-140 thousand tones, pepper 150-170 thousand tones, beans 39-46 thousand tones, carrot 56-68 thousand tones, apple 245-300 thousand tones, plum 600-700 thousand tones, strawberry 33-35 thousand tones, raspberry 75-90 thousand tones, peach 65-77 thousand tones, etc.

Tendencies in Organic Agricultural Production Development- In the past ten years, the popularity and economic importance of the consumption of organic products has been growing, and arable land where organic products are grown is growing in size, year in year out. The leading EU countries, in terms of the size of the land where organic products have been grown in 2008, were Spain (1.3 million ha), Italy (1.0 million ha), Germany (0.9 million ha) and Great Britain (0.7 million ha). (*Barth, 2010*).

The total area of land used for organic production in the Republic of Serbia is still modest with tendency towards intensive growth. According to data submitted by four authorized certification organizations in 2009, the total area used for organic production covered 2,876.5 ha.

According to the *Organic Agriculture in Serbia* report the total arable land covered with organic production in Serbia were around 8,500-9,000 ha. Authorized certification organizations certified 1,610 ha used for perennial organic plants and their products (apples, raspberries, blackberries, plums, sour cherries), while around 800 ha of such orchards in the process of conversion. Simultaneously, 1,240 ha have been certified or are in the process of conversion for growing hardy annuals (vegetables, soy beans, wheat, and corn). Around 2,300 ha are covered with meadows and grazing land which are in the process of conversion, or have already been certified for organic production. The largest area covered with organic production is in South and West Serbia and in Vojvodina.

The total number of producers or farms where organic production methods have been implemented is around 3,000, mostly small individual producers – the largest number of them has less than 6 ha. However, the number of producers with large land areas is growing, and those are mostly raspberry producers and some fruit and vegetable producers.

The leading producers of organic products are: "Zdravo organic" Selen a, "Foodland", "Royal Eco Food", "Sirogojno Company", "Zadrugar", "Radoslovi" Niš, "Mondi", "Hemel", "Midi organic", "Biofarma", "Agrounik", BMD, "Suncokret", "Biosil", etc. (*Organic Agriculture in Serbia*, 2011).

The Serbia's objective is to increase the total area of land certified for organic production to 50,000 ha by 2014, according to the National Agricultural and Rural Development Plan.

This is, simultaneously, great opportunity for compost placement. Given that organic products are becoming more and more appreciated in the domestic and foreign markets, trends in compost use in Serbia look very optimistic.

Flower and decorative plant production is modest in Serbia, and the market needs are mostly met by imported plants. According to data provided by the Serbian Statistics Office areas covered with flowers and decorative plants in the last six years have been between 1,000 and 1,360 hectares. The ownership structure is dominated by individual producers with around 90% of land, while the public sector has only 10% of such land. Produced are mostly cut flowers (carnations, roses, gerberas, chrysanthemum, tulips, gladiolus and freesias) and seedlings (begonias, petunias).

Due to favorable climate and the length of the vegetation period Serbia has good conditions for flower plantations in large open spaces rather than just in covered, protected areas.

Trends in the use of some types of fertilizers and compost – Different standards exist regarding the use of some types of fertilizers and compost. Although there are significant differences, most frequently used compost is between 6 to 10 tons of dry matter by hectare a year.

For re-cultivation considerably more compost is used, between 100 and 400 tons of dry matter per hectare.

The use of compost as fertilizer and soil conditioner in the Serbian market has been in its introductory phase. Domestic production is underdeveloped and the total consumption is symbolic, the production includes only smaller producers who produce compost for their personal use.

Expected trends in vegetable and fruit production, tendencies in organic agricultural production development and flower production and gardening will not have a limiting effect on the growth of compost production in Serbia.

Namely, the total area of land in Serbia - around 276-285 thousand hectares covered by different vegetable plants, around 240 thousand ha of orchards, organic production of food on the expected 50 thousand ha, and flower production on around 1.5 thousand ha, and home gardening, may absorb considerably larger amounts of compost.

Beginning with average EU27 standards pertinent to compost use (compost used on around 3% of arable land where 4-6 tons of dry matter is used by hectare a year) only fruit and vegetable production in Serbia could absorb around 125 thousand tons of compost (mostly lower quality compost), and almost the same amount (around 110-120 thousand tones) could be used for organic food production, home gardening and flower production (mostly better quality compost).

Still, due to differences in agro-technical measures applied in Serbia and EU countries, and the fact that this is basically a new product for the local market, realistically, in this initial phase, in the period 2012-2014, it would be possible to sell around 100-110 thousand tons of compost a year in Serbia. For this reason it is realistic to expect somewhat lower, but relatively high potential for selling compost in Serbia.

BUSINESS FINANCIAL ANALYSIS

It has been planned to produce two basic types of compost in the facility in D. municipality: Compost No. 1 ("bio waste", quality) which is a lower to mid quality product and Compost No. 2 which is a product of better quality ("green compost" quality).

The price of compost will be formed based on market research and sales possibility: for compost No. 1- 90 € by tone and compost No. 2. - 260 € by tone.

Based on the scope and structure of compost production (Table 5) and prices, the potential revenues of the facility in D. municipality have been formed (Table 6).

Table 5. Total annual production, in tonnes

Type	Unit Measure	1. year	2.-15. Year
Compost 1	Tones a year	595	703
Compost 2	Tones a year	60	224
Total		655	927

Table 6. Total revenues, in €

Type	Price per ton in €	1. year	2.-15. Year
Compost 1	90	53,550	63,270
Compost 2	260	15,678	58,240
Total		69,228	121,510

Total revenues were projected based on the assumption that in the first year around 60% of the facility's capacity is exploited (due to the period which needs to elapse for full capacities to be activated), and as of the second year it would be 121.5 thousand € a year.

Costs of doing business for the compost facility in D. municipality would include the following basic categories: costs of waste transport to the place where it will be processed (around 38 thousand € a year), costs of fixed assets depreciation (2% for buildings and 10% for equipment), costs of investment maintenance of fixed assets (1% annual rate for buildings and 2% for equipment) and costs of salaries of 5 employees in this facility (around 28 thousand € a year).

Cash flows have been formed based on the above mentioned premises: a) income statement with operating results- they are in this specific case positive in all years of exploitation, except in the first year when small losses will happen due to the fact that the capacities will not be fully used; b) the financial flow shows liquidity and shows that this project is liquid in all years of exploitation even in its first year, which means that the expected small losses in the first year will not threaten its liquidity; and c) economic flow which represents a basis for the calculation of net present value and internal rate of return as key indicators of profitability.

Project's net present value (*Net Present Value – NPV*) represents the so-called elimination criterion for project evaluation. Namely, its negative value means that a project cannot return what has been invested in it, which makes it unacceptable for investors, while its positive value means that the invested funds will be returned and provide added value (*Guide to cost-benefit analysis of investment projects*). In this concrete case net present value is 3.565 €, which means that the project of the composting facility in D. municipality is positive and acceptable for investing.

Project's internal rate of return (*Internal Rate of Return – IRR*) is an indicator showing the level of its profitability. The level above the threshold shows that the project is acceptable, that is, sufficiently attractive for investors and that it can be financed. This rate is usually used as the so-called discount factor and in this calculation it is 10%. Since the project's internal rate of return is 10.2%, this means that it is above the set threshold and thus the project of the facility for compost production in D. municipality is acceptable for investors from the standpoint of this indicator as well.

The Compost production facility in D. municipality will, under the given assumptions, return the invested funds in the eighth year of exploitation.

The sensitivity analysis of the project has shown the following: a) The project of the composting facility in D. municipality is highly sensitive to changes in total revenues— reduction of revenues as low as below 5% (more precisely – 0.5%) makes this project unacceptable (*NPV* negative, and *IRR* goes down below threshold rate), b) The project of the composting facility in D. municipality is highly sensitive to changes in direct material costs: increase of direct material costs of as low as 5% makes it unprofitable, while the same increase of these costs increases *IRR* to 11.0%; and finally c) The project of the composting facility in D. municipality is relatively sensitive to changes in investments: 5% increase of investments makes it unprofitable: *NPV* is negative, and *IRR* is below the threshold value of 10%.

From the standpoint of the level of use of capacities, the break-even-point of the project for composting facility in D. municipality is relatively low – it is 64.7%. This means that it is sufficient to achieve this level of use of capacities and that if other conditions remain unchanged, the project will enter the zone of positive business results.

RESULTS AND DISCUSSION

The operation of compost production facilities is state-of-the-art in many EU countries, but not Serbia. In Serbia, compost production is at the beginning of the road, but has huge potential. However, organizing compost production is followed by a series of risks such as:

- The basic market-related risk is the risk pertinent to sale, primarily in the initial phase. This is given the fact that compost is relatively new product in the domestic market and that consumers haven't developed a habit to use it. Therefore, the first phases of development of compost production should include specific marketing – promotional-educational efforts until demand is raised to the required level. In later phases, given the estimated needs for compost in the domestic market, sale shouldn't be the problem.

- A key to the success of a composting operation is a marketing or distribution program for compost products. To develop long term markets, the products must be of consistently high quality. Other essential marketing factors include planning, knowledge about end users, following basic marketing principles and overcoming possible regulatory barriers and product stigma. Compost characteristics desired by end users vary with intended uses, but most compost users look for the following elements:
- Quality (moisture, odor, feel, particle size, stability, nutrient concentration, product consistency, and a lack of weed seeds, phototoxic compounds and other contaminants)
- Price (should be competitive with other fertilizers, although high quality and performance can justify a higher price)
- Appearance (uniform texture, relatively dry, earthy color)
- Information (product s benefits, nutrient and pH analysis, and application rates and procedures)
- Reliable supply (*Mohee, Mudhoo, 2005*)
- In the domain of market-related risks, prices may also represent a significant risk. Due to limited production, the pricing level which would secure positive business results is relatively high: 90 € /t for lower quality compost and 260 €/t for better quality compost. These are the prices which may be obtained in developed markets, but is very uncertain whether they can be obtained in the domestic market, especially in the period when customers are getting used to the new product.
- The risk related to supply market exist, that is the risk whether there will be sufficient amounts of available biodegradable waste of appropriate type, since it is the basic source of inputs the facility needs. The risk concerns both the total amounts and their composition in terms of the percentage of the organic component.

- Financial risks may be, primarily, tied to a high degree of sensitivity of financial indicators: the project is extremely sensitive to every change of costs, and even changes in investments. Given the mentioned reserves about the prices, the risk tied to the sensitivity to changes of revenues is particularly high. Any deviation from the projected prices would make the project unacceptable.

To avoid failures and to speed up the process, experiences from Europe can be used. Compost-related national regulations as well as compost quality certification schemes has to be established for ensuring the usefulness of compost and for achieving the desired levels of health and environment protection. Moreover, there is a need to work towards a sustainable compost management system, which requires institutional, financial and economic sustainability.

CONCLUSIONS

Improving the waste management system is one of the main components of initiating the Green Economy in Serbia, and within it, spreading the practice of composting by using an adequate technology, could be quite important.

Serbia still hasn't developed an organized system of waste management which would cover generation, collection, transport, storage, treatment and final disposal. Biodegradable waste hasn't been separated and bio hazardous and industrial waste often finds their way to landfills. The existing degree of recycling, or the use of waste is insufficient. However, as Serbian laws are harmonized with the EU laws and practice, the issue of waste management will be getting more and more attention. As part of that, composting, as a type of recycling, will appear as one of available options for enhancing solid waste management. At the same time the composting could be an important segment in developing Green Economy in Serbia.

Starting from the possibilities of collecting certain types of organic solid waste as well as the local marketing potentials, the organizing compost production, in the case of small sized municipality in Serbia, shows that opportunities exist to successfully commercialize of all produced compost. Furthermore, the financial analysis points out that this could be a sustainable, financially cost-effective project.

However, organizing compost production will face certain number of challenges, primarily in terms of market-related and financial risks. It is clear from this analysis that strong local government involvement and financial support is therefore necessary for leadership and infrastructural deployment of compost production in Serbia.

REFERENCES

1. Amlinger F., Götz, B., Dreher P., Geszti J., Weissteiner, C., (2003), Nitrogen in bio waste and yard waste compost: dynamics of mobilization and availability a review, *European Journal of Soil Biology* 39, pp. 107-116.

2. Barth J., (2010), *Markets for compost and digestate in Europe-Situation, requirements, future development,* ECN and INFORMA, On line at: http://compost.it/biblio/2010_beacon_conference_perugia/2nd_day/5.c%20-%20 Barth.pdf

3. Council Directive 1999/31/EC of 26 April 1999 on the landfill of waste (OJ L 182, 16.7.1999), The European Landfill Directive, On line at: http://eur-lex.europa.eu/LexUriServ/LexUriServ.do?uri=OJ : L:1999:182:0001:0001:EN:PDF

4. Diener R.G., Collins, A.R., Martin, J.H., Bryan W.B., (1993), Composting of source-separated municipal solid waste for agricultural utilization a conceptual approach for closing the loop. *Applied Engineering in Agriculture* 9 (5), pp. 427-436.

5. Guide, (2008), *Guide to cost-benefit analysis of investment projects, European Commission Directorate General Regional Policy,* On line

at: http://ec.europa.eu/regional_policy/sources/docgener/guides/cost/guide2008_en.pdf

6. Hoitink H.A.J., Stone A.G., Han D.Y., (1997), Suppression of plant diseases by composts, *HortScience*, 32(2), pp. 184-187.

7. Marz U. et al, (2011), *Organic Agriculture in Serbia At a Glance*, Deutsche Gesellschaft für Technische Zusammenarbeit (GTZ), Serbia

8. Mohee R., Mudhoo A., (2005), Analysis of the physical properties of an in-vessel composting matrix, *Powder Technology*, 155, pp. 92-99.

9. *National Agriculture and Rural Development Program 2011 – 2013*, (2011), Ministry of Agriculture, Forestry and Water Management of Republic of Serbia

10. *Organic Agriculture in Serbia At a Glance* (2011), Deutsche Gesellschaft für Technische Zusammenarbeit (GTZ) GmbH Economic Development Program ACCESS, 2011,

11. Smith, A., Brown, K., Ogilvie, S., Rushton, K., Bates, J. (2001), *Waste management options and climate change*. Final report to the European Commission, DG Environment. Luxembourg: Office for Official Publications of the European Communities

12. Statistical Office of the Republic of Serbia, On line at: http://www.stat.gov.rs/

13. Strategy, (2010), *Waste Management Strategy for the period 2010-2019*, Official Gazette of Republic of Serbia, n. 29/2010.

14. Study, (2011) *Feasibility Study for Building Composting Facility*, GTZ, Belgrade, Serbia

15. Study, (2013), *Sustainable Solid Waste Management & the Green Economy*, ISWA – the International Solid Waste Association

16. Study, (2008), *Compost production and use in the EU, European Commission*, DG Joint Research Centre/ITPS, Organic Recovery&Biological Treatment, European Compost Network, On line at: http:// www.compostnetwork.info

17. Study, (2010), *Secondary materials and waste recycling commercialization in Serbia 2009-2010*, USAID Serbia, on line at: https://serbia.usaid. gov/upload/documents/SerbiaRecyclingAssessment_eng.pdf://

18. Study, (2013) *Sustainable Solid Waste Management & the Green Economy* (2013), ISWA – the International Solid Waste Association, On line at: http://#q=iswa+the+international+solid+waste+association

19. Van Camp., L., Bujjarabal, B., Gentile, A-R., Jones, R.J.A, Montanarella, L., Olazabal, C., (2004), *Reports of the Technical Working Groups Established under the Thematic Strategy for Soil Protection*. EUR 21319 EN/1, 872 pp. Office for Official Publications of the European Communities, Luxemburg

20. Working Document, (2012), *Biodegradable waste subject to biological treatment*, Third Working Document, August 2012, IPTS, Seville, Spain, European Compost Network, On line at: http: //www. compostnetwork.info

II. DEVELOPMENT OF GREEN ECONOMY IN THE WESTERN BALKANS

STRATEGIC FRAMEWORK FOR GREEN GROWTH IN THE SELECTED WESTERN BALKAN COUNTRIES

Elena Jovicic[17]

Aleksandra Brankovic[18]

INTRODUCTION

Green economy, which is based upon theideaof facilitatingeconomic development that is in line with the enhancement of environmental quality, efficient use of resources and higher standards of living, is the guiding principleof sustainable development. In the contextof increasing environmental concernsand the global economiccrisis, importance of the concept of green economy is only growing, and in many countries it has been accepted as one of the developmental priorities.

These principles are also incorporated in to the main strategic goals of the Western Balkan (WB) countries. In that regard, importance of the development of the concept of green economy is reflected not only in the necessity of adapting to global changes, but also in the fact that the region of the Western Balkans is *"vulnerable to the negative impacts of the environment and climate changes with local and regional impact on environment and socio-economic development"*, and that the states need to *"promote environmentally friendly mechanisms and proactive solutions*

---

[17] Institute of Economic Sciences, Belgrade, Serbia, elena.baranenko@ien.bg.ac.rs

[18] Institute of Economic Sciences, Belgrade, Serbia

to meet the challenges and overcome problems on the road to achievement of
the standards and promotion of the norms applied in the European Union"
(Belgrade Declaration, 2013).

The issues of sustainable development in all of the Western Balkan
countries have been analyzed by several authors (e.g. Pickard (2008),
Munitlak Ivanovi et al. (2009)), while some papers focus more
specifically on particular WB countries (e.g. uki (2012), Sumpor &
Kuzmi (2011)). Obviously, there are not many papers that deal with the
comprehensive analysis which involves more countries. Also, insufficient
attention is paid to the analysis of the strategic framework for sustainable
development and green economy in the WB countries. In that regard,
one should mention the evaluation of the local sustainable strategic
planning in the Drina river basin (which encompasses municipalities
from Serbia, Montenegro and Bosnia and Herzegovina) given by
Milutinovi & Jolovi (2010), while Karakosta et al. (2012) concentrate
on the analysis of the strategic framework for renewable energy sources
in Serbia and Bosnia and Herzegovina. Country specific analyses are
given by Pucar & Nenkovi -Rizni (2007), which focus on the design of
the framework for energy efficiency in Serbia, while Nadi (2011) and
Mateši (2009) deal with the analysis of strategic documents related to
sustainable development in Serbia (the former) and Croatia (the latter).

Even fewer papers are dedicated to the issues of green growth and green
economy. However, there are papers that include some aspects related
to green growth as part of sustainable development. For example, Krsti
et al. (2012) focus on an analysis of the environmental dimension
of sustainable development of the South-Eastern European countries
applying the methodology of Environmental Performance Index (EPI),
that allowed to define the key areas of environmental policy in which
is necessary to remedy the situation, following the example of best
practice in other countries that have achieved significant results. The
analysis of green business sector in Bosnia and Herzegovina, with
emphasis on the importance of supporting green entrepreneurship
in transition economies, is presented by Silajdži et al. (2014), while
Jovanovi Gavrilovi & Mini (2012) discuss the importance of green
growth for overcoming the crisis, with particular reference to the need

for more intensive incorporation of the concept of green economy and green growth in the context of sustainable development.

Given that there are not many papers that analyze the strategic framework for green growth in the Western Balkan countries in a comprehensive manner, the authors intend to assess the progress made in the official inclusion of the principles of green economy and sustainable development in the strategic framework and relevant policy documents of the four WB countries (Serbia, Croatia, MontenegroandBosnia-Hercegovina).

BOSNIA AND HERZEGOVINA

The development and implementation of the single strategic framework for green growth in the Republic of Bosnia and Herzegovina (BH) is hindered by the country's complex organizational structure. BH iscomprised of the two entities, the Federation of Bosnia and Herzegovina (FBH) and the Republic of Srpska (RS), and the District of Br ko (DB). Competencies for most of the green growth related issues are at subordinate levels, while coordination and international cooperation are responsibilities of the central government. The situation in the FBH is even more complicated, because it is divided into ten cantons, and each has its own competencies and institutions.

Consequently, there is a lack of the central level strategic framework that deals with the green growth related issues[19], and multiplicity of strategies at subordinate levels. However, although vertical and horizontal cooperation is missing(2012b), the regulatory framework in the entities is generally aligned, due to the fact that legislation is harmonized with *acquiscommunautaire.*

In the Republic of Srpskano strategy on green or sustainable growth has been enacted. However, several strategies that are in force are based upon these principles. The most comprehensive one is the *Nature protection strategy*(2011a), whose main goal is "*protection, promotion and stimulation*

---

[19]   Although the preparation of the Development strategy of BH has been underway for a while, it has not yet been adopted.

of the sustainable deployment of natural resources". In order for this to be achieved, the strategy envisages a set of diverse measures and activities, which are all paving way towards a greener economy. They include, *inter alia*, setting up a climate change monitoring system, specifying clear rules for the deployment of mineral resources, development of financial mechanisms, promotion of the traditional environmental management techniques and skills, soil regeneration, control of the utilization of fertilizers etc. *Strategic plan for rural development*(2009)focuses on guiding the development of agriculture, forestry and tourism in rural areas along a sustainable pathway.Some of the proposed activities are financial and advisory support for setting up organic and production of autochthonous plants on farms, compulsory education of farmers related to the use of fertilizers, support for the development of SMEs (fiscal, employee and credit subsidies, trainings etc.), and in particular for youth and women entrepreneurship.

Sectoral strategies on agriculture, forestry, energy and tourism in the Republic of Srpskaalso tackle certain green growth related issues. Strategies on tourism and forestry are more specific in that regard. In the *Forestry development strategy* (2012b) sustainability is distinguished as one of the main guiding principles, and majority of the proposed measures aims to secure that the deployment of forests does not harm the environment. The *Tourism development strategy* (2011b) sets out the strategic goal of achieving a sustainable tourist product, and suggests measures such as the development of tourist plans based on the principle of sustainability, introduction of incentives for development of tourism in protected areas, support to the development of rural tourism and so on. As far as the *Energy* (2012a) and *Agriculture development* (2006) strategies are concerned, although sustainable development is declared as one of the guiding principles, specific measures that promote greener economy are not envisaged. [20]

The institutions of the Federation of Bosnia and Herzegovina, just like their counterparts in the Republic of Srpska, have not brought in a

---

[20]   Several other strategies that deal with the environmental issues are also in force in the Republic of Srpska, such as the Air protection strategy and the Chemical safety strategy. Source: Council of ministers of BH (2012).

specific strategy on green or sustainable growth. However, several other strategies that tackle some of the relevant issues have been developed, but not all of them have been officially adopted. The most important and most comprehensive is the *Development strategy* (2010), adopted by the government of the entity in 2010. One of the priority goals of the strategy is to achieve sustainable growth and development, particularly in the sectors of agriculture, energy and transport[21]. Another comprehensive document is the *Federal environmental protection strategy* (2009). It encompasses four strategies - on nature protection, air protection, waste management and water management – and an action plan. Among the principles the strategy is based upon, two are of crucial importance for achieving green growth: the principle of sustainable development and the "polluter pays" principle. The strategy also entails a goal of achieving sustainable deployment of natural resources, and proposes a number of measures, such as the introduction of incentives, promotion of traditional know-how, introduction and monitoring of the climate change indicators, incentives for renewable energy sources, limiting pollution emissions etc. However, it seems that the implementation of the strategy has not been particularly effective, *"owing to the lack of financial, institutional and human resources"* (Council of ministers of BH, 2012). Among the sectoral strategies there are some, such as those on *Water* (2011) and *Agricultural land management* (2012), that acknowledge the importance of sustainability and envisage a set of relevant measures, while others, such as the *Development strategy the textile, apparel, hide and footwear industries* (2013), do not consider any of the issues that are important for achieving green growth.

---

[21]   Envisaged activities in the area of agriculture and rural development focus primarily on introducing sustainable farming techniques, supporting entrepreneurship in rural areas (especially female entrepreneurs), promoting rural tourism, and developing distinctive products with geographical origin. As far as energy and other natural resources are concerned, a broad set of measures has been proposed, including activities oriented towards the completion of the regulatory and strategic framework, development and introduction of economic instruments, and utilization of the renewable energy sources. Transport and communications related measures have been less exhaustive, as they primarily focus on introducing the monitoring system.

Within the Federation of Bosnia and Herzegovina there are several strategies at the cantonal levels, but we did not consider them in the chapter, because they ought to contain the provisions that are aligned with the framework set at the federal level.

As regards the Br ko District, sustainability is defined as one of the guiding principles of its *Development strategy* (2009), protection and improvement of the environment is set out as one of the strategic goals. In order to achieve it, a set of measures has been proposed, such as the introduction of the environmental monitoring system, landfill reconstruction, and greening the city of Br ko.

In conclusion, we can observe that the strategic framework for green growth at the central government level is missing. One of the underlying reasons is probably that responsibilities for these issues are concentrated at the sub-central levels of government. Even though certain activities have been undertaken in order to develop a comprehensive development strategy for Bosnia and Herzegovina, which would entail aspect relevant for green growth, it has not yet been adopted.

As opposed to the central government level, there is a proliferation of various strategies at the levels of entities and the Br ko District. Although none of them is entitled the green or sustainable growth strategy, many of them deal with the relevant issues. In some cases orientation towards the green growth is firm, manifested in the strategic goals and the set of the proposed measures. In many cases, however, the incorporation of the green economy approach is rather generalized and partial: for example, achieving sustainability is often mentioned in the vision and/or in some of the strategic goals, but without proposing any specific measures in that respect. Also, available reports suggest that implementation of the proposed strategies has not been satisfactory, often due to the lack of financial and, in some cases, human, resources[22]. Another interesting finding is that several strategic documents have been commissioned and prepared, but have not yet been adopted; this

---

[22]   See e.g. Ministry of foreign trade and economic relations of BH (2012a), Ministry of foreign trade and economic relations of BH (2012b) and Council of ministers of BH (2012).

may point to the inefficiency of the decision making process, which consequently impedes the completion of the green growth strategic framework at the level of the entities.

CROATIA

In assessing the strategy framework of Croatia, it can be concluded that the umbrella document focused on the country's sustainable development and green economy is the *SustainableDevelopment Strategy*(2009). It covers eight key areas, focusing primarily on the green economy within the *Environment and Natural Resources, Promoting Sustainable Production and Consumption, Ensuring Energy Independence and Increasing the Efficiency of Energy Use* and *Protection of the Adriatic Sea, Coastal Area and Islands*. The action plans for specific areas were developed with the aim to implement the defined goals (Action Plan for the Education for Sustainable Development, Action Plan on Sustainable Production and Consumption, Action Plan for Environmental Protection). The *Strategy*, including certain amendments and supplements, mostly reflects the EU Sustainable Development Strategy. This is due to the fact that Croatia, when it was candidate for the EU membership, took a serious approach when it comes to incorporation of the EU development principles into its own strategies and policies, which is the obligation of all EU Member Countries.

In 2009 the country adopted another strategy document associated with the concept of sustainable development and green economy- *Energy Strategy* (2009). The Strategy is based on a creation of the system for balanced development of relationship among the security of energy supply, competitiveness and environmental protection in order to enable a safe, high quality and affordable energy supply to the economy of Croatia and its citizens. In defining its major goals, the Strategy was built on a common EU energy policy. Specifically, the following were marked as major priorities: 20% reduction in emissions of the greenhouse gases, 20% share of renewable energy in gross total energy consumption in 2020, 10% share of renewable energy used in all forms of transport in relation to the immediate energy consumption in land transport, 9% reduction in total energy consumption by 2016, by applying energy efficiency measures. In addition to the common goals, the country has set a national goal that stipulates that the share of electricity generated from renewable energy sources, including large hydropower plants, in total electricity consumption for the period until 2020, should be maintained at the level of 35%. In addition, the Strategy envisaged some significant financial investments- up to 15 billion Euros in the period 2009-2020.[23]

In 2011 Croatian Government adopted the document *"Strategic Guidelines for Green Economy Development"*, which should constitute the basis for introduction of effective inter-sector activities, as well as to boost production and investment, with particular emphasis on the principles of sustainable development and environmental protection, renewable energy and energy efficiency (Government of Croatia, 2011). In order to initiate the activities necessary for creation of the conditions for development of green economy, the Strategy has envisaged the elaboration of a set of action plans.

The next step on the path to the sustainable development is a presentation of the *Framework for Low-Emission Development Strategy for Croatia* by the Ministry of Environment and Nature, in collaboration with the United Nations Development Programme (UNDP), in May 2013 (Grgasovi , V, 2013). According to this document, the strategy will be based on a long-term and multisectoral planning through the principles of sustainable development and implementation of the policies to mitigate climate change, and opening up "a chance to, by improving the existing infrastructure and technological solutions, innovations, transfer of advanced technology, significant structural changes in all sectors, encourage the investment cycle, the growth of industrial production,

---

[23] The Croatian government is currently working on the process of adoption of the revised Energy Strategy of the Republic of Croatia until 2030, the draft was proposed in mid-May 2013. Two goals of the strategy which are extremely important for green economy are improving energy efficiency and increasing the use of renewable energy sources (the goal is 30% share of energy generated from renewable sources in the total energy use to be achieved until 2030). For this purpose, the Strategy proposes certain measures, such as the construction of new hydropower plants and encouraging investment in other renewable sources.

developing new businesses, economic competitiveness and creation of new jobs of sustainable perspective" (Grgasovi , V, 2013, p.9).

After the EU accession on 1 July 2013, Croatia has followed the practice of all other member states, and has developed and adopted the *National Reform Programme* (The Government of Republic of Croatia, 2014). Sustainable development and green economy are elaborated in the 4th chapter *Progress towards 2020 targets*, which provides an overview of the adopted laws, adopted programs and action plans, as well as measures planned for the upcoming period.

Some areas of the green economy and sustainable development are also covered in the *Waste Management, Environmental and Regional Development Strategies.*

Obviously, Croatia has undertaken a serious and systematic approach to creating the strategic framework for the implementation of the green economy and sustainable development policies. Such activities were intensified over the previous five years, led by the process ofaccession to the European Union.

The Europe 2020 Competitiveness Report 2014 (World Economic Forum, 2014) also shows that Croatia has achieved some success when it comes to the implementationof the principles andobjectivesof a green economy. In terms of sustainable growth and environmental sustainability Croatia occupies the 15th position, and the country's performance is close to the EU average[24] (World Economic Forum, 2014). Croatia is also mentioned in the report on the implementation of the EU energy Efficiency Directive (Coalition of Energy Savings, 2014) as one of only three states[25] that have succeeded to provide credible plans which demonstrate how the governments will achieve their savings targets. In other words, Croatia presented *"assessable and good quality report, where most measures and claimed savings appear correct"* (World Economic Forum, 2014, p. 4).

---

[24] As regards other pillars of competitiveness Croatia is at the bottom among the EU member states, usually placed between the 24 and 27th position. Source: World Economic Forum (2014).

[25] Denmark, Ireland, Croatia

MONTENEGRO

Montenegro is constitutionally defined as an ecological state. The declaration proclaiming that Montenegro is an ecological state was originally voted by the Assembly in 1991, and later confirmed in the Constitution of 1992. The first article of the current Constitution states: *"Montenegro is a civil, democratic, **ecological** and the state of social justice, based on the rule of law"* (Republic of Montenegro, 2007a). Accordingly, the green economy and sustainable development are declared to be ones of the main national priorities.

Over the past ten years, Montenegro has taken a number of initiatives and adopted a series of legislative documents with the objective to form the policy framework for the implementation of the necessary reforms and promoting sustainable development.

Chronologically speaking, the first strategic document addressing the issues of importance for country's sustainable development was the document *Montenegro Ecological State Development Directions* (The Government of Montenegro, 2011a), adopted by the Government in March 2001. This document, while emphasizing the specificity of Montenegro's natural characteristics, integration of economic, environmental and social concepts, formulates potential directions for the establishment of country's ecologically sustainable development.

National sustainable development strategy (2007a), which covers the 2007-2012 period, is the most important strategic document in the initiative for green development. The document defines the main objectives of the development strategy: the acceleration of economic growth and development and reducing regional development disparities; poverty reduction and ensuring socially equal access to services and resources; ensuring effective control, pollution reduction and sustainable management of natural resources; improvement of the management system and public participation; and preservation of cultural diversity and identity.

To ensure effective implementation of these goals, the country has prepared an *Action Plan* (2007a). Initially, the Action Plan was designed to encompass the period of 2007-2012, and the progress in achieving the main objectives of the National Strategy was supposed to be monitored within the regular annual report by the Office for Sustainable Development[26]. However, in 2011 the Montenegrin Government adopted a revised and updated *Action Plan*(2011d) in which the measures were expanded and the timelines for their implementation were more precisely defined.

To support the implementation of the National Strategy, in late 2010 the Government introduced the *Communication Strategy of Sustainable Development of Montenegro for the period 2011-2013*(2011c) together with the *Action Plan for 2011*. The Strategy defines a set of objectives whose implementation should contribute to the promotion of sustainable development at all levels, as well as the establishment of effective mechanisms of communication among all involved participants. Emphasis is placed on the necessity of building partnerships between the public, civil society and the business sector in order to achieve synergy effects and to satisfy the need for decentralization of the communication process. In order to accomplish numerous goals and take all necessary measures, the strategy proposes a gradual approach to the development of communication activities. However, the implementation of this strategy has not been satisfactory[27]. Since the first phase of implementation of the *National Sustainable Development Strategy* has been completed, another review is scheduled for the period 2013-2014, after which an improved strategy for the period 2014-2020 will be proposed for government approval. *NSSD 2014-2020* should represent an umbrella document for the development of Montenegro, indicating a set of principles and goals that would provide the basis for

---

[26]   Since June 2011 known as the Department of International Cooperation and Sustainable Development of the Ministry for Sustainable Development and Tourism

[27]   The first implementation report states that in 2011 ¾ of the total number of the adopted measures remained unimplemented; while in the case of measures which had begun to apply a significant number have not yet been fully realized. Successfully implemented measures are primarily related to the establishment of an institutional framework and its implementation is mainly due to the fact that they do not require additional funding. As for the measures that are not yet implemented, the main obstacle is the lack of funds allocated for financing

defining innovative policies designed to speed up the economic growth, based on the principles of sustainable use of natural resources and environmental protection as well as to promote and improve the social integration and human capital development.

In order to fulfill the obligation to establish a vision of socio-economic development with the individual necessary investments and development methods needed for their implementation, the Government of Montenegro adopted the *Montenegro Development Directions 2013- 2016* (The Government of Montenegro, 2013*).* This document was created on the model of the *Europe 2020 Strategy*, and as the primary development interests identified "smart growth", "sustainable growth" and "inclusive growth". With regards to the sustainable development and the green economy concept, in the chapter "Sustainable growth" a set of related goals has been defined including proposed methods for their implementation.

In addition, there are other strategies that incorporate in their key goals the concept of sustainable development and green economy. For example, the *Regional Development Strategy* (2011b) as a part of the strategic goal - Regional development and environmental protection, defines three priority topics: sustainable management and use of natural resources; low carbon footprint; and infrastructure for environmental protection (municipal infrastructure). The realization of the set goals is anticipated primarily through the capacity building of local government units, improved co-ordination and strengthening of cooperation between the municipalities; connecting with the existing initiatives; - the use of available combined funding sources including national and local sources, EU funds and international funds for climate change / low carbon footprint etc.

Energy Development Strategy (2007b) (adopted together with the *Action Plan*) is also essentially connected with the concept of green economy and sustainable growth. Relying on the key energy policy guidelines, the *Strategy* defines the specific objectives and mechanisms for the transition towards a safe, competitive and environmentally acceptable supply of energy services to the consumers. In addition, this can be considered as a starting point in reaching a European model of sustainable and strategic development of the energy sector, as well as for the adoption of the necessary legislative and institutional support that would lead to the successful realization of the country's energy policy at the time of integration of the country into the European and international framework[28].

The following strategic documents can be mentioned in respect with green growth and sustainable development as well: the Spatial Plan the Transport Development Strategy, the National Strategy of Biodiversity, the Strategy on Food Production and Rural Development and others.

Based on the analysisof the strategic framework, it can be concluded that over the past few years Montenegro made significant progress in terms of the creation of the green growth policies. By adoptinga set of strategies, relevant documentsandimplementing a seriesof measures, Montenegro strengthened its commitment (at least in respect to the establishment of the strategic framework) to develop as an ecological state, which respects the principlesand objectivesof sustainable development and green economy. However, there aremany challengesandproblemswhenit comes to theirimplementation. On one hand, the insufficient level ofmutualcoherenceof strategic documents and the lack of financial information (budgets, funding sources, etc.) could be considered as main weakness, while, on the other, the main obstacles tothe realization ofthe strategies are the absence of clear delineation of responsibilities and competencieswithin the public administrationand theabsence of a genuinewillingness to implement the defined measures (Government of Montenegro, 2011a, p.8-15).

SERBIA

The principal document within the strategic framework for green growth in the Republic of Serbia is the *National sustainable development strategy*(2008). It defines sustainable development in its broadest terms, as "*targets-oriented, long-term (continuous), comprehensive and synergetic process withimpacts on all*

---

[28]   The Montenegrin Government is currently working on the process of adoption of the revised Strategy for energy development until 2030, the draft document was proposed in mid-May 2013. Two objectives of the strategy, such as improving energyefficiencyand increasing theuse of renewableenergy sources are of the great importance in terms of green economy. For example, one of the goals is to achieve a 30% share of energy produced from renewablesources by 2030.

aspects of life (economic, social, environmental andinstitutional) at alllevels". The Strategy is based upon three pillars: I Knowledge-based sustainability, II Socio-economic conditions and perspectives and III Environment and natural resources. A broad set of priority programs for each of the pillars is described, while specific activities that are to be accomplished are envisaged by the *Action plan*(2010a)[29]. Founded upon this strategy, other, more specific, strategic documents have also been prepared and adopted.

Among them, there are several strategies that are aimed at directing activities of the government[30] and businesses[31], as well as attaining broad public participation[32], in achieving the green growth objectives[33].

A group of strategic documents that are in place deals with the environmental and natural resources issues relevant for achieving green growth. The most comprehensive is the *National strategy for sustainable use of natural resources*(2012), which complements the *National sustainable development strategy*. It defines a set of measures aimed at accomplishing the three main goals: establishing sustainable use of natural resources, mitigation of adverse environmental impacts and achieving a more efficient use of natural resources. The *Biodiversity strategy*(2011b)and the

---

[29]   Activities specified within the first pillar encompass a broad set of measures oriented towards achieving economics growth (in terms of GDP growth), fiscal sustainability, proper education, development of IT technologies etc. Within the second pillars, proposed measures are related to improving the living standard of population and addressing social issues (social security, poverty, social inclusion and alike), but also to improving public health, regional and local development and ensuring public participation in the decision making processes. As far as the third pillar is concerned, measures tackle all of the aspects necessary for improving the state of the environment and efficiency in the use of resources, including the sectoral policies.

[30]   National environmental approximation strategy (2011f).

[31]   Corporate social responsibility strategy (2010b) and Strategy for the introduction of cleaner production(2009).

[32]   Strategy for implementing the Aarhus convention (2011g).

[33]   In this respect one should also mention the National CDM strategy for the waste management, agriculture and forestry sectors (2010c), which provides guidelines for the businesses in these sectors on the possibilities and modes of participation in the clean development management projects.

accompanying action plan envisage the introduction of measures aimed at controlling the use of chemicals (such as pesticides and fertilizers), mitigating the effects of the climate change and attaining environmental policy integration, but fail to suggest specific activities. The main goal of the *Waste management strategy*(2010d) is to reduce pollution and degradation of the environment. In that regard, activities envisaged by the strategy are highly relevant for achieving green growth, and particularly important are those that promote recycling and reuse of waste.

Among the sectoral strategies that are still operational, the most relevant for accomplishing green growth are those related to the sectors of energy and industry. Within the priorities of the *Energy development strategy*(2005), two are directly connected with the green economy: increase in the use of renewable energy sources and energy efficiency. This is to be achieved through the reduction in heat losses, use of energy saving appliances, and support to the deployment of various types of renewable energy sources in the production of electricity and heat, and more specific measures are given in the action plan. As regards the *Industrial development strategy and policy* (2011d), it also directly draws on the green growth, since its primary objective is the *"creation of the new competitive sustainable industrial policy"*. Specific activities are listed in the *Action plan*(2011a), and the most relevant are those related to the energy efficiency and the environmental protection: education, introduction of the mandatory energy management system, introduction of incentives for green jobs and recycling, adoption of programs for the ecologically compatible and energy efficient industry, mitigating harmful environmental effects etc.

Remaining strategies that are in place in the Republic of Serbia are not particularly relevant from the viewpoint of the green economy, because, although they may declare to be based upon the principle of sustainable development, they do not specify any specific measure (e.g. *Free zones development strategy* (2011c)). On the other hand, the *National employment strategy* (2011e) does not envisage any activities related to achieving green growth; however, it tackles the issues related to the social inclusion of various marginalized groups.

We can conclude that, over the previous couple of years, the Serbian government has been very active in creating the strategic framework for green growth. Nearly a dozen of strategic documents have been in place as of mid-2014, and several more are being prepared[34]. The clear hierarchy has been established, with the National strategy on sustainable development being the roof strategy, upon which other strategic documents have been prepared. Although there are complementarities among these strategic documents, sometimes certain activities are overlapping. Another problem is that some of the activities proposed in the action plans have not been addressed in due course. These issues, to some extent, may result from the fact that the Serbian governments, and especially ministers in charge for the issues that are crucial for green growth, have changed several times over the previous couple of years, so that the order of priorities may have changed as well.

As regards the evaluation of the strategic framework, the available reports generally praise the commitment of the Serbian authorities in developing the strategic and regulatory framework for green growth. Although there are not many extensive evaluations of the implementations of the relevant strategies, the general conclusion is that the greatest challenges derive from insufficient funding, lack of administrative and/or technical capacity, as well as unsatisfactory public awareness and participation[35].

CONCLUSION

All of the observed Western Balkan countries are committed to the principles of green economy. Over the previous years they have made substantial effort in establishing the institutional, legislative and strategic framework for green growth.

In this chapter we give a brief overview of the relevant strategic documents that have been in place as of 2014. From the viewpoint of green growth, they include several types of strategies. The most

---

[34] E.g. draft versions of the Agricultural and rural development strategy and the Energy development strategy up to 2025 are available on the web-sites of the competent ministries.

[35] For example, check out UNEP (2013), UNDP/UNEP (2012) and European Commission (2013).

relevant are those that directly aim to lead economy along the pathway of green (or sustainable) development, and they are often entitled as *Sustainable development strategies.* We can also observe the existence of another type of comprehensive strategic documents that are relevant for green growth, and these are the development strategies. Although they are oriented towards achieving core economic growth, they often contain provisions for attaining a greener growth. Strategic documents on environment, nature, biodiversity etc. are also important in directing the economy towards sustainability. Then, there are sector-specific strategies, among which energy, agriculture and forestry strategies are of particular significance.

As far as the sustainable development strategies are concerned, they have been put in place in Croatia, Montenegro and Serbia. On the other hand, neither Bosnia and Herzegovina nor any of the constituting entities have yet adopted such a strategy. Based on the conducted analysis, we can conclude that these strategies are generally devised to serve as umbrella documents that broadly encompass all the issues relevant for achieving sustainable development, while other, more specific strategic documents are prepared in line with the guiding principles of the sustainable development strategy.

We can also observe that both the sustainable development and sector-specific strategies incorporate common principles. This is due to the fact that their cornerstones are the relevant UN and EU documents related to the green and sustainable growth. The EU accession is perhaps the single most influential force that promotes the green economy concept in the observed WB countries. All of the countries pledge for the EU membership[36], and have been harmonizing their national legislation with the *acquis communautaire.* In that respect, their strategies usually call upon the main principles and goals set out in the EU strategic documents, and in particular in the EU's *Sustainable development Strategy* and the *Europe 2020 strategy*(Table 1). We can observe that the Serbian strategy sets out the same list of pillars the *Europe 2020* strategy is founded on, while Croatian strategy seems to follow a pattern of the EU's *Strategy for sustainable development.*

---

[36]   Croatia achieved this goal in 2013, when it became the 28th EU Members State.

Table 1. Priorities and pillars of strategies on sustainable development in the EU, Croatia, Montenegro and Serbia

Country		Priorities/Pillars
EU	Strategy for sustainable development	(1) Limit climate change and increase the use of clean energy (2) Address threats to public health (3) Manage natural resources more responsibly (4) Improve the transport system and land-use management
	Europe 2020	(1) Smart growth(development of knowledge and innovation) (2) Sustainable growth (greener, more resource efficient and more competitive) (3) Inclusive growth (strengthening employment, social and territorial cohesion)
Croatia		(1) Increase in the number of inhabitants (2) Environment and natural resources (3) Sustainable production and consumption (4) Social and territorial cohesion and justice (5) Energy independence and efficiency (6) Improving public health (7) Integration of the transport network (8) Protection of the Adriatic sea, coastal area and islands
Montenegro		(1) Economic development (2) Environment and natural resources (3) Social development
Serbia		(1) Knowledge-based sustainability (2) Socio-economic conditions and perspectives (3) Environment and natural resources

Sources: European Commission (2001), European Commission (2010), Government of the Republic of Croatia (2009), Government of the Republic of Montenegro (2007) and Government of the Republic of Serbia (2008).

Unfortunately, shortcoming in the implementation of the green growth related strategic provisions are also common for all of the observed countries. According to the available reports that evaluate implementation of these strategies, the lack of financial funds and inadequate administrative capacity, and also the lack of awareness and insufficient public participation, are the main factors that have so far compromised their successful implementation.

ACKNOWLEDGMENTS

The authors acknowledge the financial support of the Ministry of Education, Science and Technological Development of the Republic of Serbia (research projects 47009 and 179015).

REFERENCES

1. Assembly of the Br ko District of BH, "Development strategy of the Br ko District for the period 2008-2017", 2009.

2. "Belgrade Declaration on green economy and sustainable development in the region of South East Europe", 2013, http://www.merz.gov.rs/cir/dokumenti/beogradska-deklaracija-o-zelenoj-ekonomiji-i-odrzivom-rastu-u-regionu-jugoistocne-evrope-0.

3. Coalition of Energy Savings, "Implementing the EU energy Efficiency Directive: Analysis of Article 7 member states reports", 2014, http://energycoalition.eu/sites/default/files/20140422%20Coalition%20for%20Energy%20Savings%20Art%207%20Report%20FINAL.pdf.

4. Council of ministers of BH, "Answers to the list of EU questions on Chapter 27 Environment", 2012. http://www.dei.gov.ba/dei/dokumenti/uskladjivanje/default.aspx?id=10919&langTag=bs-BA (accessed 18.05.2014).

5.   uki , P, "Sustainable Development Under Impact of the Crisis –
     Global and National Dimensions", in *Economic Analysis*, Vol. 45,
     No. 1-2, 2012.

6.   European Commission, "Serbia 2013 Progress Report", Commission
     staff working document, COM(2013) 700 final, 16.10.2013, http://
     ec.europa.eu/enlargement/pdf/key_documents/2013/package/
     sr_rapport_2013.pdf (accessed 21.05.2014).

7.   European Commission. "Commission Communication of 15 May
     2001 - A Sustainable Europe for a Better World: A European Union
     Strategy for Sustainable Development (Commission proposal to the
     Gothenburg European Council)". 15 May 2001, COM(2001) 264
     final. 2001.

8.   European Commission. "Communication from the Commission of
     3 March 2010 - Europe 2020 - A Strategy for Smart, Sustainable
     and Inclusive Growth". 3 March 2010, COM(2010) 2020 final.
     2010.

9.   Government of the Federation of BH, "Agricultural land
     management strategy of the FBH", *Official gazette of the FBH*
     (10/2012), 2012.

10. Government of the Federation of BH, "Development strategy of the
     FBH for the period 2010-2020", 2010

11. Government of the Federation of BH, "Development strategy of the
     textile, apparel, hide and footwear industries of the FBH", *Official
     gazette of the Federation of BH* (65/2013), 2013.

12. Government of the Federation of BH, "Environmental protection
     strategy of the FBH", 2009.

13. Government of the Federation of BH, "Water management strategy
     of the FBH for the period 2010-2022", 2011.

14. Government of the Republic of Croatia, "Rural Development Strategy of the Republic of Croatia for the period 2008-2013", 2008, http://www.mps.hr/default.aspx?id=3652.

15. Government of the Republic of Croatia, "Strategic Guidelines for Green Economy Development", 2011, http://www.mzoip.hr/doc/propisi/153._-_1.3.pdf.

16. Government of the Republic of Croatia, "Strategy for Sustainable Development of the Republic of Croatia", *Official gazette of the Republic of Croatia* (30/2009), 2009, http://www.mzoip.hr/doc/Strategy_for_Sustainable_Development.pdf.

17. Government of the Republic of Croatia, "The National Reform Programme", 2014, http://ec.europa.eu/europe2020/pdf/csr2014/nrp2014_croatia_en.pdf.

18. Government of the Republic of Croatia, Energy strategy of the Republic of Croatia, 2009, http://www.mingo.hr/userdocsFigures/White%20Paper%20Energy%20Staregy%20of%20the%20Republic%20of%20Croatia.pdf.

19. Government of the Republic of Montenegro, "Communication Strategy of the Sustainable Development of Montenegro", 2011c, http://www.kor.gov.me/en/sections/Communication-Strategy-of-Sustainable-Development.

20. Government of the Republic of Montenegro, "Energy Development Strategy of Montenegro by 2025", 2007b, http://www.energetska-efikasnost.me/uploads/file/Dokumenta/Energy%20Development%20Strategy%20of%20Montenegro%20by%202025.pdf

21. Government of the Republic of Montenegro, "National strategy of sustainable development", 2007a, http://www.mrt.gov.me/odrzivi/odrzivi-nacionalna-strategija/129428/Nacionalna-strategija-odrzivog-razvoja-Crne-Gore-2007-2012.html

22. Government of the Republic of Montenegro, "Revised action plan of the National sustainable development strategy", 2011d, http://www.kor.gov.me/ResourceManager/FileDownload. aspx?rId=79237&rType=2.

23. Government of the Republic of Montenegro, "Second report on the implementation of the National strategy of sustainable development for the period April 2008 – September 2009" 2009, http://www. gov.me/files/1264587687.pdf.

24. Government of the Republic of Montenegro, "The analysis of achievements and challenges of the ecological state", 2011a, http:// www.stakeholderforum.org/fileadmin/files/Analiza_ENG.pdf

25. Government of the Republic of Montenegro, "The Montenegro Development Directions 2013-2016", 2013, http://www.mf.gov. me/organizacija/sektor-za-ekonomsku-politiku-i-razvoj/121434/ Pravci-razvoja-Crne-Gore-2013-2016-godine.html

26. Government of the Republic of Montenegro, "Regional Development Strategy of Montenegro", 2011b, http:// www.mek.gov.me/ResourceManager/   FileDownload. aspx?rid=70518&rType=   2&file=Strategija%20regionalnog %20razvoja%20Crne%20Gore%202010-2014%20godine. pdf. http://www.mek.gov.me/ResourceManager/FileDownload. aspx?rid=70518&rType=2&file=Strategija%20regionalnog%20 razvoja%20Crne%20Gore%202010

27. Government of the Republic of Serbia, "Action plan for implementation of the Industrial development strategy and policy of the Republic of Serbia for the period 2011-2020", *Official gazette of the Republic of Serbia* (100/2011, 61/2013), 2011a.

28. Government of the Republic of Serbia, "Action plan for the implementation of the National sustainable development strategy for the period 2009-2017", *Official gazette of the Republic of Serbia* (31/2010), 2010a.

29. Government of the Republic of Serbia, "Biodiversity strategy of the Republic of Serbia for the period 2011–2018", *Official gazette of the Republic of Serbia* (13/2011), 2011b.

30. Government of the Republic of Serbia, "Corporate social responsibility strategy of the Republic of Serbia for the period 2010-2015", *Official gazette of the Republic of Serbia* (51/2010), 2010b.

31. Government of the Republic of Serbia, "Energy development strategy of the Republic of Serbia up to 2015", *Official gazette of the Republic of Serbia* (35/2005), 2005.

32. Government of the Republic of Serbia, "Free zones development strategy", *Official gazette of the Republic of Serbia* (22/2011), 2011c.

33. Government of the Republic of Serbia, "National employment strategy for the period 2011-2020", *Official gazette of the Republic of Serbia* (37/2011), 2011e.

34. Government of the Republic of Serbia, "National environmental approximation strategy of the Republic of Serbia", *Official gazette of the Republic of Serbia* (80/2011), 2011f.

35. Government of the Republic of Serbia, "National strategy for sustainable use of natural resources", *Official gazette of the Republic of Serbia* (33/2012), 2012.

36. Government of the Republic of Serbia, "National strategy on the inclusion of the Republic of Serbia into the Clean development mechanism of the Kyoto protocol for the waste management, agriculture and forestry sectors", *Official gazette of the Republic of Serbia* (08/2010), 2010c.

37. Government of the Republic of Serbia, "National sustainable development strategy", *Official gazette of the Republic of Serbia* (57/2008), 2008.

38. Government of the Republic of Serbia, "Strategy for implementing the Convention on access to information, public participation in

decision-making and access to justice in environmental matters – the Aarhus convention", *Official gazette of the Republic of Serbia* (103/2011), 2011g.

39. Government of the Republic of Serbia, "Strategy for the introduction of cleaner production in the Republic of Serbia", *Official gazette of the Republic of Serbia* (17/2009), 2009.

40. Government of the Republic of Serbia, Waste management strategy for the period 20102019", *Official gazette of the Republic of Serbia* (29/2010), 2010d.

41. Government of the Republic of Serbia, "Industrial development strategy and policy of the Republic of Serbia for the period 2011-2020", *Official gazette of the Republic of Serbia* (55/2011), 2011d.

42. Government of the Republic of Srpska, "Agriculture development strategy of the Republic of Srpska up to 2015". 2006.

43. Government of the Republic of Srpska, "Energy strategy of the Republic of Srpska up to 2030", *Official gazette of the Republic of Srpska* (28/2012), 2012a.

44. Government of the Republic of Srpska, "Forestry development strategy of the Republic of Srpska", *Official gazette of the Republic of Srpska* (23/2012), 2012b.

45. Jovanovi Gavrilovi , B. and Mini , N., "Green Growth as a Generator for Overcoming the Crisis", in *Economic Analysis*, Vol. 45, No. 1-2, 2012.

46. Krsti , B., Jankovi Mili , V., Jovanovi , S., "An analysis of the environmental dimension of sustainable development of South-Eastern European countries based on EPI methodology", in *Themes Journal for Social Research*, No.02/2012.

47. Mateši , M., "Principles of sustainable development in strategic development documents of the Republic of Croatia", in *SocijalnaEkologija*, Vol. 18, No. 3-4, 2009.

48. Munitlak Ivanovi , O., Golušin, M., Dodi , S., Dodi , J., "Perspectives of sustainable development in countries of South - eastern Europe", in *Renewable and Sustainable Energy Reviews*, 2009.

49. Nadi , D., "Sustainable development and principles of Sustainable development in strategic documents of the republic of Serbia", *Yearbook FPS (Godišnjak FPN)* No. 06, pp. 213224, 2011.

50. Pickard, R., "Sustainable Development Strategies in South-East Europe", Council of Europe Publishing, ISBN 978-92-871-6371-4, 2008.

51. Pucar, M i Nenkovi -Rizni , M, "Legislative and policy in energy efficient designing and renewable energy sources- application in Serbia", in *Spatium*, No. 15-16, 2007.

52. Silajdži , I., Midži Kurtagi , S., Vu ijak, B., "Green entrepreneurship in transition economies: a case study of Bosnia and Herzegovina", in *Journal of Cleaner Production*, In Press (DOI: 10.1016/j.jclepro.2014.07.004), 2014.

53. Sumpor, M., Kuzmi , M., "Sustainable Development Aspects in Cross-Border Cooperation Programmes: The Case of Croatia and Montenegro", *European Regional Science Association - ERSA Congress*, Barcelona, 2011, http://www.ekf.vsb.cz/export/sites/ekf/projekty/cs/weby/esf-0116/databaze-prispevku/clanky_ERSA_2011/ERSA2011_paper_00425.pdf

CREATION OF GREEN JOBS: OPPORTUNITY TO REDUCE HIGH UNEMPLOYMENT IN WESTERN BALKANS[37]

Vladimir Simovic[38]

Ivana Domazet[39]

INTRODUCTION

In the period during, and immediately after the global economic crisis, the Western Balkan countries were challenged by the problem of rising unemployment. While governments of these countries are trying to address this issue by implementing various economic policy measures, it seems that on this occasion they ignore the potential of the green economy and the opportunities for opening of green jobs. In this area, particularly interesting are job positions that could be created within the industry of electronic waste recycling in the offing. The amount of e-waste is increasing at an exponential rate in global terms, which is a natural consequence of the fact that the modern society is migrating towards the information society, which implies the growing use of information technologies (Draškovi , Zubovi and Domazet, 2013, pp. 106-123). The lifespan of these technologies is getting shorter, and the natural result of that process is an increase in the amount of electronic waste. Global e-waste is growing at a rate of 5% per

---

[37] This paper is a part of research projects numbers 47009 (European integrations and social and economic changes in Serbian economy on the way to the EU) and 179015 (Challenges and prospects of structural changes in Serbia: Strategic directions for economic development and harmonization with EU requirements), financed by the Ministry of Science and Technological Development of The Republic of Serbia.
[38] Institute of Economic Sciences, Belgrade, Serbia, vladimir.simovic@ien.bg.ac.rs
[39] Institute of Economic Sciences, Belgrade, Serbia

year, making it the fastest growing waste on the planet. Each year, the amount of electronic scrap is increasing by 50 tons (Draškovi , Domazet, 2013, pp. 234-238). Every hour 4,000 tons of electronic waste is being disposed on our planet. Consequently, the economic potential of electronic waste recycling is enormous, as very valuable materials that can be re-used in the production process may be obtained by it.

On the other hand, one should not ignore the environmental side of the whole process, since the electronic waste contains a large amount of hazardous substances that, if not disposed properly and recycled, may have very negative impact on the environment. It is expected that electronic waste recycling industry in the near future becomes one of the fastest growing economic activities on a world scale just as a direct consequence of the rapid development of IT industry (Statistical Office of the Republic of Serbia, "Upotreba informaciono-komunikacionih tehnologija u Srbiji u 2013. godini", Belgrade, 2014). As a natural result of this process, it is expected that electronic waste recycling industry to absorb a large amount of the workforce from the labor market. This fact represents an excellent development opportunity for the countries of the Western Balkans.

The first part of this paper pinpoints the problem of unemployment and provides the associated statistics in the Western Balkans(Domazet, Filimonovi 2012). The second part focuses on the process of recycling of electronic waste and its significance in the modern economy. The third part is done research potential industry to recycling electronic waste in Serbia as a possible absorber part of the unemployed in this, as well as other countries of the Western Balkans. The results are summarized in the conclusion.

EMPLOYMENT IN SERBIA AND WESTERN BALKAN COUNTRIES

During the crisis period (from 2008 to the end of 2013) the number of individuals who are employed at the employer in Serbia, according to the data published by the Statistical Office of the Republic, decreased by 284 thousand. The percentage reduction in the number of employed persons in the same period, cumulatively totals 14.21% and 2.37% on average per year. Comparative data on the number of employees and job seekers in the same time intervals are presented in the Table 1. The trend of reducing the number of employees is present in 2013 as well, which is an indicator that the combined effects of the crisis and failures in privatization process are still present.

Table 1. Trends in the number of employed and
unemployed population in Serbia - period2000-2013

Year	Employment in 000*	Index (2000=100)	Total unemployment**	Index (2000=100)
2000	2,097	100.0	721,8	100
2001	2,102	100.2	768,6	106.5
2002	2,066	98.5	842,6	116.7
2003	2,041	97.3	947,3	131.3
2004	2,050	97.8	945,0	130.9
2005	2,069	98.7	991,7	137.4
2006	2,026	96.6	1005,4	139.3
2007	2,002	95.5	928,3	128.6
2008	1,999	95.3	819,5	113.5
2009	1,889	90.7	824,2	114.2
2010	1,796	85.6	837,7	116.1
2011	1,746	83.3	833,3	115.4
2012	1,727	82.4	869,0	120.4
2013	1,715	81.8	888,4	123.1

* indivuduals who are employed at the employer
** job seekers

Source: Statistical Office of the Republic of Serbia, "Projekcije radne snage Republike Srbije 2010-2050", Belgrade, 2011.

The data in Table 2 indicate that the number of inactive population in 2013, compared to the previous year, has decreased, while the number of active population in the same period, hasincreased. Individually observed, the reduction in the number of inactive, while increasing the number of the active population is a good indicator. What is specific in relation to previous years is that, according to data published as part of the Labour Force Survey, the number of employees in the 2013 compared to the previous year has increased, while the number of unemployed individuals decreased. The increase in the number of employees, according to the survey results, is also shown in the category of self-employed and day-laborers in agriculture.

Table 2. Labor market trends inSrbiji 2008-2013

	Year					
	2008	2009	2010	2011	2012	2013
Active population	3,267,107	3,119,429	2,964,966	2,924,352	2,929,481	2,966,838
- Employed	2,821,724	2,616,437	2,396,244	2,253,209	2,228,343	2,310,718
Thereof - self-employed and day-laborers in agriculture	954,307	840,602	775,717	411,512	406,711	425,420
- Unemployed	445,383	502,982	568,723	671,143	701,138	656,120
Inactive population	3,083,221	3,230,909	3,352,921	3,373,209	3,348,215	3,157,129

Source: Statistical Office of the Republic of
Serbia, Labor Force Survey, 2014

Table 3 depicts trends in the number of employees on a monthly basis, according to the records of The Statistical Office of the Republic of Serbia, as well as trends in the number of unemployed persons for the same period according to the records of the National Employment Service. Differences that are shown in Tables 2 and 3, concerning the number of unemployed individuals according to the data released by the National Employment Service, and those published within the Labour Force Survey conducted by the Statistical Office, in addition to methodological differences, come from the fact that individuals who are registered in the records of the National Employment Service in order to achieve certain benefits (health insurance, assistance for the unemployed, social support, etc.) often work in grey market and are not really looking for a job.

Table 3. Trends in the number of employed and unemployed population in Serbia - period 2010-2013 (in 000)

	Employed				Unemployed			
	2010	2011	2012	2013	2010	2011	2012	2013
January	1,851	1,775	1,739	1,724	752	751	764	779
February	1,846	1,776	1,739	1,725	767	764	777	790
March	1,817	1,755	1,730	1,725	779	774	783	792
April	1,815	1,753	1,734	1,724	772	770	775	793
May	1,813	1,751	1,733	1,722	763	764	763	784
June	1,811	1,749	1,736	1,718	747	756	755	776
July	1,808	1,747	1,736	1,715	737	749	753	772
August	1,806	1,744	1,734	1,709	724	746	752	761
September	1,775	1,738	1,724	1,705	721	743	751	759
October	1,773	1,737	1,725	1,705*	718	738	753	760
November	1,773	1,736	1,725	1,704*	722	735	755	763
December	1,771	1,739	1,724	1,703*	730	745	761	770

Source: Statistical Office of the Republic of Serbia, "Projekcije radne snage Republike Srbije 2010-2050", Belgrade, 2011.

From the data presented in the Table 3 we can observe that in the second half of 2013 there has been a reduction in the number of employed individuals with respect to first half of the same year. Comparing with the data pertaining to the year 2012, we note a downward trend and more drastic decline in the number of employed population. When it comes to tracking the trends in the number of unemployed individuals on a monthly basis in 2013, there were no significant monthly fluctuations.

Table 4. Trends in the number of employed and unemployed population in Serbia -period 2008-2013 (in%)

	Year					
	2008	2009	2010	2011	2012	2013
Total	14,4	16,9	20,0	23,6	24,6	23,0
Male	12,6	15,5	19,2	23,1	23,9	21,7
Female	16,7	18,6	21,0	24,3	25,6	24,6

Source:Statistical Office of the Republic of Serbia, Labor Force Survey, 2014

According to the data published by Statistical Office of the Republic of Serbia, which are presented in the Table 4, in 2013, women's participation in the overall structure of unemployed persons in the population group aged 15-64 years (Working population) was 24.6%, which is a decrease compared to the previous year. Available from the table, we can also observe that the unemployment rate for men in 2013 compared to the previous year decreased by 2.2 percents.

The trend of activity and inactivity, as well as employment and unemployment rates in the period from 2008 to 2013 are displayed in Table 5 Data analysis indicates a drastic increase in the unemployment rate during the crisis period, from 14.4% in 2008 to 23% in the first half of 2013. In contrast, the data presented in the table showed a significant decrease in the unemployment rate in 2013 compared to the previous year by as much as 1.5 percent.

Table 5. The rates of activity / inactivity and employment
/ unemployment period2008-2013(in %)

	Year					
	2008	2009	2010	2011	2012	2013
Rate of activity	62.7	60.6	59.0	59.4	60.1	61.6
Rate of inactivity	53.7	50.4	47.2	45.4	45.3	47.5
Rate of employment	14.4	16.9	20.0	23.6	24.6	23.0
Rate of unemployment	37.3	39.4	41.0	40.6	39.9	38.4

Source: Labor Force Survey (2008-2014)

According to officials, new layoffs in the public sector are expected in the following period in order to prevent the collapse of the economy and reduce public spending. In addition, if Serbia concludes a new three-year deal with the International Monetary Fund, according to official statements, a decrease in the number of employees in public sector by about 100,000 can be anticipated in next two years. In that regard, the assumption that labor market trends in the future will be unfavorable sounds reasonable.

The situation is similar in other countries of the Western Balkans. According to the statement of the Agency for Statistics of Bosnia and Herzegovina, the number of registered unemployed in February 2013 amounted to 554,489.

Table 6. Numberofrecorded unemployed individuals
in BosniaandHerzegovina - period2011-2013

Bosnia and Herzegovina	2011	2012	2013
Regist redunemloyment	527,667	543,647	554,489

Source: Agency for Statistics of Bosnia and Herzegovina

It may be observed that the number of registered unemployed individuals
for a period of one year (2012-2013) rose to 10,842. Unemployment
structure in Bosnia and Herzegovina, according to different criteria, is
presented in Table 7.

Table 7. Structure of unemployed persons in Bosnia
and Herzegovina, based on different criteria

Year	2012	2013
Total	543.647	554.489
Male	271.318	276.233
Female	272.329	278.256
University degree	30.294	34.681
Male	10.853	12.273
Female	19441	22.408
College degree	7,579	7.656
Male	2.864	2.915
Female	4.715	4.741
High School degree	135.299	141.224
Male	54.181	57.421
Female	81.118	83.803
High skilled / Skilled	193.913	196.715
Male	117.312	119.068
Female	76.601	77.647

Semi skilled	13.482	13.060
Male	7.710	7.454
Female	5.772	5.606
Unskilled	163.080	161.153
Male	78.398	77.102
Female	84.682	84.051

Source: Agency for Statistics of Bosnia and Herzegovina

If the unemployed individuals in Bosnia and Herzegovina compared to the qualification structure, it can be seen that the most of unemployed belong to the high skilled and skilled category, or 196,715 in total, followed by unskilled individuals, with 161,153 in total, and then those with secondary education - 141,224.The minimum number of unemployed persons have college degree - 7,656, followed by those with a university degree - 34.681 (including Masters and PhDs).Among the unemployed, 278,256 are women, which makes 50.2% of the total number of unemployed.Most of them are unskilled – 84,051, followed by women withhigh school degree – 83,803 and those who are high skilled and skilled with 77,647 in total.

According to the latest official data, in Croatia there is 17.2% of the unemployed in working-age population. The number of unemployed individuals in the period 2011-2013 increased from 305,333, as there were in 2011, to 345,112, as it was recorded in 2013. In just two years the number of unemployed increased by 39,779 (Table 8).

Table 8. The number of registered unemployed persons in Croatia - period 2011-2013

2011	2012	2013
305.333	324.324	345.112

Source: Croatian Employment Service

Although the number of unemployed population has increased, the rise in the number of unemployed men was greater than the increase in the number of unemployed women (Table 9).

Table 9. Gender structure of unemployed persons
in Croatia during 2011and 2012Croatian

Gender	2011	2012
Male	141.408	152.079
Female	163.925	172.245

Source: Employment Service

The increase in unemployment was observed in all levels of education, but the slightest increase occurred in the group of unemployed people who have the lowest education level, while the largest increase was among the unemployed who have the highest level of education.Thus, the average number of unemployed who have completed primary school increased by 0.4%, while the average number of unemployed who have completed college or university degree increased by 20.6%.According to the National classification of activities, the largest number of applications received for the vacancies was reported from the education sector (14%), followed by the provision of accommodation, preparing and serving of food (13.2%), and the processing industry (11.9%).

According to the State Statistical Office of Macedonia, 273,860 unemployed persons, ie 28.8%, was recorded in 2013. This is the lowest unemployment rate compared to the previous years. In 2010 the unemployment rate was 32%.

Table 10. Number of registered unemployed individuals
in Macedonia in the period 2010-2013

2010	2011	2012	2013
321,341	281,144	243,403	217,858

Source: The State Statistical Office of Macedonia

Since 2013, the Agency for Employment of Macedonia, keeps records of unemployed individuals by breaking the number of active and passive unemployed persons. According to this classification, at the end of 2013, there were 96,200 active and 121,658 passive unemployed persons.

Table 11. Unemployment structure in
Macedonia according to qualification

Qualification structure	Number of unemployed
Unskilled	104,977
Semi-skilled	8,689
Skilled	38,397
High-skilled	0
High school degree	32,302
College degree	4,128
University degree	20,799
Master degree	764
PhD	17

Source: The State Statistical Office of Macedonia

As for the persons employed, out of 678,467 in total, 522,820 of them work in the private sector, while the remaining 155,647 are employed in public or other sectors. Most people are employed in the processing industry - 122,502.

According to the Employment Agency of Montenegro, at the end of 2011, there were 30,521 unemployed persons (14,317 women). Unemployment rate stood at 11,55%. Unemployment in 2012 recorded an increase of 711 individuals and the total number of unemployed in that year was 31,232. The total number of unemployed at the end of 2013, was 34,514realizing an increase of 10.5% compared to the number of unemployed in 2012.

Table 12. Number of registered unemployed individuals
in Montenegro in the period 2010-2013

2010	2011	2012	2013
32.026	30.521	31.232	34.514

Source: Employment Agency of Montenegro

Table 13. Unemployment structure in
Montenegro according to qualifications

I and II level degree	III, IV, V level degree	VI, VII, and VIII level degree
6.814	17.823	5.884

Source: Employment Agency of Montenegro

The qualification structure of the unemployed in 2011 is shown in Table 13.

In 2013 unemployment among women increased from 47.4%, as it was in 2012, to 48.8%. There was an increase in unemployment among the youth categories of unemployed - at the age of 25 years there was a growth of 13.7%, and in the group aged 25 to 30 years, the growth was 35.4%.

RECYCLING OF ELECTRONIC WASTE AS A "NEW" INDUSTRY

To put it simply, e-recycling is the process of recycling or reuse of computer equipment and other electronic devices. The fact that technology is developing rapidly in recent decades and that the lifetime of the technology is getting shorter, results in the emergence of an increasing amount of various electronic devices which, after being outdated, become waste that should be disposed properly and reused. For example, 40 percent of commercial computers reach their end-of-life after three years, another 40 percent after five years, and the remaining 20 percent after seven years(EPA, 2011).

The problem of large amounts of e-waste, logically, first hit the most developed economies which, thanks to their heavy investment in new technologies, were very quickly faced with a large amount of "old" technology that had to be appropriately treated. This circumstance has led to the appearance of national initiatives for the development of e-recycling. Even in the most developed economies such as the U.S., e-recycling is a relatively new phenomenon. For this reason, even those countries do not have a sufficiently developed infrastructure necessary for the successful implementation of this process. According to International Association of Electronics Recyclers (IAER) estimation, in U.S. there was only 7,000 employees within the electronic waste recycling industry in 2003, while the whole industry has created an annual revenue of about $ 700 million (Kang, H.-Y, Schoenung, J.M, 2005, pp.368-400), which is obviously a bit number, given the size of the market and the amount of electronic waste that it generates annually. For example, in 2005 electronic waste accounted for about 5% of the total waste that citizens and businesses in the U.S. generate annually. The National Safety Council reported 63 million computers were obsolete in this country in 2005 (Shelton, 2010).

In the past 10 years, the electronic recycling industry records a growth, so it is estimated that at present it generates annual revenue of about $ 5 billion, and employs about 30,000 workers, with a tendency of further growth. The U.S. Environmental Protection Agency (EPA) estimates that out of the total amount of e-waste, that is annually generated on the territory of this country, only 15% to 20% are being recycled, which creates considerable ambence for the development of this industry in the future. Of all the developed countries, Japan ranks first in the world in the amount of electronic waste that is recycled. This country recycles about 85% of the total e-waste. It is estimated that in the next decade, the amount of electronic waste in the world scale may rise up to 500%. Currently, the largest producer of e-waste are the U.S. and China, with an estimated volume of about 3 million tons of e-waste every year.

The process of electronic waste recycling can be represented as shown in Figure 1.

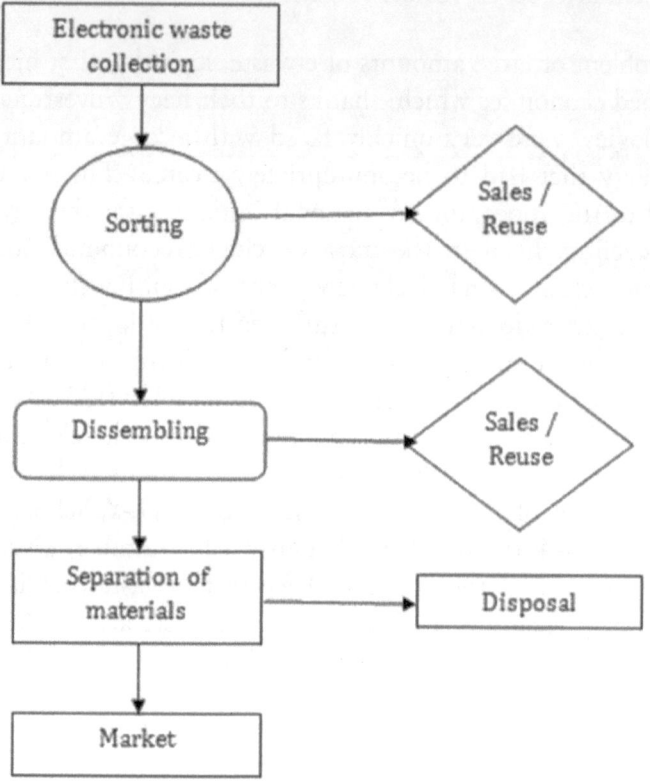

Figure 1. Display of the process of electronic waste recycling

Source: Kang, H.-Y, Schoenung, J.M,2005.

The first step in the recycling of electronic waste is definitely an organized collection of electronic waste. This step in the process of e-recycling is the most critical, since unfortunately only a small amount of electronic waste is being collected and recycled in an organized way.

In the process of sorting e-waste, one of the two scenarios is possible. Electronic devices which prove that they still have useful value, can be sold as used, which is, at least temporarily, delaying the process of their recycling. In the second case, if the product as a whole is no longer of practical value for customers, it is decomposed into components, which formally starts its recycling process.

At the stage when the electronic device is separated into components also are two possible scenarios. According to the first scenario, the parts of the device that turn out to be functional may be sold on the market, which returns them into use. In the event that the parts of electronic device are non-functional, we proceed to the next stage of the recycling process, and it involves the separation of materials.

In the process of separation of materials, using the specialized equipment, various materials that make up the electronic device are being separated. In terms of re-use, the materials can be classified into the following:

1. Recyclable (can be re-used by returning into production process)
2. Non-recyclable (can notbe returned into production process, used for energy – burnig, or can be safely stored)
3. Dangerous – hazardous (materials that are harmful to humans and their environment)
4. Harmless (materials that are harmful to humans and their environment)

Recycling of electronic waste has great economic potential, because the realization of this process leads to very valuable of materials (gold, aluminum, copper), which can be restored to the production process. In the condition of the limitations of these natural resources, this model of their return into the production process is of paramount importance. By recycling one million cell phones one can get 16 tons of copper, over 750 lbs of silver, 75 lbs of gold, and 33lbs of palladium. For example, it is estimated that in one year, the U.S. alone throws mobile phones in which the value of gold and silver are estimated to be approximately $ 60 million. Recent studies showed that precious metal recovery contributes to over 80% of the personal computer materials' market value, despite the small quantity of them found in computers (Streicher-Porte, M. et al. 2005).

In addition to its economic viability, electronic waste recycling is extremely important because of its positive effect on the environment. Electronic waste is considered to be hazardous waste because it contains elements such as lead, cadmium and mercury, which can have unforeseeable bad effects on the environment and human health. Recent studies are confirming extremely negative impact of this kind of waste on human health (Leung, A. et al. 2008). For example, CRT monitors or monitors with cathode ray tubes contain an average of about 4.5to 9 pounds of lead. Good example is the fact that about 40% of lead in landfills comes from consumer electronics.

In 2004 in Serbia, about 60 companies were involved in recycling, mainly through recycling of scrap metal, paper and PET packaging. Today, in Serbia there are about 280 companies that process secondary materials on different technological levels. Among these companies there are three factories for the recycling of electrical and electronic waste. These plants are "BiS Recycling Center" in Omoljici near Pancevo, "SE Trade" in VisnjickaBanja in Belgrade and "Eco-metal" in the municipality Vrdnik near Novi Sad. Although over one million euros were invested in each of these factories, that was not enough to effectuate the full recycling in them. Recycling of non-recyclable of material requires large financial investments, special infrastructure and sophisticated technology whose value reaches several hundred million euros. What is common to all three plants is that they recycle recyclable elements in devices such as plastic, metal and glass. By recycling of one computer that weighs 66 pounds, 55 pounds of high quality material returns to production. Waste of second and third category accounts for 10 pounds, and 1 pound of material that can not be recycled in our country remains(Ereciklaza, 2014).

Non-recyclable components such as motherboards, CRTs, processors and hard drives, are stored in special containers and finally exported overseas, because the final recycling is performed by a small number of recycling companies in the world.

EXPLORING THE POTENTIAL FOR DEVELOPMENT OF THE INDUSTRY OF ELECTRONICS RECYCLING IN SERBIA

With the aim of investigating the potential for the development of electronic waste recycling as one of the possible generators of new jobs in the future, in February 2014, the survey on a sample of 100 participants was organized and conducted in Serbia. The aim of this study was to identify the real extent of the quantity of electronic waste generated by individuals (households in Serbia), but also to make insight in the the level of development of awareness regarding the importance of recycling of electronic waste among the population of Serbia. For the purpose of research realization, a questionnaire was designed and distributed to the respondents, and the results are processed and systematized.

In the first category, which is covered by the research, the respondents were asked to answer the question about the amount of electronic waste they are producing annually. Electronic waste is divided into several categories: cell phones, TV sets, white ware, computers, other electronic devices unmentioned. The results shown in Table 14 were obtained by further processing.

Table 14. The amount of electronic waste produced
in Serbia that respondents produce annually

e-waste category	The amount of electronic waste per participant per annum in pieces
Cell phones	0.70
TV sets	0.11
White ware	0.17
PC's	0.07
Other e-devices	1,20

Source: Author's research

As shown the results presented in Table 14, the average citizen of Serbia, on an annual basis, "produces" a significant amount of electronic waste. If we multiply the data on the amount of electronic waste from Table 14, by the number of households in Serbia (2.48 millionsaccording to the census of 2011)and then with an average weight of certain categories of electronic waste that are included in the survey (Table 15), we acquire the data that the citizens of Serbia annually produces about 29,000 tons of various electronic waste.

Table 15. The average weight of certain categories of electronic waste

e-waste category	The average weight of certain categories of electronic waste per piece	Estimate of the annual amount of waste of households in Serbia (in tons)
Cell phone	0.09kg	156
TV	12kg	3,274
Household appliances (white ware)	50kg	21,080
PC (monitor and chassis)	15kg	2,604
Other electronic devices	0.5kg	1,488
Total:		28,602

Source: Author's research

Available data from companies that are currently engaged in recycling of electronic waste in Serbia show that less than 10% of disposable electronic waste is recycled in this country. We should not ignore the fact that the amount of electronic waste exponentially increases from year to year, taking into account the advancement in technology and its increasing presence in the lives of all citizens. This circumstance suggests that the electronic waste recycling industry can represent a significant economic branch in the future, that could have a significant impact on reducing unemployment, but also give a significant contribution to the total gross national income.

We should not disregard that even the most developed countries still do not have adequately regulated issue concerning recycling of growing amount of electronic waste. As a consequence of this fact, a large amount of electronic waste ends in Nigeria and other poor countries through "black" channels. In this way, they literally become a junkyard of rich and developed countries, and in them the recycling process takes place with irreverence of minimum requirements and the conditions for its execution. Bearing this fact in mind, Serbia and other Western Balkan countries could work on strengthening of their capacities intended for recycling of electronic waste, and then, by synchronized action, intervene on the world market as the major buyers of electronic waste of developed countries. Thereby, the full utilization of processing capacity and good impact on employment and gross domestic product in the long term could be ensured. In addition, by e-waste recycling one can obtain valuable raw materials, that could be sent back on the world market either in the form of semi-finished or as finished products. This would indirectly encourage development of other activities, and the positive economic effects would be multiplied.

Within the second category of issues covered by the survey, we analyzed the current situation in terms of the quantity of electronic waste annually submitted by citizens for recycling to the one of authorized recycling centers in the territory of the Republic of Serbia. Electronic waste is classified in the the same categories as in the previous question in order to obtain comparable results. The results are provided in Table 16.

Table 16. The amount of electronic waste by categories which the examinees annually submit to the recycling centers in Serbia

e-waste category	The amount of e-waste that is submitted to recycling in pieces
Cell phones	6
TV sets	1
White ware	1
PC's	2
Other e-devices	5

Source: Author's research

The results point to the fact that less than 10% of electronic waste, that is annually "produced" by citizens of Serbia, is being recycled, which opens a range of other issues. First of all, the question is what happens with the electronic waste that is no longer in use and that is not is being recycled in a proper manner?The only logical answer to this question is that a large quantity of such waste ends inadequately disposed (very often in the nature), creating a large potential and real danger to the environment. Some estimates suggest that in Serbia, about 40,000 tons of electronic waste ends up in landfills, in various warehouses and dumps. Bearing in mind that the amount of of electronic waste will rise steadily in the future, this issue shoud be carefully approached in order to find an appropriate soultion. The solution to this problem lies solely in proper disposal and recycling of electronic waste in approved recycling centers.

Table 17. The willingness of the citizens of Serbia to
hand over their e-waste to recycling centers

Are you willing to submit your e-waste for recycling?	Number of exeminees
Yes, with the appropriate remuneration.	52
Yes, with no charge.	36
No.	12
Total:	100

Source: Author's research

The next question that arises as a logical reaction to the fact that Serbia recycles only a small percent of the annualy produced electronic waste is why is it so? In clearing up the answer to the last question, a third category of questions to which the respondents included in the survey gave answers, can significantly help. Namely, within this category, the willingness of the average citizen of Serbia to submit their electronic waste for recycling by an authorized recycling center, was tested. The results of this part of the survey are shown in Table 17.

The fact that 36% of respondents are willing to donate their electronic waste to the recycling centers free of charge, suggests that citizens are aware of the fact that electronic waste is a big burden for them and that it should be properly disposed of and recycled. A certain number of respondents expected an adequate financial compensation for the submittion of electronic devices, which leads to the conclusion that we should develop an appropriate system of compensation payments to individuals who are willing to submit their electronic waste for recycling. Category of respondents who answered negatively to the possibility of handing electronic waste for recycling is in the minority, but its existence points to the need to educate the general public about the importance and necessity for recycling of electronic waste.

CONCLUSION

This paper highlights the great potential for development of the industry of electronic waste recycling in Serbia and other Western Balkan countries. The development of an entirely new industry, due to its great potential conditioned by modern technology trends and increasingly short life span of products and technologies, will inevitably lead to the creation of new jobs in the area of green economy, which will contribute to solving the problem of high unemployment in these economies.This claim is confirmed by the fact that in most developed countries, where the process of recycling of electronic waste is still not at a high level, there was a significant increase in the number of employees within the industry over the past 10 years.

The paper points out the fact that the citizens of Serbia, in line with global trends, produce growing amount of electronic waste. In one of the first researches on the quantity of electronic waste produced by the citizens in Serbia, based on the sample the survey was carried out, we have elaborated the estimation of annual production of electronic waste in this economy. Also, we have indicated the fact that less than 10% of e-waste is being recycled in Serbia, which is below the average compared to the developed economies, in which this process is not yet fully developed as well.

In addition, we have proposed the measures which may lead to an increase in the level of recycling of electronic waste in Serbia, and thus also in other countries of the Western Balkans. Those measures imply the strengthening of capacities for the development of recycling centers, where even non-recyclable elements contained in the e-waste could be recycled; the raise of awareness of the necessity of e-waste recycling and more organized approach to collecting of electronic waste. Over time, the increasing amount of electronic waste which is recycled in the domestic market, articulated a proposal to the Western Balkan countries, individually or through regional cooperation, to intervene on the world market of electronic waste as its importers, which would create conditions for maximum utilization of existing facilities and construction of new ones. In that way, the impact on employment would be even better.

Since this situation in other countries of the Western Balkans is similar due to analogic socio-economic environment, we can generally conclude that these countries have a great potential in the field of development of electronic waste recycling industry, which can become a significant absorber of excess manpower from the labor market, and hence one of the economic growth generators.

REFERENCES

1. Domazet, I, Filimonovi , D, "Working Potential of the Elders in Serbia and Proposal of Reactivation Models", New Challenges in changing Labour Markets, Institute of Economic Sciences, Belgrade, 2012, pp. 133-152.

2. Draškovi , B, Domazet, I, "Instrumenti finansiranja ekoloških troškova I koriš enje prirodnih dobara I vrednosti u zašti enim rezervatima prirode u Srbiji", Ecologica 70, 2013, pp. 234-238

3. Draškovi , B, Zubovi , J, Domazet, I, "Management and Utilisation of Natural Resources in Special Nature Reservesin", MonographSustainable Technologies, Policies, and Constraints in the Green Economy, Ed. Andrei Jean-Vasile et al. IGI Global, USA, 2013, pp. 106-123.

4. "Electronics Waste Management in the United States Through", U.S. EPA, 2011, EPA 530-R-11-002http://www.epa.gov/wastes/conserve/materials/ecycling/docs/fullbaselinereport2011.pdf

5. Kang, H.-Y, Schoenung, J.M, "Electronic waste recycling: A review of U.S. infrastructure and technology options", Resources, Conservation and Recycling, no. 45, 2005, pp. 368–400

6. Leung, A. et al. "Heavy Metals Concentrations of Surface Dust from e-Waste Recycling and Its Human Health Implications in Southeast China", Environmental science & Technology, 42 (7), 2008, pp.2674-2680http://www.ereciklaza.com/sta-je-reciklaza.htm#, (Accessed on April 20, 2014)

7. RZS, "Upotreba informaciono-komunikacionih tehnologija u Srbiji u 2013. godini", Statistical Office of the Republic of Serbia Belgrade, 2014.

8. RZS, "Projekcije radne snage Republike Srbije 2010-2050", p 10. Statistical Office of the Republic of Serbia, Belgrade, 2011.

9. Stoši , I, Domazet, I, Hani , H. "Effects of Privatization and Restructuring on Manufacturing Industry: The Evidence from Serbia", Metalurgia InternationalVol.XVIII, No.7, 2013, pp. 77-82.

10. Shelton, R, "E-Waste recycling", SNU-Tulsa Research Journal, Volume 3, Issue 1, 2010.

11. Streicher-Porte, M. et al. "Key drivers of the e-waste recycling system: Assessing and modelling e-waste processing in the informal sector in Delhi", Environmental Impact Assessment Review, vol. 25, issue 5, 2005.

12. www.bhas.ba (Accessed on April 06, 2014).

13. www.statistika.hzz.hr (Accessed on April 03, 2014)

14. www.avrm.gov.mk (Accessed on March 29, 2014)

15. www.zzzcg.org (15, 2014)

THE INSURANCE SECTOR AND CLIMATE CHANGES: THE FORMATTING OF EU POLICY FOR THE WESTERN BALKANS

Ivan Piljan[40]

Dusan Cogoljevic[41]

INTRODUCTION

The issue of climate changes is an existing social problem for modern civilization. At the same time, it is an environmental problem, as well as an economic, political, social, cultural, and health issue. This involves a global environmental problem and for that reason, we are to discuss global climate changes which affect countries, nations, and continents regardless of location or the degree of liability in creating and maintaining these changes.

In the Western Balkans, the issue of climate changes has been a subject of interest for decision-makers and interested parties in the last couple years, though various studies deal with this problem from the perspective of science. Sociologists and political scientists, when analyzing the climate changes issue, mostly do so in the context of the negotiation process and a new global regime for climate changes. The question of adaptation is generally the subject of research of papers in different areas, but it is rarely done from the perspective of adapting to climate changes.

---

[40] Assistant Professor, Faculty of Business Economy and Entrepreneurship, Belgrade, Serbia, piljanivan@gmail.com

[41] Assistant Professor, Faculty of Business Economy and Entrepreneurship, Belgrade, Serbia, dusan.cogoljevic@vspep.edu.rs

The climate changes issue is not easy to define in the frame of only one scientific area, regardless whether it is natural or social sciences. Considering the causes and consequences of this social issue and problem of nature, equal to the issue of survival of nature and civilization, the question of the context and basis upon which this problem can be scientifically analyzed is raised.

According to all the indicators of various research papers of insurance and reinsurance companies, the insurance sector has started to be more involved in risk management connected to climate changes. The question of determining the potential long and short term effects of climate changes on the business activities of insurance and reinsurance companies represents a priority and its final goal is finding measures to minimize risk and damages.

That is the reason why the insurance sector has to cover, along with risk assessment, climate changes and in such a way adequately adapt its product - insurance.

CLIMATE CHANGES

The climate changes issue is an existing social problem for modern civilization. At the same time, it is an environmental problem, as well as an economic, political, social, cultural, and health issue. Today, in modern scientific thought and in social and natural sciences, there is no serious scientific paper, article or book which can negate the existing of climate changes. Moreover, there is no disagreement about the global environmental issue, and due to thus, we are to discuss global climate changes which affect countries, nations, and continents regardless of location or the degree of liability in creating and maintaining these changes. This involves dramatic climate changes where altered forces of nature do not spare any victims. It is evident, however, that there is certain disagreement in science related to the problem of the impact of anthropogenic factors on climate changes creating. Regardless of these inconsistencies, the future of modern civilization, people, nations, as well as the flora and fauna is mostly determined by the future development of climate changes and by the question whether the human race, which has directly or indirectly had an impact on this, can turn the situation around and benefit directly, as well as give support to nature and the natural world.

There is a simple solution for this problem, but the consequences of such a solution are in its idealistic significance: industry closure is not a solution which can bring prosperity to civilization but, rather, it may create an economic and political global catastrophe. On the other hand, a disastrous state of affairs whereupon high temperatures destroy everything is not far from the aforementioned idealistic sense. A devastated climate results in the destruction of the economy, agriculture, and consequently, political instability. In whichever direction it is considered, a catastrophe is inevitable if the climate changes issue is approached from the perspective of exclusivity and inflexibility. Thus, more flexibility in the traditional regard of politics as well as economics of ecology and environmental problems, or in other words, disregarding the traditionally rigid and conservative understanding of the climate problem and its impact on social and natural development is a solution which may be successful. The winning combination, in fact, may be to create two paths, two strategies for resolving the climate changes issue, whereupon both roads are an alternative to each other, as well as support. The solution is also mitigation (climate change mitigation) and adaptation (to changed climate conditions). Mitigation has for its goal a limitation of climate changes by reducing gas emissions by way of the greenhouse effect. On the other hand, adaptation is related to the adapting of environmental, social and economic systems as a response to real or expected climate changes and their effects and processes. It is also related to changes in processes, practices and structures in order to mitigate potential damage or benefits which climate changes produce. To be more precise, a strategy of adapting to climate changes can be viewed as a necessary response of the international community to the existing problems which climate changes cause. For countries which are especially vulnerable to existing climate changes consequences, adaptation strategies are very important due to the fact that if they fail to adapt, there may be "significant losses, social unrest and a relocating of the population, even sickness and death".

The issue of adaptation is mainly the subject of scientific studies which rely only on theoretical concepts without putting these theories into practice, or else the adaptation concept is observed completely separately from adaptation which is the subject of studies in other areas. In this sense, adaptation consists of three parts: the theoretical part, as a response to risks and vulnerability; the political answer to the problem of adaptation to climate changes (policy), and practice, or the involvement of relevant factors in the process of adapting to climate changes. Each study of the problem of adapting to climate changes raises the question whether adapting to climate changes which is today predominantly carried out by way of different policies is the solution for the impact of climate changes, especially in developing countries and for developing an analysis of the relevant political instruments and approaches in the framework of the Convention and the theoretical approaches which are related to adapting to climate changes.

During the last ten years, beside the fact that a large number of theoretical approaches and policies in the area of climate changes have been developed, the largest number of them has been related to only one approach defined by the Convention – mitigation. Thus, adapting to altered climate conditions has become the subject of increased interest at the beginning of the 21th century. However, most studies access the question of adaptation from the perspective of natural or social sciences, while the multidisciplinary or interdisciplinary approach is mostly absent.

Even though developing countries are the most vulnerable to climate changes, the question of adapting was mainly in the focus of interest of developed countries. Also, it should be taken under consideration that the question and approach to adaptation and sustainable development is not the same for developed and developing countries.

In the Western Balkans, the climate changes issue has been a subject of interest of decision-makers and interested parties during the last couple of years, while various studies have analyzed this issue from the perspective of science. Sociologists and political scientists, when analyzing the climate changes issue, mostly do so in the context of the negotiation process and the new global regime on climate changes. The question of adaptation is generally a subject of research from different areas, but it is rarely done from the perspective of adapting to climate changes.

The concept of adapting to climate changes has not been researched in Serbia until today's day.

Climate changes adapting as a concept on an international level is, at the same time, a component of the sustainable development concept in developing countries. There is the question of the economic, political and financial possibilities of incorporating the project of adapting to climate changes within the development politics of developing countries. Thus, controversies in accepting and incorporating adaptation on climate changes in traditional insights on the aims and efficiency of the sustainable development concept as a global response to the ecological, political, social and economic challenges of modern mankind are possible.

The climate changes issue is not easy to define in the frame of only one science, no matter whether this concerns natural or social sciences. Considering the causes and consequences of this social problem and challenge of nature, as well as the question of the survival of nature and civilization, the question of context and basis in which this problem can be scientifically analyzed is raised. The political and economic causes of climate changes expressed in traditional materialistic and quantitative indicators implicate that social sciences such as sociology, politics, economy, social and political ecology take part in researching the climate changes phenomenon and the future social consequences, although the possible contribution of natural sciences should not be overlooked. Natural sciences, unlike social, can determine with precision and even predict the dynamic of the development of climate changes and the consequences on the flora and fauna.

THE IMPACT OF CLIMATE CHANGES

The risks which climate changes bring with them are real and their impact is gradually more present. In fact, according to the UN, all its urgent appeals were linked with the issue of climate. The UN Security Council in 2007 held their first discussion on climate changes and the consequences on international safety.

The climate changes science is now better appreciated. The insights of the Intergovernmental Panel on climate changes shows that, even if emissions were reduced to half the 1990 level in 2050, it would be difficult to avoid an increase in temperature of 20C over the pre-industrial level. Such an increase in temperature would be a serious security risk which would increase if the warming effect continues. The effects of climate changes are situations such as the melting of glacier peaks and glaciers, with extreme weather conditions becoming more frequent and more intense. Investing in the mitigation of climate changes and ways of adapting to the inevitable should keep pace with the responses to international safety threats related to climate changes.

It is estimated that the restoring of the climate would cost the world economy as much as 20% of the global GDP per year, while the costs of an effective widespread activity could be limited to 1%.

Climate changes are best understood as multiple threats which deteriorate the existing trends, and increase tension and instability. The key reason for this is that climate changes threaten to encumber those countries and regions which are already weak and war-torn. It is important to acknowledge that those risks are not only of a humanitarian nature, but include political and security risks which directly affect European interests. Moreover, in accordance with the concept of human safety, it is clear that the numerous questions related to climate changes which impact international safety are mutually connected and demand comprehensive political answers (Grozdani , Radovi -Markovi , Jevti , 2013, pp. 92-112).

The EU is in a unique position to respond to the climate changes impact on international safety, considering its leading role in development, global climate politics and the wide range of tools and instruments at its disposal. A safety challenge plays a part in the power of Europe due to its holistic approach to the prevention of conflicts, crisis management and post-conflict renovation, but also because of the fact that it is the main proponent of effective multilateralism.

EU CLIMATE STRATEGIES

On January 10, 2007, the European Commission introduced a new energy policy and climate changes policy. This package of measures united various proposals to the EU Council to determine the goals of the future climate changes and energy policy. The key elements of this package are the following: setting the target of reducing GHG emissions, strengthening the emissions trading scheme, energy efficiency incensement, a larger usage of renewable energy and a greater support to new technologies.

As one of the world's largest emitters of greenhouse gases and one of the creators of the global climate politics agenda, the EU undertook a specific obligation to realize an agreement about the new global climate regime for the period after 2012. If it is necessary to come up with a solution of the contract on an international level in the following decades, the foundation must be laid down in the shortest possible period. The debate on the climate policy has still not reached an international consensus, and has not even succeeded in forming a strong coalition which would be able to take action on a global level. This causes a serious worry considering the reports of the Intergovernmental Panel on climate changes whose assessment of the state of the global climate removes any doubt of the seriousness of the situation and assessment of possible risks and possible adverse effects (Droge, 2010, pp.105-116).

The EU state member governments have committed to reduce greenhouse gas emissions for a minimum of 20 percent. In assessing EU climate strategy, it is important to make a difference between its effects within the EU and out of this region. The EU Council has emphasized that the set goal of 20% is the minimal level which would be increased to 30% in international negotiations at the moment when all industrialized countries agree with a common goal. Tightening targets in terms of reducing carbon dioxide emission is imperative, especially as it will increase the credibility of the EU climate policy. An important goal is to reduce global warming by an average level of 20C. Accomplishing these goals will not be an easy task, due to the fact that based on previous data and considering the differences in economic development, by 2050 industrialized countries should reduce carbon dioxide emissions by as much as 80%. The EU is at the moment responsible for one-sixth of the global emissions of carbon dioxide and one fifth of greenhouse gas emissions of industrialized countries (Annex I of the Kyoto Protocol).

Gas emissions trading is a basic management mechanism on the EU level, in order to provide a harmonizing with the goals of reducing carbon dioxide emissions. This system demands that companies respect the allowed emissions. The favorable side effects are an increase of energy safety (by increasing the share of renewable energy) and an increase of competitiveness on international markets (the strengthening of efficiency and innovations). Participation in the gas emissions trading system provides the companies some reliability in planning, as well as sending an important message to other countries. Long-term trading can play an important role on the international level if countries accept binding targets. Thereby, the EU could be a leader in this field, supporting other countries to follow it. Also, the system of allocation and gas emissions trading should be transparent in order to prevent an obstruction of competition and endanger the energy supply (Ganter, 2010, pp.117-128).

Increased energy efficiency is especially possible to accomplish by determining sector levels – strengthening the development of new technologies and developing consumer standards for electric devices and vehicles. A large potential of energy savings is improving the existing objects – insulating buildings. International cooperation in this area is extremely important, both on the technological level and in the area of forming innovation politics. To increase energy efficiency, the EU Council considers it very important to introduce the proposed measures, not only to EU countries but others as well. Developing countries and newly industrialized countries could be offered the possibility of planned cooperation in the transportation, construction and energy sectors, and the developing of common standards in reducing energy consumption can be promoted.

In the area of support for technological strategies, the EU has to offer support to renewable energy, while there are obvious differences in certain technologies. While the costs of hydropower and wind energy, and some aspects of biomass production are almost competitive, others such as solar, geothermal and ocean energy lag far behind. At this point, policy creators should estimate whether it is better to spend the available funds on promising but expensive technologies with no time limits (such as solar energy) or alternative technologies with the potential of being launched on the market in the near future. The European Commission has no mandate to intervene with national decisions regarding energy mix: member states have a sovereign jurisdiction over their energy supplies. This does not exclude the Council's approval to the set goal of the participation of renewable energy in the energy mix, which directly impacts the energy mix on the level of the member states.

Increasing the participation of renewable energy and promoting the development of technologies based on this will help European companies to maintain their competitiveness on a continuously expanding market. Viewed long-term, the tendency to accomplish these goals will stabilize or even reduce dependence on energy imports.

The EU is an important and influential factor in the global climate policy arena. The basis of the EU climate strategy offers an exceptional stimulus to other states to participate in gas emissions trading and technological cooperation.

Thus, it is necessary to urgently take action in order to reduce greenhouse gas emission and mitigate the impact of climate changes. However, even if efficient steps for emission reduction are taken immediately, it seems as if the inevitable minimal increase of the average global temperature is 20C, what would have as a consequence rising sea levels, increasing natural disasters, and a spreading of desert areas. Another possible consequence could be an increase of conflict due to insufficient natural resources such as food and potable water in various parts of the world. Yet, most developing countries have insufficient funds and no alternatives of livelihood sources or efficient adaptation to changes. Even though they are the least responsible for climate changes, the countries of the Global South are the most vulnerable to their influence, among which are also the countries of the Western Balkans. That is the reason why developing countries should demand from the industrialized world to face their historic responsibility and give proposals for a mitigation of climate changes. Adaptation is identified as one of the key elements for the intensification of a future response to climate changes. A discussion on adaptation policies largely means a debate on who pays for what and which financial mechanisms should cover the expected costs, as well as how financial commitments should be shared. As other elements for the mitigation of climate changes consequences, new political possibilities for collecting means for adaptation are imposed, such are taxation on carbon, auction of gas emission rights, taxation of international air traffic and initiatives for climate insurance.

CLIMATE CHANGES AND CHALLENGES POLICY IN WESTERN BALKANS STATES

In Albania, one of the external factors which influence improvements in climate changes policy is EU accession. Internally, investing in green technologies (transportation, renewable energy sources and energy efficiency), together with ecotourism, organic agriculture and forest certification are among the important movers of sustainable development (Drakenberg, 2011). The Ministry of the Environment, Forestry and Water Administration (MoEFWA) is responsible for enforcing activities in the climate changes area. Related to international obligations on protecting the environment in the area of climate changes, Albania has ratified the Kyoto Protocol in 2005 and submitted its First National Communication to the UN Framework Convention on Climate Changes (UNFCCC) in 2002. The Second Communication was prepared in 2009 and in April 2013 MoEFWA announced the preparing of the Third National Communication in cooperation with the UN Development program (UNDP).

In the NSDI draft for the period 2013-2020, Albania set the goal of reducing GHG emissions by 16 percent by 2020, compared to the basic year of 1990 and a goal of reducing the amount of HCFC from 120 to 108 tons by 2014, with a long-term goal of reducing to 29 tons by 2040. Regarding the adaptation measures, MoEFWA, in cooperation with UNDP and the Austrian Development Agency, have prepared an Albanian Document for a carbon financing policy in 2009 which puts

Albania in a competitive place of the mechanisms for pure development and future carbon markets, based on the high quality of the Albanian project activities.

Bosnia and Herzegovina ratified the UNFCCC in September 2000 and the Kyoto Protocol in April 2008. Soon after these obligations, the country had institutional plans for solving climate changes challenges (Laganin, 2010). The Ministry of Physical Planning, Civil Engineering and Ecology is a major institution which is engaged with climate changes issues. It is a key point for UNFCCC and the Global Environment Fund (GEF). Furthermore, a steering committee for climate changes with 32 member states was founded (Laganin, 2010). The initial financial support for preparing preliminary documents for the First National Communication of the UNFCCC in 2009 came from GEF, and Bosnia and Herzegovina (BiH) is now working on the Second National Communication. The initial communication indicates the need to develop national strategies and action plans for the mitigation of climate changes, and it is significant to connect the two strategies with national economic and development plans, and also to enable a direct inclusion of subjects and authorities on the local level.

At this moment, BiH has no comprehensive multiethnic climate policy and significant effort to integrate climate politics in different sectors is needed. Harmonizing with real EU climate achievements is in the early phase and the country has accomplished a limited progress related to the 2013 EC-BiH preparations. Also, there is a lack of research in relation to the issue how climate changes impact forest and biodiversity productivity on regional and local levels. A reliable model for evaluating possible national actions has still not been developed (Vojnikovi , 2010).

The major institutional challenges which hinder the development of a climate changes policy are insufficient funds for the increasing costs of climate activities management, a poor regulatory framework, a lack of transparent business procedures, corruption and a poor infrastructure (Vojnikovi , 2010). Thus, the question remains how to create the necessary strategies and how to adhere to the accomplished with the support of international experts and financing from for example the following: GEF, UNEP, UNDP and from bilateral donors.

The Former Yugoslav Republic of Macedonia (FYROM) ratified UNFCCC as a Non-Annex I party in December 1997 and the Kyoto Protocol in July 2004. It presented two national communications to UNFCCC (2003 and 2009) and at this moment it is preparing the Third Communication. The National Action Plan for the mitigation of climate changes was presented within the 2012 Second National Communication (UNEP). There is also a plan prepared to introduce the monitoring and reporting as well as verification of GHG emissions within the EU Emissions Trading System (EU ETS) in 2012, and in effect, the country has started to build its relevant capacity.

Mitigation measures have been introduced in certain national strategies, and there is a comprehensive Communication Strategy on climate changes with a detailed Action Plan. A Case Study on the potential of mitigation in the transportation sector has been accepted and scenarios of mitigation for the evaluation of possible GHG reductions have been planned in accordance with forthcoming requests by UNFCCC and the EU. Within the National Sustainable Development Strategy (2010), improvements in the area of the energy sector which contributes to national sustainable development have been identified. The National Investment Strategy of Environmental Protection (2009) identifies carbon financing as a potential tool for attracting foreign investments (National strategy for adaptation of health sector on climate changes (2011)). Also developed was the National Strategy for Pure Development Mechanisms during 2008-2012 (2007) and National Indicators of Climate Changes.

Montenegro ratified UNFCCC in October 2006 as a Non-Annex I party, and the Kyoto Protocol in March 2007. In 2010, the Initial National Communication to UBFCCC was submitted and in 2014 the government planned to finalize a Second National Communication. The Ministry for Sustainable Development and Tourism is a major competent authority in the area of climate changes (adoption of policies and regulations) and the Agency for Environmental Protection is an executive authority for implementing legislation. National strategic and state legal frameworks were to some extent engaged in climate changes issues, even if Montenegro is still in the early phase of preparing to fight against climate changes.

In separate national and environmental strategies, including the National Strategy for Sustainable Development (2007) and the National Policy of Environmental Protection (2008), Montenegro set general goals in the climate changes area. Climate changes are weakly integrated in the policy and plans of agriculture, the spatial planning waste sector, but in the sector of forestry, air quality and energy, the integration of climate changes policy is somewhat improved. Between 2010 and 2011, Montenegro improved its legislation framework related to the energy sector by developing a Law on Energy, a Law on Energy Efficiency, Energy Politics of Montenegro until 2030 and a Draft of a Strategy of Energy Development of Montenegro to 2030. The current energy goals of Montenegro are 33% of the share of renewable energy sources in use by 2020 and an improvement of energy efficiency of 9% by 2018. The strategies include a combining of heat and electricity, an improvement of industrial boilers, a replacement of coal with liquid petroleum gas in industrial furnaces and a production of high-temperature heat.

Serbia stands out regarding improvements in climate changes policies, as it was noted in the EC Report of Progress. Serbia ratified UNFCCC in March 2001 as a Non-Annex I party, and the Kyoto Protocol in January 2008. The Ministry for Energy, Development and Environmental Protection (MEDEP) is the focal point for UNFCCC and the Kyoto Protocol. Since ratifying UNFCCC, Serbia has made a significant effort to meet the requirements of the Convention. The preparation of the First Report of a Biennial Update has started, an obligation toward UNFCCC, and development guidelines have been prepared for the Nationally Appropriate Mitigation Action (NAMA). The First National Communication with UNFCCC was submitted in 2010 and the government is now working on the Second Communication.

Preparing a strategy for climate changes and an associated Action Plan stipulates the including and questioning of basic needs in terms of adapting to climate changes in the aim of a sustainable way to reduce GHG emissions. The Strategy and Action plan will determinate the level of GHG together with the goals of reducing GHG emissions by 2020 and 2030. Regulations in certain sectors, including energy, waste, air, transport and industry, contribute to mitigating climate changes, while the policy in the forestry sector includes certain measures for adapting. In the transportation sector, Serbia has the goal to restore an efficient international rail system, it is carrying out road repair, increasing the level and efficiency of river transportation and has also ceased the production of leaded gasoline. Furthermore, it is ready to invest in waste technology, while in the agricultural sector, the use of biogas for heat production and for large livestock operations is a key step to reducing agricultural emissions. In the area of forestry and land use, the optimum strategy is afforestation.

The National Program of Environmental Protection (2010) and the Sustainable Development Strategy (2008) considers climate changes to be a significant challenge for environmental protection. Developed were the Strategy for Energy Development until 2015, the Strategy for Scientific and Technological Development and the Strategy for Forestry Development, which are related to the importance of mitigation and the adaptation of activities of economic development in energy and forestry. In 2010, Serbia adopted the first Action Plan for Energy Efficiency (LOCSEE-RS, 2013). As a Contracting Party of the Energy Community, Serbia has ambitious targets until 2020, including 27% of renewable energy sources and 10% of a biofuel share in the transportation sector. The targets for energy efficiency are similar to those of the other Contracting SEE parties (9% by 2018).

THE INSURANCE SECTOR AND CLIMATE CHANGES

Climate changes have a strong negative influence on the insurance sector, which is reflected through a slow development of this sector and the transferring of a larger part of the risk on the state and individuals. The differences between the amounts of unpaid premiums and amounts paid from insurance policies based on the claims incurred have decreased, which leads to a decrease of the ability of the insurance market to absorb the damages connected with climate changes, which has negative repercussions for the availability of insurance services with an acceptable premium. According to one scenario (UNEPFI, 2006, p. 15), which takes into consideration the latest scientific knowledge on the influence of climate changes, the impact of climate changes on insurance companies could be disastrous. Namely, if nothing is undertaken in regards to reducing gas emissions, in the decade to the year 2015, the insurance industry would be facing the problem of the inadequacy of insurance premium determination; in the decade to 2025, certain markets would become uninsurable (as it occasionally happens in the coastal areas of the USA); in the decade to 2035, property insurance would become extremely limited, and in the decade to 2045 (by when it is estimated that at least once per year the damages would exceed one trillion dollars), numerous insurance companies would become insolvent. Climate changes are no longer merely a theoretical question, as they represent a realistic situation which has already had a significant impact on global insurance sector business activities, and based on a Ernst & Young study (Strategic Business Risk, 2008, p. 4) climate changes are the most significant risk which insurance companies would be facing in the following years (Njegomir, Markovi , 2009, p. 106-120).

According to all indicators, parallel with the global warming process, there has also been a significant increase of damage assessment damage caused especially by weather.

By the definition of risk, risk in insurance depends on the occurring of adverse events, the exposure and sensitivity of insured property and persons to adverse events and insured values. Any changes in any of these three components could impact the increasing or reducing of risk. The increasing of damage assessment for insurance is conditioned, to a large degree, by socio-economic changes, such are an increasing concentration of values and also an increase of the concentration of population in areas exposed to catastrophic events, by increasing insured assessments as a consequence of an increase of the population, the assessment of insured goods, the liberalization of the insurance market and a higher frequency of insurance, changes in insurance coverage and also an increased probability of the occurrence and intensity of damage by way of disastrous events. Due to an analysis of all parameters in the previous period, we can conclude that climate changes are not the only damage claims paid out by insurance companies, but they have a significant influence - as natural disasters caused by nature forces ensue from global warming. Furthermore, it is evident that there is an intensifying of natural disasters linked with weather excess (such as floods, draughts, storms), while viewed long-term, the damages incurred by natural disasters due to geophysics factors (such are earthquakes, tsunamis, volcanic eruptions) are constant. Even though it is difficult to quantify the existing and future effects of climate changes on the damages caused by natural disasters, it is evident that extreme catastrophic events and their frequent occurrence caused by climate changes incur great damages for the insurance market.

In terms of climate changes impact on the insurance sector, an especially challenging area is the effect of hurricanes that hit the coastal area of the USA. The proof that climate changes impact the occurrence of these natural phenomena is the fact that the 10 most devastating hurricanes and thus, most damaging for the global insurance market happened in the last 10 years. For example, in 2005, the hurricane season distinguished by the largest number of the named hurricanes ever, caused damages for the insurance market damages estimated at about 87 billion dollars. Thus, the catastrophic hurricane Katrina caused a total economic damage to the amount of 125 billion dollars (62 billion dollars were covered by insurance) (Schadenspiegel, 2007). The mentioned hurricane season led to a change of insurance company standards which was reflected in various factors, including record hurricane damages, changes of perception in terms of hurricane activity, changes in the domain of risk modeling and changes in assessing the needed capital of rating agencies which consequently led to a different approach to the strategies of capital management and the method of determining premiums. The scientific assumptions are that the possibility of hurricane occurrence is connected to long-term changes in the surface temperature of the sea, which typically appears in 20 to 50 year-cycles.

The most sensitive sector of climate changes is the sector of property insurance especially in the area of impact on generating natural disasters and this sector has suffered the most difficult consequences of these changes. Climate changes have not only influenced property insurance but also other insurance types and even the complete business activities of insurance companies. After some catastrophic events, it is possible to initiate claim proceedings against architects, engineers, designers and other professionals from the area of construction if they failed, during the designing and constructing of buildings, to take under consideration the new weather conditions caused by climate changes, and thereby directly affect life and health. Floods, draughts, storms, heat waves and precipitation followed by hail, all caused by climate changes, have a strong impact on insurance in agriculture and forest holdings. In Europe, there is already a limited offer of insurance coverage for forest holdings due to a proliferation of winter storms during the last years which led to the implementation of more restrictive conditions and insurance premium tariffs. Climate changes also influence motor vehicle insurance, as well as Casco insurance. There is also a direct connection between traffic accidents and weather conditions, as during warmer weather, the number of traffic accidents increases by 18% (TOPICS geo, 2004, p. 25). Extreme weather conditions contribute to vehicle damage due to falling trees, roof parts, hail precipitation, floods, etc.

Climate changes, besides their influence on insurance businesses, have a large influence on changes in the investment climate. There is a significant influence on the investment strategies of insurance companies which in turn has an influence on long-term financial profitability and solvency. Thus, these changes influence not only both sides of the balances of insurance companies, the assets and liabilities, by way of generating adverse events, but they also influence property values by way of financial market reactions. Climate changes mostly impact the stock market and real estate, corporate bonds, etc. Also, the worth of companies whose business activities or products are sensitive to climate changes could be endangered, which could cause sudden market shocks, as climate factors are not integrated in market prices, which could consequently endanger performances of the investment portfolios of insurance companies. Applying creative strategies in protection against risk, insurance companies not only protect and improve the performances of their investment portfolios, but they also improve their market reputation and additionally support companies in limiting the negative influences on the environment, which is in the interest of insurance companies. This is the reason why numerous insurance companies, such are AIG, Swiss Re and Allianz, are placing their funds in the projects of developing the use of renewable energy sources, in improving energy efficiency, in waste management projects, recycling and afforestation (Njegomir, Markovi , 2009, pp. 106-120).

The influence of climate changes on insurance companies is reflected in the risk which they take for their clients and through their investment activities, representing a risk only for the insurance sector. On the other hand, if adequate measures of adaptation are applied, climate changes bring multiple possibilities for improving insurance companies' business activities. Collectively, the risks and possibilities which climate changes incur for the insurance sector are given in the following table.

Table 1. Climate changes risks and possibilities
for insurance companies

Type of Insurance	Risks arising from climate influences, policy implementations or their failure	Possibilities arising from proactive policies or climate influences
Property	-accumulation of extreme events endangers solvency/liquidity -providing of coverage becomes difficult -lack of capital/reinsurance -inadequate risk assessment -bad informing; public sector reaction -greater costs of restoration	-higher demands for insurance and alternative risk transfers -differences in risks could be included in insurance premium. -Kyoto projects insurance -administrative recoveries from disasters - insurance prototypes provided
Liability	-unexpected claims caused by duty of attention -malfunction of products due to new conditions -transportation disorders	-higher demands for insurance due to the existing of duty of attention -insurance coverage for professional services connected to carbon dioxide market -"green" transportation products such as insurance policies for motor vehicles with low mileage

Life/ Health/ Savings	- periodic impact on human health - underestimate expected period of human life due to warmer winters in northern hemisphere -reduced available income due to catastrophes	-higher demands for health insurance -growing wealth in developing countries due to technology transfer
Other insurance types	-increased damages due to business closure -disorders in the area of entertainment -increased damages in agricultural production -new technologies in energy sector	-alternative risk transfer -exploring and development of carbon dioxide low emission technologies -consulting services -insurance of carbon dioxide emissions trade -trade risks for export of technology -carbon becomes insurable asset

Source: Climate Change & Financial sector: An Agenda for Action
(June 2005: 26)

Some examples of innovative solutions applicable in insurance companies are the following: insurance policies for hybrid and alternative fuel motor vehicles (Sompo Japan Insurance), insurance policies for motor vehicles with lower gas emission (Tokio Marine & Nichido), development of insurance policies for motor vehicles on the pay-as-you-go principle which assumes premium payment depending on the level of motor vehicles use (insurance company AGF, a member of the Allianz Group), insurance policies for windmill fields (the AXA Group which has earned 14 million dollars from these insurance policies in 2006) (Mills, 2007).

Climate changes cause fundamental changes in the domain of catastrophic events probability as well as changing the conditions of insurability of certain risks and they have the potential to influence the determining of insurance premiums (greater insurance premiums in the areas especially exposed to the effect of catastrophic events but also stimulating insurance premiums for clients which achieve positive effects on global warming reduction), as well as the policy of fund reservation and solvency (Vujovi , 2009, pp. 23-24).

We can say with certainty that climate changes influence the business activities of reinsurance companies in a similar way as insurance companies. Considering the fact that the role of reinsurance is mostly limited to taking responsibility for covering rare but extreme events, climate changes have an even greater influence on the business activities of reinsurance companies. These are the reasons why reinsurance companies were the first ones which alerted the world about global warming and the first to support research studies in order to gain statistically more credible long and medium term weather forecasts. In the current conditions, reinsurance companies have two alternatives available: eliminating certain risks from reinsurance coverage, which is unacceptable considering the fact that in those conditions insurance coverage for such risks would fail, or an increase of reinsurance premiums which would lead to an impracticality of insurance implementation. A shortage of reinsurance capacity which inevitably ensues from climate changes effects requests finding new solutions in insurance risk management. This is why reinsurance companies try to apply more sophisticated risk modeling and more disciplined risk-taking, based on research of climate changes phenomena and adaption measures such as season hurricane predictions, understanding of the sensitivity of new industries, and other research in order to use the possibilities of new markets. Innovative solutions include the appliance of an alternative transfer of insurance risk on the capital market and also using the role of the state in providing insurance and reinsurance coverage. Public attention is directed, in modern times, to actually finding new forms of partnerships of the public and private sectors, whereas the state should be a partner and not an alternate of the private insurance sector.

CONCLUSION

In Western Balkans countries, it is important to strengthen institutions, capacities and policies in the area of climate changes. An analysis of institutional structures and political and economic sectors should be integrated in the evaluation of potential climate changes strategies for mitigation or adaptation. Also, of a crucial importance is the improving of civil society participation in raising awareness, as this area is incomplete at the moment. Even the efforts to harmonize with EU legal standards are actively carried out, and public institutions are focusing on implementing climate activities in the international arena. The problem is the fact that some of these activities are not focused in a unique way or are insufficient and request further coordination, cooperation and financing, as well as long-term vision. Various projects contribute to that (e.g. LOCSEE) which bring significant benefit to the region with regards to progress toward integration and the attempt to coordinate low carbon strategies with intersectoral focus in the EU.

The key question in the following period will be how to manage climate changes effects. This question will primarily have to be solved by insurance and reinsurance companies which are most directly threatened by the consequences of global warming and which during the following years would have to confront the challenges of developing and implementing strategies and business solutions in the context of risk management caused by climate changes and the need for continuously seeking solutions for capital growth for risk coverage. In regards to the climate changes which are undoubtedly bringing changes regarding risk insurability, it is not only insurance companies engaged in the problem of property insurance which are affected, but also insurance companies which provide life, health and liability insurance. Viewed long-term, the investments of insurance companies are threatened by the negative consequences of global warming.

The insurance business is a specific business, cyclical by nature. Considering that in the last years of the 20th century there has been a decrease in premiums, and an increase of frequency and intensity of damages, it is inevitable that insurance companies consolidate or unite and that premium rates increase, depending on the given risk.

With globalization, the world is becoming more connected and events in one country can have an influence on the events in another, and it is clear that today there is a need for more diverse insurance policies. Today, a liberalization of insurance is obvious in many countries.

As the concentration of greenhouse gas increases constantly, also due to globalization, it is evident that the question whether climate changes are going to happen is unnecessary, but rather, the focus should be on the speed of the consequences of those changes and how serious they may be. Even if greenhouse emission stops at the present value, some consequences would be unavoidable.

We cannot precisely predict what the climate will be in the future. This is the reason why intelligent risk management directs us to take action today, which can enable mitigation and adaptation to global warming, as taking no action is much more expensive than taking any action.

Based on long-term analysis of large natural disasters, it has been confirmed that the trend of damage incurring is growing. This is a consequence of large socio economic development which includes an increase of value concentration, population and settlement growth and an industrialization of the areas exposed to bad weather conditions.

The insurance industry must actively start the process of adaptation if it wishes to survive and should start with the following activities:

Scientific studies connected to climate changes must be intensified, with more investing of time and money, such as, for example, a discussion on issues connected to climate changes and extreme weather conditions from the insurance perspective, predictions on how climate changes will influence finances, etc.

Insurance and reinsurance companies must take a new approach in issuing insurance policies by looking ahead and not remain based only on statistical data, as was the case. Pricelists and models for allocation of capital must be constantly updated in order to be a reflection of the most current scientific proof and not only the extreme ones, as was the tendency in the past.

In the following period, insurance and reinsurance companies must take under consideration risks as products of probability and intensity and view them more objectively with the appliance of developed scientific methods in their identification, analysis, measurement and control.

From the standpoint of society, it is necessary to increase pressure on governments with the aim of bringing more restrictive laws related to construction, where this is necessary, and also to make those conditions better linked with the conditions and terms of insurance policies. Insurance companies should cooperate with governments and agencies for assistance in case of accidents, as this is the only way to reach the right solutions.

Observed long-term, people engaged in strategies will want to consider the future insurability of risk connected to weather conditions. If insurance companies are prevented from charging adequate risk payments (e.g. due to certain regulations) or if insurance companies are prevented in some other way, such as due to market pressure, it could happen that insurable risks become non-insurable.

REFERENCES

1. Adaptation and Vulnerability to Climate Change: The Role of the Finance Sector, Geneva, United Nations Environment Programme Finance Initiative, (2006).

2. Climate Change & Financial sector: An Agenda for Action (2005), A publication of the Allianz Group and WWF.

3. Drakenberg (2011). Albanija – Životna sredina i klimatske promene, kratka politika. Sida - podrška zaštiti životne sredine i klimatskim promenama. Gothenburg Univerzitet i Švedski Univerzitet poljoprivrednih nauka, Novembar 2011. godine. (Dostupno na: http://sidaenvironmenthelpdesk.se/wordpress3/wp-content/uploads/2013/03/Albania-ECCPB-Alb-Nov-2011.pdf)

4. Droge, S. (2010): Klimatske promene-studije i analize: Klimatska strategija EU, Beograd: Evropski pokret u Srbiji, pp. 105-116.

5. Ganter, S. (2010): Klimatske promene-studije i analize: Finansiranje adaptacije na klimatske promene, Beograd: Evropski pokret u Srbiji, pp.117-128.

6. Grozdanic, R. Radovic-Markovic, M. Jevtic, B. (2013), New technologies, green growth and jobs, Rural Entrepreneurship: Opportunities and challenges, Beograd: VŠPEP, pp. 92-112.

7. Laganin, O. (2010). Uspostavljanje politike o klimatskim promenama u Bosni i Hercegovini. Presentacija UNFCCC Focal Point. Jugoisto na Evropa Forum o klimatskim promenama. Available on: http://www.seeclimateforum.org/upload/document/establishment_of_cc_policy_in_bih_by_unfccc_focal_.pdf

8. Mills, E. (2007), From Risk to Opportunity: Insurer Responses to Climate Change, Boston, MA, Ceres.

9. Njegomir, V. Markovi, D. (2009): ŠKOLA BIZNISA Nau ni asopis: Klimatske promene i njihov uticaj na osiguranje i reosiguranje, Beograd, pp. 106-120.

10. Strategic Business Risk: Insurance 2008. New York, Ernst & Young in corporation with Oxford Analytica.

11. Schadenspiegel: 50 years, Munich Re, Munich, Germany, (2007).

12. TOPICS geo: Annual review: natural catastrophes 2003 (2004).

13. Vujovi , R. (2009): Istraživanja i projektovanja za privredu: Uticaj globalizacije i klimatskih promena na stanje rizika i tržišta osiguranja, Beograd, pp. 23/24.

III. VARIOUS ASPECTS OF GREEN ECONOMY IN THE WESTERN BALKANS: ANALYSIS AT THE COUNTRY LEVEL

NEW OPPORTUNITIES FOR GREEN BUSINESS DEVELOPMENT[42]

Bozo Draskovic[43]

Jelena Minovic[44]

INTRODUCTION

Special Nature Preserves (SNPs) are areas where the condition of nature remains unchanged or just slightly changed, which are important because their uniqueness, rarities or exemplar features, and are the habitats of endangered wild species of flora and fauna at the same time. These areas are usually without settlements or with sparsely populated locations,

---

[42]   This paper is a part of the research projects No. 47009 (European integrations and social and economic changes in Serbian economy on the way to the EU), and No. 179015 (Challenges and prospects of structural changes in Serbia: Strategic directions for economic development and harmonization with EU requirements), financed by the Ministry of Science and Technological Development of the Republic of Serbia. The paper is a result of a the research realized within the project "Economic aspects of costs and benefits of the environmental policy in the Republic of Serbia", financed by the Environmental Fund of the Republic of Serbia.

[43]   Institute of Economic Sciences, Belgrade, Serbia, bozo.draskovic@ien.bg.ac.rs

[44]   Institute of Economic Sciences, Belgrade, Serbia

where people live in harmony with nature. These areas are intended for preservation of the existing natural features, genetic fund, ecological balance, monitoring of natural phenomena and processes. Scientific research in these areas is permitted, but visits of excursionists are controlled in order to preserve traditionally inherited natural values (Draškovi , 2013).

In this study, we gathered and analysed data on the management financial analysis for three Special Nature Preserves (SNPs) in Serbia: Zasavica, Uvac and Stari Begej – Carska Bara. Nonetheles, SNPs Uvac and Stari Begej – Carska Bara have been defined as the natural resources of great importance, while SNP Zasavica is a natural resource of the first category for the Republic of Serbia. The key natural resources are Zasavica river and river valley Uvac that serve as the basis for SNP Zasavica (SNP Zasavica, 2012, and Draškovi , 2013), (Nature Preserve Uvac, 2007, and Draškovi , 2013). At the same time, SNP Stari Begej - Carska Bara has been included in the list of marshlands of international importance (Republic Agency for Spatial Planning, 2009, and Draškovi , 2013). SNP Zasavica is the special natural treasure with more than 800 species of flora. The most valuable and most important plant in the preserve is the *Aldrovanda* vesiculosa, commonly known as the waterwheelplant, for which Zasavica is the only habitat in Serbia. The special value of the preserve is the established presence of a globally endangered species of fish *Umbra krameri*, the European mud minnow, for which the waters of Zasavica are one of the two remaining habitats in Serbia. The most valuable and important bird in the preserve is the razorbill seabird, a highly endangered species on the planet. An old species of pig is cultivated in Zasavica – Mangalitza, old sorts of cattle – Prairie Ox, as well as Balkan Donkey (SNP Zasavica, 2012, and Draškovi , 2013). SNP Uvac has been founded as the area for protection of the population of the European Griffon Vulture (*Gyps fulvus*), one of the most massive species of ornitofauna in Serbia. The griffon vulture is a scavenger bird, one of the more significant factors in the food chain and cleaning of nature through prevention of the spread of infectious diseases. Key natural resources of Uvac are: waters, land, woods, wildlife and fish. Flora of the Uvac preserve includes more than 500 species of plants, among which a large number of rare, endemic, medicinal or edible herbaceous and woody plants. There are well preserved fragments of high stands of beech, spruce and fir tree (Nature Preserve Uvac, 2007, and Draškovi , 2013). SNP Stari Begej - Carska Bara is an area that was declared the area of international importance for birds in 2000, and thus represents an important habitat for nesting birds. Species of birds that are distinctive for the entire area are herons, cormorant, stork, geese and ducks, birds of prey, gulls, cuckoos, swallows, starlings and crows. Preserve is also inhabited by mammals whose living is conditioned by their natural environment of water habitats, marshes and riparian forests. The area is rich with the resources of surface and underground waters (Republic Agency for Spatial Planning, 2009, and Draškovi , 2013). Vegetation of SNP Stari Begej - Carska Bara consists of water macrophytes, wetland vegetation, woodland vegetation, meadows, steppe grasslands (Republic Agency for Spatial Planning, 2009, and Draškovi , 2013), (Draškovi and Minovi , 2013).

522 120 hectares of land, forests, pastures, marshes and wetlands, which comprise 5.91% of the Serbian territory, fall under the ecological protection regime in the Republic of Serbia. Protected areas are managed by different entities, from non-governmental organisations through private companies to public companies owned by the State (Draškovi , 2013).

Draškovi and Minovi (2013) presented the results of the comparative analysis of the population and visitors for three SNPs: Zasavica, Uvac and Stari Begej - Carska Bara. These authors have shown that the natural wealth that is found within these three preserves is so vast that it *"cannot be expressed in money"*, followed by the conclusion that the State should finance the survival of these preserves and that none of these SNPs should be made private or sold. Draškovi , Domazet, and Minovi (2013) explained what are the problems of value and valorization of natural resources, as well as the benefits and costs.

The goal of this study is to show that there are great potentials for the green business development in the SNPs of Serbia. The paper emphasizes natural resources of each preserve, as well as their importance and value for the Serbian green business development. Deficiencies of the analysis referred to above have also been listed, as well as the problems Serbian SNPs face. In addition, techniques and opportunities for the development of environmental accounting and green business in

Serbia have been described. The result of our research shows that the management of SNPs Zasavica and Uvac achieved positive economic effect in the process of preserve management, while the management of SNP Stari Begej – Carska Bara operated at a loss.

The structure of this paper is as follows: 1. Introduction,2. The concept of environmental accounting and sustainable development, 3.Financial analysis of management for all three SNPs, 4.Opportunities for development of the green business and environmental accounting within the SNPs, and 5.Conclusion.

THE CONCEPT OF ENVIRONMENTAL ACCOUNTING AND SUSTAINABLE DEVELOPMENT

Researches on the possibility of constituting a separate segment of accounting called ecological or green accounting were initated in recent decades. The motivation for the implementation of Environmental accounting (English: Environmental Accounting – EA) under the term of ecological or green accounting as synonyms (English: Green Accounting – GA) arose primarily from the desires and needs of some developed countries in the first place, to create methodology and techniques for monitoring the implementation of the sustainable development concept (Draškovi , 2013).

Environmental accounting with the accounting records of natural resources has initially begun to apply in some countries since 1970. A country that has pioneered the application of this type of accounting is Norway. After almost two decades of the development and experimental application, in early 90's the United Nations, OECD, followed by the World Bank and Eurostat initiated and supported the groups of experts who had the task to define key elements of the methodology for the establishment of a consistent system of environmental accounting. As a result of this work, the initial methodology was drafted called the System of Economic and Environmental Accounting (SEEA). Thereupon the United Nations issued instructions for the implementation of environmental accounting under the code EA1993 (Belopavlovi and Stevanovi , 2012).

In fact, in the late twentieth and early twenty-first century, the movements and awareness of the need to observe economic and social development from the point of its sustainability are growing. The content of the concept of sustainability lies in observing the relations of current consumption of resources and their survival in the future. A key task of environmental accounting should be to collect and quantify the economic parameters of the acquirement in order to establish how threatened is the sustainable development from the perspective of exhaustion and degradation of resources in the future. The point is to bear in mind that the non-renewable resources are limited and ultimately exhaustible, in relation with the current development and exploitation of resources (Draškovi , 2013).

One of the definitions of the sustainable development: "Development that meets the needs of the present without compromising the ability of future generations to meet their own needs"(WCED, 1987). Here we are primarily referring to the sustainable employment of natural wealth, i.e. wealth inherited from past generations, nature (USEPA, 1995).

Minovi and Draškovi (2012) used the numerical simulations to show the unsustainability of the economic and environmental development of Serbia within the set assumptions. Therefore, some of the future researches might relate to the definition of sustainable development for the protected natural areas through the inclusion of external costs. Similar to the studies Draškovi and Minovi (2012)[45], and Minovi et al. (2013)[46], sustainable development model for Serbia's SNPs could be made - the so-called "prey-predator" model, with the help of numerical simulations. Development of the "prey-predator" model for all three special nature preserves would clearly identify in each preserve the population of predators, on the one hand, and prey population, on the other. In that way, one would gain the insight into the intensity of their

---

[45] Draškovic and Minovic (2012) drafted the "prey-predator" model for retal trade market in Serbia.

[46] These authors used their numerical simulations for the proposed models on the examples of economy and finances. At the same time, the type of "prey-predator" model is being used in ecology, physics, computer sciences, demographics and sociology (Draškovi and Minovi , 2013).

mutual interaction, and could assess benefits and losses made by the same for each SNP (Draškovi and Minovi , 2013).

The essence of the sustainability concept is the need to constantly maintain preserves of natural capital over time. Environmental accounting assumes application of the principle that national accounting should include into recording and balancing all elements of the property (assets) at the state level, as follows: natural capital, human capital and manufactured, i.e. produced capital. In current accounting practice and methods developed for its implementation, in the national accounts the records are primarily kept in terms of the produced capital as the basic element of production and the level of development at both micro and macro level – the State. These accounts represent the basis for reporting and tracking the changes in GDP. At the same time, the above-mentioned developed accounting technique does not include consumption of the natural capital and assets, which are often treated as free resources or as an external social cost. The problem in recording these costs, either as exploitation of the natural resources, or as natural resources that are being degraded due to the economic activity and pollution, becomes ever more pronounced. Therefore, it became increasingly clear that, with the reduction in reserves of non-renewable resources, we must take much more care when spending natural capital. Other natural, specific resources, expressed by the term human capital, are not considered from the standpoint of book-keeping, efficient "consumption" and renewal by any accounting. As in the case of the natural capital, there are no harmonized approaches to the human capital either, that would provide directions for its empirical book-keeping, accounting for and incorporating as a segment of the total social accounting, social wealth and welfare state (Draškovi , 2013). Lange (2003) constitutes four basic components of the ecological or green accounting:

- Accounting of the reserves (assets) of natural resources, primarily related to the reserves of natural resources and monitoring of their changes in the national accounting.
- Flow of materials and pollution accounting (energy and resources flow), which provides information about the level of industrialization and the use of energy and materials as inputs

in production, final products and services, and generation of pollution and solid waste on that basis.

- Environmental and resources protection, cost management that is identified in the conventional national accounting, incurred by industry, government and households, aimed to protect the environment or manage resources.

- Eco-friendly macroeconomic aggregates, which include indicators of environmental sustainability adjusted to the net domestic product (NDP).

- The establishment of environmental accounting and its integration with standard accounting is still at the level of theoretical considerations.

FINANCIAL MANAGEMENT ANALYSIS FOR ALL THREE SNPS

SNP Zasavica is managed by a social (now non-governmental) organisation the Scout Association of Sremska Mitrovica. SNP Uvac is managed by the state-owned company founded in order to manage the preserve, under the name "Uvac Preserve" Ltd, with the head office in Nova Varoš, while the company Fishpond Estate "E ka" manages SNP Stari Begej - Carska Bara. Nature preserves are not *de facto* separate legal entities; regulations define them as the areas of particular interest, which are then controlled by some legal entity. There is no separate environmental accounting kept in the preserves, or in the national parks and other forms of organised protection of the environment, natural assets and treasures, which is the shortcoming of the entire system, so it is not just a problem of one SNP.

The data in Tables 1, 2 and 3 include two key sets of financial information. One relates to the structure of income generated from the use of each SNP - Zasavica, Uvac and Stari Begej - Carska Bara, respectively. The second group of data refer to the information about the costs related to maintenance and protection of natural resources and capital of each analysed SNP. What lacks in green accounting is the valuation quantification of the individual values, which would involve indicators for evaluation – cash statement (SNP Zasavica, 2012), (Nature Preserve Uvac, 2007).

Table 1. Structure of income and expenses of
SNP Zasavica for the period: 2009-2011.

000 RSD	2009	%	2010	%	2011	%
Total income	40.962		39.766		79.578	
Own income	5.915	·14,4	9.290	23,4	13.812	17,4
Subsidies and donations	28.380	69,3	27.661	69,6	47.700	60,0
Domestic donations	22.930		22.707		47.700	
Local government	5.850		4.500		5.000	
RS Budget	16.880	41,2	9.887	24,9	37.670	47,3
Autonomous Province	200		8.321		130	
Water Fund					4.900	
Foreign donations	5.450		4.953			
Income from tourism, visits	3.157	7,7	3.239	8,1	6.401	8,0
Total expenses	40.343		39.085		79.200	
Cost of wages	5.962	14,8	7.236	18,5	8.064	10,2
Material expense	12.023	29,8	13.956	35,7	19.815	25,0
Costs of maintenance	6.173	15,3	5.704	14,6	6.291.	8,0
Costs of marketing, improvement and protection	1.166		2.188		6.911	
Income from tourism, visits	3.157	7,7	3.239	8,1	6.401	8,0
Number of staff	19		19		19	
Book value of assets	24.451		29.889		67.559	

Source: Accounting of the Scout Association of
Sremska Mitrovica, and Draškovi (2013).

Total income of SNP Zasavica increased in the observed period (2009-2011) by 94.6%. Own income, or income earned from managing the preserve, which mainly consists of income from services provided to tourists, i.e. ticketing of visitors, and income from the manufacture and sale of the specific eco products, recorded the increase from RSD 5.9 million in 2009 to RSD 13.8 million in 2011. At the same time, there was a growth in income from donation and subsidies, from RSD 28.4 million in 2009 to RSD 47.7 million in 2011. Share of subsidies and donations in total income came to 69.3% in 2009, 69.6% in 2010 and 60% in 2011. The most important source of funds from subsidies is the budget of the Republic of Serbia, which participated in total income of the preserves with RSD 16.9 million in 2009, or 41.2%, RSD 9.9 million in 2010, or 24.9% and RSD 37.7 million or 47.3% in 2011. High share of budget resources is related to the investment projects in building the preserve infrastructure. The share of own income in total preserve's income amounted to 14.4% in 2009, and increased to 23.4% in 2010, so that in 2011 it would reduce to 17.4% of the total income. Income from tourism, tickets paid by visitors, had a share of 7.7% in 2009, 8.1% in 2010 and 8% in 2011.

Total expenditures, with regards to all years that have been analysed, were lower than total income. That means that operating profit came to approx. 619 thousand Dinars in 2009, 680 thousand Dinars in 2010 and 378 thousand Dinars in 2011.

Salaries of persons working in the preserve watchmen service, who provide tourist services and maintain the preserve, represent the expenditure which annually ranges from 7 to 8 million Dinars, and the share of this item in total expenses was 14.8% in 2009, 18.5% in 2010 and 10.2% in 2011, respectively. By total size and relative share in total expenses, material costs were the single largest item, so that in 2009 these costs amounted to RSD 12 million, in 2010 to RSD 13.9 million and in 2011 to RSD 19.8 million. The costs that were allocated to maintain the preserve had the following shares in total expenses: 15.3% in 2009, 14.6% in 2010, and 8% of all expenses in 2011.

Data on the book value of assets of SNP Zasavica refer to investments in Visitors' Centre, supporting equipment such as watchmen's lodge, ticket offices, boarding of tourists to the preserve tour boat and benches. Value of these assets increased from RSD 24.4 million in 2009, to RSD 29.9 million in 2010, so that in 2011 the growing trend continued to reach the amount of RSD 67.6 million. Based on these data, one can conclude that the funds received as subsidies are largely invested in fixed assets. The book value of assets does not include the value of woods, meadows, wetlands and marsh reeds as natural treasures.

Table 2. Structure of income and expenses of
SNP Uvac for the period: 2009-2011.

000 RSD	2009	%	2010	%	2011	%
Total income	22.688		15.960		24.353	
Own income	9.873	43,5	9.327	58,4	9.340	38,4
Subsidies and donations	90		121		111	
Domestic donations						
Local government						
RS Budget	12.000	52,9	5.750	36,0	14.000	57,5
Autonomous Province						
Water Fund						
Foreign donations						
Income from tourism, visits	725		762		902	
Total expenses	11.457		11.636		12.373	
Cost of wages	8.442	73,7	8.659	74,4	8.666	70,0
Material expense	1.407	12,3	1.792	15,4	2.121	17,1
Costs of maintenance	989	8,6	966	8,3	1.366	11,0
Costs of marketing, improvement and protection	619	5,4	219	1,9	220	1,8
Income from tourism, visits						
Number of staff	15		16		15	
Book value of assets	4.922		18.608		29.822	

Source: Accounting of the Association Uvac Preserve
Ltd from Nova Varoš, and Draškovi (2013).

Total income of SNP Uvac had a cyclic movement in the observed period. In 2010, income decreased compared to 2009 by RSD 22.7 million to RSD 15.9 million. In 2011, total income increased to RSD 24.3 million. The preserve's own income comprised of income from managing natural resources and assets was relatively levelled out p.a. and ranged in average approx. RSD 9 million. Total income was significantly influenced by Republic of Serbia's budgetary funds, which amounted to RSD 12 million in 2009, or 52.9% of the total income, then decreased to RSD 5.7 million in 2010, with a share in total income of 36%, so that in 2011 these funds would increase to RSD 14 million, with the share in total income of 57.5%. Contrary to the above, the share of own income ranged from 43.5% of the total income in 2009 to 38.4% in 2011. The data show that the preserve faces the problem of financing maintenance, protection and development when state subsidies decline.

Share of income from tourism / tickets paid by visitors, in the total income is marginal, and amounted to RSD 725 thousand in 2009 or 3.2% of the total income, RSD 762 thousand in 2010 or 4.8% and RSD 902 thousand or 3.7% of the total income. Total expenses, according to the data obtained from the management of SNP Uvac, were lower than total income in all analysed years. In other words, operating profit totalled approx. RSD 11 million, RSD 4.3 million and RSD 11.9 million in 2009, 2010 and 2011 respectively. Information about the profit referred to above can be misleading if the analyst does not take into account the fact that retained earnings were invested in maintaining the preserve's capacities, particularly investments in building the Visitor Centre and maintaining the trails and access roads to the preserve.

Salaries of persons working in the preserve watchmen service, who provide tourist services and maintain the preserve, represent the expenditure which annually ranges from RSD 8.6 million and the share of this item in total expenses was 73.7% in 2009, 74.4% in 2010 and 70% in 2011 By total size and relative share in total expenses, material costs were single largest item after the cost of wages. They totalled RSD 1.4 million in 2009, RSD 1.8 million in 2010, and RSD 2.1 million in 2011. The costs that were allocated to maintain the preserve had the following shares in total expenses: RSD 989 thousand in 2009 or 8.6%, 966 thousand in 2010, or 8.3% and RSD 1 million or 11% in 2011. Costs recorded as expenses for marketing, improvement and protection of SNP had 5.4% share in 2009, 1.9% in 2010 and 1.8% in 2011. The data on the accounting value of assets of SNP "Uvac" refer to investments in Visitors' Centre, tourist boats, and supporting equipment such as watchmen's lodge, ticket offices, boarding of tourists to the preserve tour boats and benches. Value of these assets increased from RSD 4.9 million in 2009, RSD 18.6 million in 2010 to further increase which reached the amount of RSD 29.8 million in 2011. Based on these data, one can conclude that the funds received as subsidies are mostly invested in fixed assets. Book value of assets does not include the value of woods, meadows, ambient and other natural resources and assets of the preserve.

Table 3.Structure of income and expenses of SNP Stari Begej - Carska Bara for the period: 2009-2011.

000 RSD	2009	%	2010	%	2011	%
Total income	5.187		7.333		7.500	
Own income	3.987	76,9	3.233	44,1	3.322	44,3
Subsidies and donations	1.200	23,1	4.100	55,9	4.178	55,7
Domestic donations	1.200		4.100		4.178	
Local government						
RS Budget	500		1.000		2.000	
Autonomous Province	700		3.100		1.986	
Water Fund					172	
Foreign donations						
Income from tourism, visits	3.987		3.233		3.322	
Total expenses	10.560		13.980		13.860	
Cost of wages	7.200	68,2	9.720	69,5	10.520	75,9
Material expense	1.820	17,2	2.900	20,7	2.290	16,5
Costs of maintenance	980	9,3	940	6,7	920	6,6
Costs of marketing, improvement and protection	560	5,3	420	3,0	130	0,9
Income from tourism, visits	3.987		3.233		3.222	
Number of staff	13		17		15	
Book value of assets	457		1.302		1.928	

Source: Accounting of the company Fishpond "E ka", and Draškovi (2013).

Total income of SNP Stari Begej - Carska Bara increased in the observed period (2009-2011) by 44.6%. Own income or income earned from managing the preserve, mainly consisting of the income generated from tourist services, i.e. ticketing of visitors, recorded a real decline from RSD 3.9 million in 2009, to RSD 3.3 million in 2011. At the same time, income from donations and subsidies grew, from RSD 1.2 million in 2009, to RSD 1.4 million in 2011. Growth of donations and subsidies shares in the total income increased in the observed period by RSD 2.98 million or 2.48 times. Share of own income in total income of the preserve was 76.9% of the total income in 2009, while in 2011 it decreased to 44.3% of the total income. Conversely, the share of subsidies and donations increased by 23.1% of the total income in 2009 to 55.7% of the total income in 2011.

Total expenses, according to data obtained from the preserve management, were higher than total costs in all analysed years: in 2009 by more than RSD 5 million, in 2010 by RSD 4.6 million and in 2011 by RSD 6.3 million. The source used to cover the losses in management of the preserve remained unknown.

Salaries of persons working in the preserve watchmen service, who provide tourist services and maintain the preserve, represent the highest expense. These costs exceeded total income achieved by the Preserve in all analysed years: in 2009 by approx. RSD 2 million, in 2010 by more than RSD 2.4 million, and in 2011 by somewhat higher than RSD 3 million.

In the total structure of expenses, costs of staff wages have a tendency of growth, from 68.2% in 2009 to 75.9% in 2011. At the same time, the number of persons employed increased from 13 in 2009 to 15 in 2011. The average gross salary of employees was RSD 46 thousand in 2009, RSD 48 thousand in 2010, to reach RSD 58 thousand in 2011. In the structure of expenses, material costs for functioning of the SNP participate with a minimum of 16.5% in 2011 to a maximum of 20.7% recorded in 2010. It is characteristic that investment costs to maintain the preserve were very low, ranging through years from RSD 920 to RSD 980 thousand per year, i.e. within the range of 6.6% to 9.285% of the total costs.

Data on the accounting value of SNP Stari Begej Carska Bara assets refer to investments in supporting equipment such as watchmen's lodge, ticket offices, boarding of tourists to the preserve tour boats and benches. Value of these assets increased from RSD 457 thousand in 2009, to RSD 1.9 million in 2011. Based on these data, we can conclude that the funds obtained from subsidies were scarcely invested in fixed assets, i.e. most of the funds are invested to finance the preserve watchmen service, which is responsible for the control and preservation of the use of natural resources and assets within the preserve.

Table 4 shows that the management of SNP Zasavica generates positive economic effect in the process or preserve management. In case of SNP Uvac, presented profit is the excess of "income" over expenses, and in fact these funds are obtained from the budget of the Republic of Serbia for investment in the construction of the Visitors' Centre in Kokin Brod. In case of SNP Stari Begej – Carska Bara, total income is lower than total expenses; therefore the management of the Fishing Estate "E ka" operates at a loss when it comes to managing the preserve.

Lack of the analysis is characterized by the fact that the financial aspects of the analysis don not include issues related to property records, i.e. natural resources that are found within the preserve, which include waters, swamps, woods, marsh reeds, and biodiversity.

Table 4. Income-to expenses ratio of SNP Zasavica,
Uvac and Stari Begej - Carska Bara, respectively,
for the period: 2009-2011. in 000 RSD

Zasavica	2009	2010	2011
Total income	40.961.625	39.765.792	79.578.313
Total expenses	40.342.978	39.085.342	79.200.258
Profit/loss	618.647	680.450	378.055
Uvac			
Total income	22.688.000	15.960.000	24.353.000
Total expenses	11.457.000	11.636.000	12.373.000
Profit/loss	11.231.000	4.324.000	11.980.000

Stari Begej - Carska Bara			
Total income	5.187.000	7.333.000	7.500.000
Total expenses	10.560.000	13.980.000	13.860.000
Profit/loss	-5.373.000	-6.647.000	-6.360.000

Source: Accounting of the Scout Association from Sremska
Mitrovica, Accounting of the company Uvac Ltd Preserve from
Nova Varoš, Accounting of the company Fishpond "E ka".

Future research should include some of these issues, in particular
the items listed above that have records obtained by monitoring. For
example, the time buckets of data regarding the quality of waters, the
numbers of some species of birds, condition of woods, marsh reeds etc.

OPPORTUNITIES TO DEVELOP BUSINESS AND ENVIRONMENTAL ACCOUNTING WITHIN SNP

Development of environmental accounting should allow various
ecological groups, companies and decision-makers in the sector of
national economic policies to implement the following:

- To provide more comprehensive monitoring and instruments of
  collection and processing of data relating to natural resources
  and assets, both those that have a market value and those that
  represent common assets and services of nature,
- To define factors that are of major impact on the relation
  between economy and ecology,
- To search for the dynamic formula which explains how can
  economic growth affect the achievement of set environmental
  goals,
- To draft concepts and form databases for the strategic planning
  of directions for development, in order to achieve sustainable
  development policy in the future and for the future generations
  (Draškovi , 2013).

In the protected areas of nature in Serbia, from national parks to landscape conservation areas, there are no models to present the natural capital in accounting. Accounting records, in accordance with the Law on Accounting and Audit, are kept at the level of organisation that manages the protected area. Such accounting records include the recording of the produced, i.e. invested capital and assets and liabilities in the balance sheets. Cash flow and income statement reflect business trends, income and expenses incurred during the conduct of business activity – management of the protected areas. A portion of recorded income achieved by the managements comes from direct and indirect use of the natural resources, i.e. natural capital. Example of direct income is the cash inflow from issuing permits for hunting or fishing, from the exploitation of plant and animal species etc. When it comes to direct exploitation of resources, in the current practice natural assets or capital are transferred to the use or market values that can be stated as monetary assets, and thus recorded in the balance sheets as income. Indirect income is related to the use of natural resources, and such use is not presented as the consumption of natural values, or assets. Typical example of indirect income from natural capital or the eco-system is the income generated from providing tourist services to the visitors. These services only refer to their ecological aspect, measured by the price of ticket to enter the preserve. Ecological aspect of the tourist service does not include the income from consumption of food and beverages, or the income from overnight stays in/or near the preserve. Income generated from donations, subsidies or direct grants of the state are also not included in the ecological income, which would, as such, be recorded in total income. The expenditure side of environmental accounting should include in the income statement all expenses recorded and related to the costs of investments in maintenance of resources of the natural area: protection, monitoring, investments in enhancing or restoring the natural capital regardless of the source of funds (own funds, donations, subsidies, budgetary funds).

The technique of establishing a parallel environmental accounting for the protected areas can only be developed if the following assumptions are taken into account. First, it is necessary to prepare, or categorise all data obtained as a result of monitoring by the specialized institutions and professional associations. The data should include a unique system of quantifying for the base year, when the initial ecological balance sheet is established, by all major groups of natural values and assets. Through monitoring we get all quantities and condition of woods, waters, air quality, geological values, the value of wood and other land, condition of flora and fauna and other groups of natural assets. All of them together make a stock of goods within the eco-system. A part of species and organisms that exist in the eco-system certainly remains not fully recorded. Though being a factor of that eco-system's balance, they cannot be recorded separately. However, we can define them by a general term as *other assets.*

The next step in the constitution of the environmental accounting for the specific protected area would be to set up the intersection between the parts of environmental accounting for the given eco-system and standard accounting system, which is effective and applicable to the corporate entities. This can be developed in two directions. One aspect deals with the recording of transfers of renewable and non-renewable natural assets from the eco-system accounting into the standard business accounting. It is to show the contribution of natural resources, real or perceived rents, creating and maintaining of the economic income. In the environmental account this process would be defined as the cost, and in the standard model of corporate accounting as income.

In cases involving exploitation of non-renewable natural resources located within the protected area, the flow between the environmental and standard accounting is one-way. Income will be recorded by the standard accounting, and losses of resources will be recorded in the environmental accounting.

Simply put, free benefits that are not recorded in the standard accounting represent clear expenses that fall under environmental accounting, which are presented as an abstract "social cost". This social, or ecological cost, will not be recorded more accurately due to the lack of a developed methodological system of environmental accounting.

CONCLUSION

The study gathered and analysed data on the financial analysis of management for three Special Nature Preserves (SNPs) in Serbia: Zasavica, Uvac and Stari Begej - Carska Bara. Subject of the analysis carried out in this paper are the possibilities to develop green business in Serbia. We described natural resources of each of the preserves, and their importance and value of the green business development in Serbia. We also stated the deficiencies of the analysis, and the problems that SNPs in Serbia face. Consequently, we described techniques and opportunities for the development of environmental accounting and green business in Serbia. The goal of this study is to show that there are great potentials for the development of green business in SNPs of Serbia. Result of our financial statements' analysis for all three SNPs indicates that the managements of SNP Zasavica and Uvac achieve positive economic effect in the process of managing the preserve, while the management of SNP Stari Begej – Carska Bara operates at a loss. The research showed that Special Nature Preserves cannot operate economically positive without state subsidies, because the demand for tourist services does not suffice to cover the costs of maintenance and protection of the values located in the preserves.

Any future research should include the issues related to the records of property, or natural assets in the preserve, which are: waters, swamps, woods, marsh reeds, biodiversity, and include them into the financial aspects of the analysis. It would be useful to have time bucket data on the quality of waters, quantity of some species of birds, conditionsof woods, marsh reeds etc.

REFERENCES

1. Associations of Scouts from Sremska Mitrovica, Accounting.

2. Belopavlovi, G., Stevanovi S., "Accounting Aspects of Environmental Protection", Institute of Economic Sciences Belgrade and BBA Beograd, editor B. Draškovi , Economic Aspects of Ecological Policy, 2012, pp.

3. Company Fishpond "E ka", Accounting.

4. Draškovi , B., Management of Resources in Protected Areas in Serbia, Publishers: Institute of Economic Sciences, Belgrade and Belgrade Banking Academy, Faculty of Banking, Insurance and Finance, Belgrade, 2013.

5. Draškovi , B., Minovi J., "Natural Resources and Their Impact on the Development of Serbia", Institute of Economic Sciences, Economic Sciences on the Crossroad: proceedings from the International Scientific Conference on the Occasion of the 55th Anniversary of the Institute of Economic Sciences, Belgrade, 2013, pp. 503-513.

6. Draškovi , B., Domazet I., Minovi J., "Issue of Values and Evaluation of Natural Resources, Benefits and Costs", Novi Sad University, Subotica Economic Faculty, Annals of the Economic Faculty in Subotica, 2013, 49(30), pp: 11-26.

7. Draškovi , B., Minovi J., "PARETO'S RETAIL TRADE TURNOVER DISTRIBUTION", DRUNPP Sarajevo, TTEM - Technics Technologies Education Management Journal, 2012, 7(2), pp: 706-715.

8. European Communities, Seriee Environmental Protection Expenditure Accounts - Compilation Guide, An introduction to Environmental Accounting As a Business Management Tool: Key Concepts and Terms (1995), United States Environmental protection Agency. Luxembourg: Office for Official Publications of the European Communities, 2002. http://epp.eurostat.ec. europa. eu/cache/ITY_OFFPUB/KS-BE-02-002/EN/KS-BE-02-002-EN. PDF

9. Lange, G.-M., "Policy Applications of Environmental Accounting", The World Bank environmental department, Washington, USA, 2003, http://siteresources.worldbank. org/INTEEI/214574-1115814938538/20486189/ PolicyApplicationsofEnvironmentalAccounting2003.pdf

10. Minovi , J., Draškovi B., "Gross Domestic Product and External Costs: The Case of Sustainable Management in Serbia", University of Pitesti, Romania, Econophysics, Sociophysics & Other Multidisciplinary Sciences Journal (ESOMSJ), 2012, 2(2), pp: 17-21.

11. Minovi , J., Radovi -Markovi M., Draškovi B., "Financial Engineering Education: The Case Study of Financial Modelling Using Games", The International Journal of Engineering Education (IJEE), Special Issue: Human Computer Interaction in Engineering Education, 2013, 29(3), pp: 634–643.

12. Nature Preserve Uvac, "Special Nature Preserve "Uvac", Management Plan 2008-2012 ", Nova Varoš, 2007.

13. Republic Agency for Spatial Planning, "Spatial Plan of the Special Purpose Area of the Nature Preserve Stari Begej – Carska bara", Autonomous Province of Vojvodina, Province Secretariat for Architecture, Planning and Building, Public Enterprise Planning Institute of Vojvodina - Novi Sad, 2009.

14. SNP Zasavica, "Special Nature Preserve Zasavica, Management Plan 2012-2022 ", 2012.

15. United States Environmental Protection Agency (USEPA), "An Introduction to Environmental Accounting as a Business Management Tool: Key Concepts and Terms", 1995.

16.   WCED (World Commission on Environment and Development), Our Common Future, New York: Oxford University Press, 1987.

GREEN TOURISM DEVELOPMENT IN SERBIA

Milutin Djuricic[47]

Milan Djuricic[48]

INTRODUCTON

It is a fact that mass tourism is occasionally a serious threat for the environment. The alternative is 'soft' or green tourism – also known as eco-tourism, gentle tourism or sustainable tourism. Basically, the goal is to abandon the set touristic destinations and turn to tourism which does not leave entire destroyed areas behind it (http://biologija.com.hr/ modules/AMS/article.php?storyid=8446,).

Sustainable tourism, an important element of modern tourism, has been recognized as a developmental chance for Serbia. The term 'sustainable' is hard to explain out of context, so we will endeavor to explain it within the frame of the tourism sector. By the nature of things, 'sustainable' tourism is contrary to efficient mass tourism based on the use of natural and other resources in order to form a low price, without environmental damage calculation and regardless of quality. Tourism with the label 'sustainable' is based on the understanding of nature and its processes and on more knowledge than ever – it is 'a new way of looking at old things'. It assumes strict control of the influence of tourism on the environment and endeavors to accomplish a balance of ecological, economic and socio – cultural components of tourism. It is especially applicable in the tourist development of protected areas (national and nature parks and reservations), which in turn becomes more popular as various segments of the travel business

---

[47] Full Professor, Business and Technical College in Užice, Serbia, djurazo1@ gmail.com

[48] Associate Professor, Faculty for Business and Industrial Management, Belgrade, Serbia, nikkec@open.telekom.rs

offer. Today, a special place is taken by eco-tourism, a modern form of tourism which, through education, volunteering activities, and learning about nature, helps the conservation and protection of nature. The term eco-tourism today is defined in various ways, but it represents a concept of tourism which includes a set of principles and a special segment of the market. Some definitions of this term are the following:

- "Ecotourism is ecologically responsible traveling and visiting of relatively untouched natural areas in the purpose of enjoying and admiring nature (and all the accompanying cultural features from the past and present) and promoting conservation, with a small negative influence of visitors but providing socio-economic benefits for the local residents which participate actively in the eco-tourist business" (Ceballos – Lascurain, 1996).
- The International Ecotourism Society/TIES in 1991 defined eco-tourism as 'responsible traveling in nature areas, protecting the environment and keeping the welfare of the local population.'
- The IUCN (World Conservation Union) in 1996 defines eco-tourism as 'environmentally responsible traveling and visiting of relatively untouched nature areas, enjoying nature and respecting it (as all the other accompanying cultural features from the past and present), and promoting preservation, with a low influence of visitors and providing useful socio-economic participation of the local population.'
- The international standard for eco-tourism, GREEN GLOBE (2004), defines ecotourism as the following: 'Ecologically sustainable tourism with a primary focus on researching natural areas tightly connected to preserving, respecting and conserving the environment'.
- Some define ecotourism as tourism based on nature which through results in sustainable development brings a protection of natural areas, educating visitors about sustainability and creating benefits for the local population. It is a small but rapidly growing industry which acts within the frame of the market niche which manages market forces and regulations. Ecotourism, on the market, is mostly individual or small-scale tourism (tourist groups up to 25 persons and hotels with less than 100 beds) in which small and medium enterprises operate.

Ecotourism is a very important component of sustainable tourism in Serbia, based on nature, and includes the rural and cultural element of tourism. It may become the tool for accomplishing total sustainable development of tourism and an adequate approach for the repositioning of Serbia as a tourist destination on the international market by creating a desirable Figure of the country with natural and cultural resources.

HISTORIC DEVELOPMENT OF GREEN ECOTOURISM

Many people link ecotourism with the author Miller (1978) which in his research proved that national parks are the most attractive, complex and powerful eco-tourist destinations. In more than three decades, this term has become one of the most frequently used in modern tourist literature, although the issues which it addresses are beyond its capacity and are the subject of more comprehensive studies.

Larman, J. and Durst, B. observe modern ecotourism as a system whose active elements are all the participants in the tourist business:

- tourists which use the wealth of a natural environment;
- tourism workers which according to the system of active preservation and conservation of certain natural parts provide long-term use of resources, and
- the local population which uses the environment for ecotourism and should provide a good quality of life for themselves.

Larman and Durst consider ecotourism as: "…natural tourism which the tourist carries out by visiting destinations and combining one of the three basic motivations (education, recreation and adventure) to visit various destinations…" (Larman and Durst, 1987, p. 5).

Larman and Durst consider ecotourism as a natural tourism which unites all human natural needs for recreation, joy, research, recovery, etc., with the original environment resources, which someone may consider their most important contribution to defining and developing of ecotourism.

On the other side, Hawkins considers that ecotourism owes its rapid development to the internationalization of ecological problems and to the aspiration of a large number of tourists from developed countries to base their travel on natural activities. According to Hawkins, natural resources are limited and must be preserved for the future generations. This testifies that only with international cooperation and large activities in the area of ecotourism can further degradation of the environment be stopped (Milenkovi , Boškovi , 2012).

As its basic function, ecotourism has the protection of natural areas, creating earnings, the education and participation of the local population in development. The Canadian Environmental Advisory Council (1991, p. 25) lists the following important characteristics of ecotourism:

1. it must promote an ecological ethos;
2. it must not degrade resources;
3. it is more eco-centric than anthropocentric;
4. benefits for wildlife and environment (social, economic, scientific, management and political) are needed;
5. it enables gaining direct experience of the natural environment;
6. it contains an educational component, and
7. it contains a cognitive and affective dimension.

It is obvious that the eco-centrism of all the participants in the tourist economy is dominant and that natural characteristics and ethics determine the physiognomy of ecotourism, with its sustainable functioning being logistically supported by elements of techno-centrism of all those which adapt themselves to natural laws. Only the responsible behavior of all the participants in ecotourism can help overcome conflicts between tourism and the environment and can create conditions for a complete harmonization of tourism and environment, or their symbiosis (Milenkovi S, Boškovi N., 2012).

Page and Dauling (2002) defined five essential principles of ecotourism which activate all its vital functions and resources, but also insist on a constant sustainability of those components in the purpose of the preservation of a cultural, social, educational and economic balance of eco destinations. These principles are the following:

1. it is based on nature;
2. it is ecologically sustainable;
3. it is ecologically educational and cultural;
4. it enables benefits for local community, and
5. it enables pleasure for tourists.

The economic dimension of ecotourism must not be ignored, as ecotourism is a chance for the development of various forms of entrepreneurship and economic development and the employment of eco touristic destinations which are mostly in underdeveloped or poorly developed areas.

Ecotourism, according to Weaver (2001), lists education as a significant component, as tourists, via a new way of hedonism or consumption of environmental products, are at the same time learning about the unity of man and nature.

The World Tourism Organization – UNWTO 2012 observes ecotourism as a concept made of all forms of natural tourism in which the major motivation of tourists is the observing and appreciation of nature and traditional cultures which dominate in natural areas. This means that the basic driving force of ecotourism is the motivation of all participants to preserve the traditional way of using the environment.

Ecotourism in Serbia has started to be studied more actively at the beginning of the new millennium. Milenkovi (2006) observes that Serbia has significant potential for developing this type of tourism. Živkovi (2009), Kosovi (2009) and others, initiated questions about the regional redistribution of ecotourism in order to determine the useful effects of ecotourism which improves the observed environment. Bela and associates (2011) document the processes of transforming ecotourism into practice, but without adverse impacts on the environment. Štrbac and Hamovi (2011) point out the economic effects of ecotourism. Stankov and associates (2011) stress the preservation of biodiversity in specific areas of Serbia, which means their protection, which should be the basis for developing ecotourism in protected areas.

It is evident that the development of green ecotourism is accompanied by certain misapprehensions, as well as limitations and possibilities – chances (Table 1).

Taking into account all the mentioned facts, there is the question whether Serbia should accept examples of good practice developed in the world or apply ecotourism to our particular conditions, taking into account the characteristics of the environment, tradition and cultural and historical heritage? Also, there is the question if the introduction of the economic value of ecotourism as an economic activity means that it can be profitable, but only as sustainable tourism. Profit gain by destroying the limited ecological resources of Serbia cannot be allowed.

Table 1. Definition of the basic model of green eco-tourism

GREEN TOURISM ATTRIBUTES		
MISCONCEPTIONS	LIMITATIONS	POSSIBILITIES
- each underdeveloped area is an ideal area for ecotourism development	- the area is unexplored in the purpose of standard verification and certificated for ecotourism	- untouched nature
	- a lack of infrastructure minimum	- archeological site and historical monuments
- the ecological awareness of the population and tourists is at a high level	- a low level of ecological awareness	- safe water and food
	- desire for a rapid rising of the life standard,	- hospitality and variety of the autochthon culture (regional, local)
- rural tourism is actually ecotourism	- a lack of clear standards and legislation	participation in projects of research, protection and conservation

Source: Adapted from: Milivojevi J., 2006

ECO DESTINATONS IN THE WORLD AND IN SERBIA

Most authors agree that the major eco-destinations in the world are the following: Panama, Costa Rica, Ecuador, Yucatan (Mexico), Dominican Republic, Alaska, Madagascar, Tanzania, Kenia, Virgin Islands, Iceland, Laos, India, Sri Lanca and Cambodia. For all these, promoting beautiful nature is at the same time a profitable business.

In several countries, eco-tourism provides a major flow of foreign currency. In Costa Rica it is more profitable than banana exporting, in Tanzania and Kenya it is more lucrative than exporting coffee and in India more than textiles and jewelry exports. It is estimated than in Kenia only one lion brings a profit of about 5,000 Euros per year to tourism, and a herd of elephants, in the same period, brings 460 thousand Euros. Thanks to eco-tourism and eco-tourists, the Hawaiian coral reef provides annual earnings of about 270 million Euros. Eco-tourists are featured by the following context: 'keep to the marked road, cooperate with foreigners, do not bring weapons, leave the place where you spent some time cleaner than it was when you came, do not disturb the environment with noise, behave as if you were in your own home, defer to instructions, do not search only for exotic things, but also, endeavor to discover other cultures and other ways of living, and be sure in the purpose of your travel'. 'Eco-tourism is one of the major factors which helps the preservation of the Galapagos Islands' – the National Park of Tapanti in Costa Rica. All these eco-destinations adhere to the regulations of the Green Globe 21 Standards, and have multiple benefits for businesses, customer/tourist and society at large (Table 2).

Table 2. Benefits from the Green Globe 21 Standards

Benefits from Green Globe 21 Standards		
Benefits for business	Benefits for customers	Benefits for society
• better environment	• better environment	• better environment
• saving of costs	• providing of minimum standard	• sustainable development
• competitiveness		• investments
• global marketing		• authorization
• documented environment	• supply from green companies	• more jobs and new employments

What is the state of affairs in Serbia?

In Serbia, the term eco-tourism is completely misunderstood, or even vulgarized. It is reduced to the abuse of nature and the logic of profitability or capital, which as a consequence can have nothing good, as nature has its own balance on which we all depend. If takes under consideration a wide range of choices and the amount of natural resources which Serbia disposes with, and which are not used in the spirit of sustainable development, thus having catastrophic consequences. All those natural treasures should be protected and improved, and then used for the improvement of life quality in our region.

To create an eco-destination and to develop eco-tourism requires an evolution of principles, directions and certification, based on standards of sustainability. In such a way, ecotourism can do the following: 1. Contribute to biodiversity preservation, 2. preserve local community welfare, 3. include others experiences of learning and understanding, 4. include responsible actions of tourists and the tourist economy, 5. direct small groups of small business systems, 6. Request the smallest possible consumption of nonrenewable resources and 7. stress local participation, ownership and entrepreneurial possibilities, especially for the rural population.

It is obvious that eco-tourism should be observed as a specific and special way of sustainable tourism. It must be planned and managed to accomplish crucial and environmental goals, which requests the following (Wood, 2002):

1. Specialized marketing to attract travelers interested in nature.
2. Managing abilities adjusted to the behavior of visitors in protected areas.
3. Guiding and interpreting services for the local population, which are directed toward questions about history, nature and sustainable development.
4. Government policies which determine earnings from tourism for creating funds for the protection of wild areas and for sustainable development of the local communities and domestic population.

5. Focus of attention on the local population, which must be given the right of approval for the development of tourism based on former awareness, the right of full participation and, if they decide so, the giving of funds and providing of training to use the advantages of such an option of sustainable development.

With a well designed systematic approach, eco-tourism can become a good developmental possibility for Serbia.

THE DEVELOPMENT OF SERBIAN ECO-TOURISM – A REALISTIC DEVELOPMENT POSSIBILITY

All former research has shown that the level of eco-tourism development in Serbia is unsatisfying, due to insufficiently developed centers of eco-tourism. Also, there is no real campaign for raising awareness about eco-tourism. On the other hand, Serbia has all the needed requirements to develop eco-tourism, rich in forests, reserves, national parks, rivers, lakes, and mountains, which is an excellent basis to resolutely move towards the development of eco-tourism. Namely, eco-tourism as a small industry, can bring significant progress to tourism in Serbia, through the open door for all those desiring peace, pure nature, as well as an improvement of the national budget. A positive example could be applying the system, as it is for example, in Costa Rica, which can bring positive effects.

Unfortunately, the development of eco-tourism in Serbia is in its very beginning. According to the assessment of the World Tourist Organization, the global share of eco-tourism in the total tourist traveling is between 2 and 4%. Considering the tendencies in Serbia and movements on the domestic tourist market, it can be estimated that this share is even smaller for Serbia. Many people see the reason for this in the insufficient motivation of the potential creators of such tourist products, as well as the moderators – tourist agencies, primarily due to low profitability. The exceptions to the rule are several protected areas - Zasavica, Carska Bara and Pali -Ludaš.

Eco-tourism has still not obtained the institutional place it deserves, in the Tourism Development Strategy (2006) or in the National Strategy of Sustainable Development (2007). Both strategies do not see eco-tourism explicitly as one of the solutions of the numerous ecological and economic problems of Serbia. Knowing that Serbia is rich in natural and cultural areas imposes the conclusion that it is necessary to develop eco-tourism in the area of Serbia which has good resources for the development of this form of sustainable tourism, which records, on global level, a high growth rate. Thereby, numerous positive effects for society as a whole can be accomplished (Figure 1).

The basis for the development of eco-tourism in Serbia can be the relationship between certain protected natural resources and the purposes of their managing (Table 3) (Stojanovi 2006). From Table 3, the goal marked as tourism and recreation (Table 1) which can be equated with the term eco-tourism, can primary be the goal in national parks (II), natural monuments (III) and protected areas (V), the secondary goal in areas of wilderness (Ib), and possibly an applicable goal of management in the area of habitat managing (IV) and a protected area for resources management (VI). Only in strict nature reserves (Ia) is eco-tourism not an applicable goal of management.

Figure 1. Green tourism as a development chance for Serbia

Table 3. Relation of protected natural resources
and managing goals (Stojanovi , 2006)

Managing goals	Protected area category						
	Ia	Ib	II	III	IV	V	VI
Scientific researches	1	3	2	2	2	2	3
Wildlife protection	2	1	2	3	3	-	2
Preservation of special and genetic variety	1	2	1	1	1	2	1
Providing of services in the environment	2	1	1	-	1	2	1
Protection of specific natural and cultural forms	-	-	2	1	3	1	3
Tourism and recreation	-	2	1	1	3	1	3
Education	-	-	1	2	2	2	3
Coordinated use of resources from natural eco-systems	-	3	3	-	2	2	1
Preservation of cultural and traditional characteristics	-	-	-	-	-	1	-

Key:

- number 1 is the primary goal;
- number 2 is the secondary goal;
- number 3 is the possible applicable goal of managing of the protected area;
- a dash (-) means the given goal is not applicable in the observed category of the protected area.

The basis for the development of eco-tourism, as a market niche of Serbian tourism, are the protected natural resources. Until today's day, some 474 natural resources have been protected – 5 national parks; 17 natural parks; 16 landscapes with outstanding features; 69 nature reserve; 3 protected habitats; 325 natural monuments and 39 natural resources with historical and cultural features. Also under protection, based on various facts, are the following: 215 plant species and 427 animal species, marked as natural rarities. These areas are the basis for the development of eco-tourism. Their surface is 530.714 ha, or 6.0 % of the territory of Serbia. The spatial plan of the Republic of Serbia (Off. Gazette of the RS, No. 88/10), stipulates that, by 2015, some 10% of the Serbian territory will be under protection, and by 2021 about 12% of the Serbian territory will be under some type of protection (Milenkovi , 2012).

Accepting the Strategy of Tourist Development of Serbia (2006) by clustering the tourist space into divided clusters, it is possible to develop eco-tourism in the way presented in Table 4.

Table 4. Tourist clusters as the basis for the development of eco-tourism in Serbia

TOURIST CLUSTER according to the Strategy of Tourist Development of Serbia (2006)			
1.VOJVODINA	II. BELGRADE	III. SOUTH-EAST SERBIA	IV. SOUTH-WEST SERBIA
-NP Fruška Gora	The least possibilities for the development of eco-tourism due to a high level of urbanization and deterioration of the environment.	-National park erdap	-Maljen and Suvobor
- Gornje Podunavlje		-Homolj mountains	- Zlatibor
- Sands of Subotica		-Natural Park Resave	- Slater
-Deliblatsko sands		- Južni Ku aj	- Natural Park Golija
- Gravitation zone of Lake Pali		- Rtanj Mt.	- National park Tara
- Ludaš Lake		- Vlasina and Krajište	- National Park Šara
-Koviljsko-petrovaradinski rit		- Stara Mt.	-Ov ar-Kablar gorge
- Vršac mountains			- National Park Kopaonik
- Carska swamp (Figure 3)			- Pešter plateau
- Obed swamp			- Canyon River Uvac (Figure 2)
- Zasavica			

Each potential eco-tourist destinations is characterized by various natural and cultural resources and has good resource potential for the development of eco-tourism. Only clustered Belgrade has no potential for eco-tourism, but it represents the largest dispersive zone for other tourist clusters through the following:

- the travelling of Belgrade residents to the eco-spaces of other clusters in Serbia;
- traveling of foreign guests to eco-tourist destinations, in the form of eco-breaks and
- an organized traveling of tourists staying in Belgrade to eco-touristic destinations, the so-called eco-passes.

The production of organic food for tourism, rich and high-quality forest resources and fruits of the forest for the production of organic food, picking and using medicinal herbs, the development of educational, exploratory eco-phyto pharmacological tourism, eco-climatic eco-tourism in clear beech forests, digging for gold in gold-bearing rivers (Mlava and Pek), eco-fishing and hunting, specific forms of eco-hostels, using a horse and carriage for traveling, eco-safari, sports and recreation, healthy climatic conditions and other specificities of eco-destinations raise the quality and complexity of eco-tourist offers.

In the purpose of a systematic approach to the development of green – eco-tourism in Serbia, it is necessary to master five basic steps:

1. Adopt and apply regulations of eco-tourism international GREEN GLOBE 21 Standards,
2. Conduct research and verification of all areas interesting for the development of green eco-tourism areas,
3. Build up a necessary infrastructure in the areas predicted for ecotourism,
4. Perform a verification of the eco-tourism system in a particular area in accordance with the requests of ISO 14001 and Green Globe 21 Standards in all elements and processes, and
5. Continually improve all processes and elements of the system.

CONCLUSION

The movements on the modern global economic market also include an ecological component. Namely, fast economic development leads to damage to the environment, and only an economic philosophy of business activities becomes unsustainable, so the concept of sustainable development starts with realization and becomes applied on the tourist market.

Green tourism as a modern form of selective tourism at the beginning of the Third Millennium has become a more significant segment of the total tourist development of numerous countries, especially those underdeveloped, which dispose with relatively untouched nature and a cultural environment which can represent a good basis for the development of eco-tourism.

Our country possesses good economic eco-tourist potential or significant natural resources which can be valorized through green tourism and a planned clustering of the tourist areas of Serbia. It can be accomplished by a systematic approach from the state level (creating initial conditions and motivation), through the active role of the local self-government, creating of necessary infrastructure for eco-tourism, intensive trainings and rising of eco-awareness of the population, adopting and applying international standards ISO 14001 and Green Globe 21 and the obligation of a certification of an integral system of eco-tourism. All these must be based on a well-designed marketing approach and followed by a constant monitoring of the conditions of the areas (spot checks, tracking via satellite, eco-police) and by a system of a constant improvement of the environment.

The designing and development of green tourism is very challenging and demands a complete dedication of the jurisdiction. Only the well motivated have the will and energy to start such a business and provide only additional earnings, as green tourism is still not promoted on the level of the entire Serbia, and there is no needed infrastructure in the protected areas which will support it. Also, the educational system in Serbia has no adequate education for implementing green tourism and organic agricultural production. Supporters of sustainable tourist development through the green tourism can see only a real tourist industry which helps an eco-tourist to understand and experience the destination in the right way. If the approach to green tourism is not systematic, it will remain an unfilled desire of nature lovers.

Serbia should adopt a new tourist aspect – green travel and protection of natural habitats from the evil of mass tourism. By responsible development, green tourism could beat poverty and encourage a balanced regional development of Serbia through the emphasis of local values and tradition. Eco-tourists make friendships with the local population, learning something about the history and nature of the visited areas. They exchange information and build constructive, educational and ethic communications, non-disturbing and non-frustrating for the local environment.

In the end, the general conclusion would be that green tourism development in Serbia is relatively profitable, thought the only real and successful way for its development is a comprehensive and responsible approach to the long-term preserving of the environment and natural resources of Serbia. Thus, they would be preserved for future generations.

REFERENCES

1. Bela, M. and ass. (2011). Ekodestinacije u funkciji održivog razvoja turizma (Eco-destinations in the function of sustainable development of eco-tourism). Ecologica 18(62): 261-4.

2. Canadian Environmental Advisory Council. (1991), A protected areas vision for Canada. Supply and Services Canada. Ottawa. 88p.

3. Ceballos-Lascuráin H.,(1996) Tourism, ecotourism, and protected areas, IUCN – The World Conservation Union 1996 ISBN: 2-8317-0124-4 DOI: 10.2305/IUCN.CH.1996.7.en

4. GREEN GLOBE 21, International Ecotourism Standard, 2004

5. Kosovi , M., (2009), Evropska Unija, globalizacija i ekoturizam (the EU, globalization and eco-tourism), Ecologica 16(55): 563-7.

6. Laarman, J. and Durst, B. (1987), Nature travel and tropical forests. Raleigh: North Carolina State University

7. Milenkovi , S. (2006) Me usobni odnosi turizma i životne sredine (the relations between tourism and the environment). Kragujevac: Ekonomski fakultet.

8. Milivojevi J., Kanjevac Milovanovi K., Koki Arsi , A., Ecotourism- – misconcepctions, terms, possibility, Festival kvaliteta 2006, Kragujevac, 2006.

9. Milenkovi S, Boškovi N., (2012), The development tendencies of eco-tourism in Serbia, Ekonomski fakultet, Kragujevac.

10. Miller, K. (1978), Planning national park for eco-development: Methods and Cases from Latin America, Michigan: University of Michigan, Centre for Strategic Wild Land Management Studies.

11. Nacionalna strategija održivog razvoja (the National Strategy for sustainable development), (2007), Off. Gazette of the RS, No. 101/2007.

12. Page, S. and Dowling, R. (2002), Ecotourism, Harlow: Pearson.

13. Prostorni plan Republike Srbije (the Spatial Plan of the RS) (Off. Gazette of the RS, No. 88/10).

14. Stankov, U., and ass. (2011), Eco-tourism - an alternative to mass tourism in Stara Planina Nature Park, the Journal of the Geographical Institute Jovan Cviji , 61(1): 43-59.

15. Stojanovi , V. (2006): Održivi razvoj turizma i životne sredine (the sustainable development of tourism and the environment), Novi Sad: PMF, Departman za geografiju, turizam i hotelijerstvo.

16. Strategija razvoja turizma Republike Srbije (the Strategy of the Development of Tourism in the RS) (Off. Gazette of the RS, No. 91/2006).

17. Štrbac, M., Hamovic, V. (2011) Ekonomski efekti ekoturizma (the economic effects of eco-tourism), Ekonomika poljoprivrede, 58(2): 241-249.

18. Weaver, D. (2001), Ecotourism as mass tourism: Contradiction or reality?, Cornell hotel and restaurant administration quarterly 42(2): 104-12.

19. Wood M.E., (2002): Ekoturizam – principi, postupci i politike za održivost (Eco-tourism – principles, proceedings and policies for sustainability), CenORT, Belgrade.

20. Živkovi , B. (2009). Ekoturizam u funkciji razvoja Homolja (eco-tourism in the function of the development of Homolj). Ecologica 16(56): 645-9. http://ecotourismserbia.rs/rs/asocijacija/ ekoturizam-u-srbiji/

21. http://biologija.com.hr/modules/AMS/article.php?storyid=8446, Date: 26.07.2011, 09;07;00.

ACHIEVING FOOD SECURITY THROUGH SUSTAINABLE AGRICULTURAL TRANSFORMATION IN SERBIA[49]

Milica Kocovic[50]

Olivera Pantic[51]

INTRODUCTION

This paper should give us first view to diagnose the state of agro-industry, which is inevitably conditioned by certain historical choices, as well as a mission of Serbia's accession to the European Union. Keeping in mind serious social and economic changes that the country has faced in the last few decades, it leads to uregent need to create appropriate solutions for the efficient functioning of all market participants. Once recognized, the trends in the transformation of agriculture initiated by the transition of CEE, will help us to point out the countries that have implemented best practices that could be implemented in Serbia as well, with the aim of balanced and sustainable development. Special attention will be focused on the work potential of family farms- small producers in Serbia and possibilities of their association in cooperative production of organically grown foods, keeping permacultural aproaches and ethics as

---

[49]   The work is a part of research projects under the codes 179015 (Challenges and prospects of structural changes in Serbia: Strategic Directions for Economic Development and harmonization with EU requirements), 47009 (European integration and social and economic changes in Serbian economy on the way to the EU) and 31005 (The modern biotechnological approach to solving the problem of drought in agriculture) funded by the Ministry of Education, Science and Technology development of Republic of Serbia.

[50]   Research assocate Institute of Economic Sciences, Belgrade Serbia, milica.kocovic@ien.bg.ac.rs

[51]   Research associate Institute of Economic Sciences, Belgrade Serbia

a leading idea, which could affect the (local and regional) development and migration to rural areas.

HISTORICAL BACKGROUND TRANSITION AND SIMILARITIES WITH CEE

The most important feature of all CEE is transition of economies. The transition process as defined by the World Bank includes:

- Privatization
- Restructuring,
- Price liberalization,
- Liberalization of foreign trade,
- Liberalization of interest rates,
- Conduct of competition policy,
- Reform of the banking system,
- Creation of financial markets and financial institutions.

Central and Eastern Europe (CEE) had begun the transition process approximately ten years before the Republic of Serbia. Policies that these countries implemented, were significantly different. All the countries were working a lot on the national level in order to modernize agriculture, because their infrastructure and organization lagged behind the countries of Western Europe, and because of thatthey were not competitive. Due to the socio-economic and cultural diversity of the countries, they had a unique experiences of transition with different effects.Common objectives of all CEE countries were reflected in: decollectivisation of land, leaving the centrally planned economy while reducing state intervention and price controls, the tendency toward a free market, creating new institutions and restructuring of the labor market. These paths from one social system to another have led to major structural changes, as well as the changes in ownership of the land. The characteristic of the initial phase of transition in all CEE countries is allocation of land resources, privatization and changes in the organizational and ownership structure which lead to: reduced production volume (almost all countries), unemployment and a rise of social conflicts, differences in income, often fall of investment, which is accompanied by a fall in exports, corruption, and ever-present gap between urban and rural areas.

Establishment of private land ownership, moved differently when it comes to the agricultural sector in CIE countries. In some countries, land were owned privately in the socialist period, next to goverment and social land.[52] In connection with mentioned special attention should be paid to solutions made by those countries in terms of agricultural policy. The establishment of private ownership of land is usually performed by the: restitution, restitution model combined with the sale of land (leasing) and restitution with the distribution of land to agricultural workers, in order to maintain social equality (Lerman, 2000) .

Table 1. Models of land privatization in CEE

State	Collective farms	State/ government owned farms
Hungary	Restitution, compensatory bonds, distribution.	Sales for compensatory bonds, selling/ leasing Restitution
Romania	Restitution, distribution.	Restitution
Bulgaria	Restitution	-
Chech republic	Restitution	Sale/leasing
Slovakia	Restitution	Sale/leasing
Slovenia	-	Sale/leasing
Poland	-	Sale/leasing
Latvia	Restitution	Restitution
Lithuania	Restitution	Restitution
Estonia	Restitution	Restitution

Source: Swinnen, Mathijs (1997).

Approaches to privatization vary in relation to different ownership structure in the post-collectivist period. The pre-transition period of the

---

[52]   Hungary, Romania, Bulgaria, Poland, Czech Republic, Slovakia, Slovenia

Republic of Serbia was characterized by dual production structure. Even in the period of existence of the state of Yugoslavia, mass collectivization of land never took place.[53] On one side there were state and social enterprises, and on the other small farms privately owned.

The characteristics of agricultural structure of Serbia in the nineties were:

- The existence of two sectors of ownership, different in terms of concentration of land, capital, organizational and technological solutions, intensity of production, productivity and market orientation, fragmented ownership structure of farms
- Prevalence of mixed ownership of farms and the high percentage of households with farms,
- A large overemployment in the public sector, with unfavorable age and educational structure of active and total agricultural population (Nikolic, 1994).

All the post-transition countries were found redundant labor force in agriculture.Leaving the policy of price support and high subsidies, led to the establishment of market prices of goods and labor, andthis led to the reducted need for labor. Among the surveyed countries, only Slovenia and Poland had approximately the same percentage of land in private hands before the start of the transition and after as well. Also interesting to note is that these two countries have exceeded GDP from 1990sin 2003.[54] When it comes to privatization and transition in general, Slovenia had an experience that could be quite inspiring.[55] Priority was given to eloquent decision makers, and the subsequent development of the companies was largely dependent on state support. Better results

---

[53] Yugoslavia was one of the first country of socialism, which introduced the principles of the market economy.

[54] In addition to these countries, it happened even in Slovakia, Czech Republic and Hungary.

[55] The Republic of Slovenia is independently developed efficient project development, relying on the knowledge of their experts. The idea was not to allow the decay of any state enterprise, the former socialist economy, but help them to adapt to new conditions! So in Slovenia they decided to expertise, knowledge and competence put to the fore, in the process of restructuring.

were recorded, in cases where the state has supported the privatization process with its measures (Stevanovic, Djorovic, 2009). Many CEE countries and current EU members have similar soil structure as the Republic of Serbia.

The structure of the land fund all of the surrounding countries belonging to the EU is such that small farms up to 3 ha prevale, which represent more than 60% of farms. Among the above mentioned countries, the largest number of farms up to 5ha are in : Bulgaria 96.8%; Romania 93.8%; Greece 76.1%. Farms in the region, 5-10ha, are represented insignificantly, above 10% in Bosnia and Herzegovina and in Greece, and in Serbia, 14% of these farms are represented in the total number. Farms larger than 10 ha, in the region and the countrieswhich were observedrepresent around 5% in the total number of farms.

Table 2. Census of Agriculture 2012., Republic of Serbia

Republic Serbia	Without land	Do 2 ha	2,01–5,00 ha	5,01–10,00 ha	10,01–20,00 ha	20,01–50,00 ha	50,01–100,00 ha	More then 100 ha
Number of farms	9486	293667	184637	89749	32486	12922	4243	1365

Source: Statistical Office of the Republic of Serbia 2012.

According to the census of 2012, we can see that the number of farms up to 5 ha is 424 304, which represents the percentage of 76% of the total number of farms where the schedule is such that farms up to 2ha in size, represent 49% of the total number of farms. According to the group of authors, the three key problems of agriculture in rural areas of transition countries are:

- size of the farm,
- low level of labor productivity,
- poor connection between the agricultural and manufacturing sectors (Stevanovic, Djorovic, 2009).

The markets of Serbia and neighboring countries are characterized by a large number of small family farms with low labor productivity on the verge of profitability. However, the complete situation of agroeconomy, was not caused by poor transition. From the period of the SFRY, the attitude towards agriculture was the decades-long negative.

At the expense of the contribution to this sector, it was invested extensively in the industry, which is now also devastated, and as a result of technological progress outdated. Although according to George Shultz's opinion Yugoslavia, among all Eastern European countries, was best preparedfor the transition process during the nineties[56], the circumstances that took place in the nineties shifted the countries of the former Yugoslavia in the tail (except Slovenia).

"We never put you in the same cathegory with the countries of real socialism. You are something else, you developed capitalism without capitalists, your employees are at the same time, producers, managers and owners. If you overcome your internal problems peacefully, you will be at the forefront of the countries in transition, as you used to be at the forefront of the reformist countries. "(Ibid.). Unfortunately, history shows us that wedid not make the best moves and that are actually completely badly "played". This led us to the position that twenty years later, we "swim" in the sea of transition (Kocovic, Radovanovic, 2014).

AGRICULTURAL SECTOR IN SERBIA

In the last decades of the twentieth century transformation of agriculture has been very rapid because of technical and technological progress and its application in agroeconomy. Mass production, chemical treatment of soil and plants, global warming and decades of "wasting the planet", led to a review of globally adopted principles. Today, it is necessary to work on adopting the decision on all fronts concerning the sustainability of poverty reduction, adverse impacts on the marine environment, while ensuring economic stability. Given that the meetings of the UNFCCC have definitely established that the climate change happen, and they are

---

[56]   Hyperinflation, recession, civil war, NATO bombing

human-induced, finally, on the global level it is insisted on sustainable development.[57] *"Green Revolution"* - initiated the need to restart the traditional forms of agriculture pushing the limits of its imagination. Understanding of agriculture in the long journey of its transformation changed. Breadth of understanding of agriculture is determined by the level of general development of the country. According to the production and technological point of view agriculture is a very complex system, which is based on the unbreakable bonds and mutual relationships of a series of activities. The Republic of Serbia is a country of great potential in agroeconomy. Taking into account the structure of the soil, geo-political position and methods of soil treatment, with a focus on finding good solutions at the macro and micro level, we believe that it is possible to achieve sustainable growth in this large agro-industrial area. Agroindustry poses a most important industry in the Republic of Serbia. In addition to agricultural production, we should mentione food industry as a closely related industry, which uses primary agricultural products as a raw materials and processed them into consumer goods. The share of agriculture from 10.6% of GDP was recorded in 2013 while the share of the food industry in the same year was 6.4% (Republic Institute for Statistics, 2014). However, the indirect benefits of agricultural production could be measured by contributions in many other industries, particularly for producers and processors of raw materials and inputs. If we look into the all benefits of this industry, it is estimated that the share of agricultural production is much larger and it is 40% of GDP (Serbian Chamber of Commerce, 2014). Although the macro-economic situation is still unstable, one of the possible ways to overcome it, is to improve the quality of rural areas with adequate incentives for the development of entrepreneurship and the small and medium-sized enterprises in the agricultural sector. In recent years a number of documents, aimed to improve the development of the agricultural sector, has been adopted.[58] Transition period in

---

[57]   Climate change related to the change of environment, that are directly or indirectly attributable to human activity, by changing the composition of the global atmosphere. Consequently, sustainable development is emerging as the only solution to the respect of environmental and social issues with economic development.

[58]   Some of them are: the Law on Agriculture and Rural Development (Ministry of Agriculture, Forestry and Water Management, 2008), the Law on Food Safety

Serbia formally begun in 2001 and it has been followed by a large number of policy adjustments and an increased urgency to re-align its economic policies to adapt to the new economic order. The reforms have been carried out by the government to support their development as well as many other measures in order to improve the business environment in Serbia. This refers to the creation of adequate infrastructure for the operation of small and medium-sized enterprises. Despite certain improvements, the SMEs development has not had such a favourable trend nor has it resulted in improving entrepreneurship activities in a desired manner, due to a negative macroeconomic environment in the country and the recession that hit the national economy (beginning with 2008). Namely, the private sector failed to perform its role as regards absorbing the unemployed workforce that was left redundant as a result of privatization of state-owned companies. Furthermore, no satisfactory results have been achieved as regards new employment, nor is there any increased interest among the unemployed in trying their chances in the private sector of industry (Radovic, Kocovic, 2014).

ORGANIC PRODUCTION AS A NEW INCENTIVE TO THE DEVELOPMENT OF AGRO-INDUSTRIAL SECTOR

Incentives with aim to develop any sector of the economy requires simultaneous work on all levels of the country. At the macro-level, this can be achieved by proper choice of public policies, and as well as encouraging desirable behavior and the adoption of the principle of the micro-level. Conditions that have to be fulfilled in agricultural areas include: structural problems, harmonization of internal market regulations, as well as many other issues that need to be harmonized with the laws in force in the EU. Special help in the transformation

---

(Ministry of Agriculture, Forestry and Water Management, 2009), the Law on Organic Production (Ministry of Agriculture, Forestry and Water Management, 2008), the National Rural Development Programme 2011-2013 (Ministry of Agriculture, Forestry and Water Management, 2011), the strategy of agriculture and rural development of Serbia from 2014 to 2024 (Ministry of Agriculture, Forestry and Water Management, 2013) and others.

process, the EU has provided by some funding through a number of programs for interested countries for accession.Special attention is given to issues of funding, harmonization and uniformity of the law. This is provided by programs: CAP, Agenda 2000, SAPARD, IPA, etc. In order for the economy to function in accordance with the modern requirements of the world market it is necessary to educate people about the possible use of EU funds at the disposal for the countries that are in the process of accession (Pantic et al, 2013). New potentials of development are reflected in the synergy of inter-sectoral action which assume connection and parallel flow of: rural development, organic agriculture, crafts, eco-tourism, cultural-tourism-generaly all the special forms of tourism, and the association of small producers through cooperatives. Having regard to the shortcomings of post-transition countries we mentioned in the paper, the reforms would include: training of all participants, education for the new possibilities, the use of new technologies with the active implementation of the marketing concept. Serbian agriculture is based on small family farms with low productivity and low labor surplus in production.

Rural population lacks of:

- Organization,
- Entrepreneurial spirit,
- Market access and education[59]

Since the small farms are most common, there is a possibility of directing towards organic production. Organic production stands out as one of the factors of the future economic growth of Serbia, whose market has the same economic principles as in any other market goods.Considering that demand is growing much faster than domestic supply, the Serbian economy could convert the potentials of organic farming into export opportunities (*Organic farming in Serbia 2013*, The National Association for the development of organic farming Serbia Organica, 2013). With

---

[59]   Based on the Labour Force Survey RSO 23% of the rural population in the active age are self-employed, 14% work in the household, and 62% have a formal zapoislenje with other people. Small business which is engaged in the work of others has 20% of the rural population.

abundance of agricultural land and agro-industrial tradition, which represent the strengths of the agricultural sector, it is expected to have in future new export opportunities, improved quality of living standards and improved position of farmers. Comprehensive management and food production based on environmental practices, a high level of biodiversity, conservation of natural resources and application of high standards of animal welfare and production methods using natural substances and methods is called - organic production (Low on Organic Production, 2010). In order to distinguish these products on the market, they are indicated with the special logo, symbol or code that is assigned only when it is found that all the proper ingredients are natural, and that all the legal requirements for its sale are achieved. Tight control of these product categories gives possibility to achieve greater safety of food sold in the market. Agricultural products classified as organic are natural, without pesticides or powders that can impair human health, they have met the requirements of environmental protection, they are also multifunctionaly useful for consumers. In Serbia, most of the land is still in the process of conversion, the procedure that ensures the achievement of the quality of land which meets the requirements for organic production.

Table 3. Area under organic crop production
in Serbia in the 2012th and 2013.

Categories	The surface of the conversion period (ha)	Surfaces with organic status	Total (ha)
2013*			
Crop production	2.973	2.360	5.333
Fruit production	357	1.527	1.884
Vegetable production	115	123	238
TOTAL	3.445	4.010	7.455
2012			
Crop production	1.734	2.850	4.584
Fruit production	1.091	4.054	5.145
Vegetable production	233	296	529
TOTAL	3.058	7.200	10.260

Source: Serbian Chamber of Commerce and the National Association
for the Development of Organic Agriculture "Serbia Organica"

* Also included period January-September 2013th

Table 3. shows the area under organic crop production in the 2012 and
2013.In 2012 largest part of the area was under organic production of
fruit growing, while in the period from January to September 2013that
number decreased twice. This situation may be explained by bad weather
and poor marketing of organic fruit in the domestic and international
markets, which affects decline in the interest of farmers for this type
of production. The area under organic vegetable productionrecorded
a slight decline, and one possible reason is the lack of the information
which the home buyers do not have.[60] The growth in the areas under

---

[60]   Those information are concerned with all the benefits of this type of plant

organic production in the period 2012-2013 is recorded only in crop production, which spread from about 4.500ha in 2012 to 5.333ha. The growth of interest in this type of production may be found in the opportunities for export marketing of agricultural products, especially grains and corn, which can make a significant inflow of funds to the farmers.

Table 4. Organic livestock production in Serbia, 2012-2013.

Categories	Period conversion Number of livestock and poultry animals	Organic status Number of animals are animals and poultry
2013*		
Large livestock (cattle, horses, donkeys)	481	2,972
Small livestock (sheep, goats, pigs)	3,473	708
Poultry (chickens, ducks, geese, turkeys)	1,432	183
Beehives	764	1,273
2012		
Large livestock (cattle, horses, donkeys)	2,164	230
Small livestock (sheep, goats, pigs)	3,404	983
Poultry (chickens, ducks, geese, turkeys)	4,276	3,600
Beehives	2,610	4,394

Source: National Association for the Development
of Organic Agriculture "Serbia Organica"

* Also included period January-September 2013th

production

Organic livestock production in Serbia is becoming more represented. Food safety and food security have been called into question in recent years, and by the organic production any doubts regarding the quality of food that is produced are eliminated. Table 4. provides an overview of the current situation in organic livestock production, it showed a significantly higher number of livestock and poultry in conversion than those with organic status.

Table 5. Area under organic farming in the neighboring countries, 2012.

Country	Area in%
Bulgaria	0.8
Croatia	2.4
Romania	2.1
Slovenia	7.3

Source: Eurostat

Table 5.shows the area under organic production in neighboring countries, where this indicator implies a share of utilized agricultural land under organic production.They include the areas that are in the process of conversion and those that have already received the organic status. According to Eurostat, Slovenia is intensively engaged in organic production, because 7.3% of its agricultural land is under organic production. In Serbia, 0.3% of the total cultivated area is under organic production, which is insufficient keeping in mind the natural resources and opportunities for its development and improvement.

AGRICULTURAL COOPERATIVES AS A KEY FOR ACHIEVING AGRICULTURAL SAFETY THROUGH SUSTAINABLE TRANSFORMATION

The reasons for the underdeveloped organic production in Serbia are manifold (*"Organic farming in Serbia 2014"*, The National Association for the development of organic farming "Serbia Organica", 2014). Small producers in Serbia are faced with a set of problems in manufacturing. First of all, farmers usually point out the lack of financial resources in order to intensify investment in machinery, storage and distribution. Insignificant part of the farmers is creditworthy and can obtain funds for investment from external sources, while most of them depend on the current market conditions, the intensity of competition and the demand for their products. Although they produce on small farms that are predominantly 2ha to 3ha in size they are intensively trying to survive on the market and stay cost-competitive. In addition to financial problems, manufacturers are facing a problem of logistics, transport, storage etc. The arrival of large retail chains in Serbia has further intensified competition, considering that the ability to import organic products, for which there is demand, is always present. Therefore, about 70% of organic producers decided to make long-term cooperation agreement with them, while a smaller percentage still sells directly to consumers, at the green market. The producers are therefore faced with: poor infrastructure, limited access to services and information, markets and finances. Access to loans for all the needed inputs might be a huge problem for small producers. But small producers' costs could be reduced if they are allowed to purchase and make an offer together in groups. It is mentioned also in FAO work in brochure for *Worlds food day* that: *accumulated research and experience show that while small farmers acting alone did not benefit from higher food prices, those who are acting collectively in strong producer organization and cooperatives were able to have advantage of market opportunities and mitigate the negative effects of food and other crisis.*[61]

---

[61]   Agricultural cooperatives: key to feeding world. Internet approach 20.06.2014.http://www.fao.org/fileadmin/templates/getinvolved/images/WFD2012_leaflet_en_low.pdf

In order to make the organic form of production optimal for all participants, it is recommended to make organizations and joint actions on the market as voluntary organization of cooperatives in order to benefit from better retail prices for inputs. In this way, there could be a diversification in organic production, so that the cooperatives cover all the necessary marketing activities of production of various crops, promotion, logistics and adequate prices for regular clients. Similar to the former *vertical systems*, in modern economy new forms of cooperatives could be economic drivers on the local level. As already mentioned, in favor of this idea goes experience of Slovenia, which used know-how approach and engaged experts to overcome the transition hazards and barriers at the start. Today's modern forms of association of cooperatives, in addition to traditional activities, could have a function of educational centers to acquire new knowledge and skills necessary in the modern turbulent conditions of free market. Small producers are strongly vulnerable and feel every market change. The essence of the model is to make a cooperation, be a link between small producers (sometimes state owned enterprises), all market participants, to the final consumer. Earlier, this relationship allowed the transfer of technology and knowledge with transformationof production, income and food chain. The model of cooperatives in the seventies and eighties in synergy with other factors contributed to the impressive growth of agricultural productivity. In the post-transition period, there were examples of new forms of association of agricultural producers. (Nikolic, Katic, 2006: 204)[62]

A cooperative is a social enterprise that balances two main goals:

1. satisfying its members' needs, and
2. pursuing profit and sustainability.[63]

Cooperatives are not limited by anything if we compare them to other organisations, they can:

---

[62] Production on the example of Bulgarian cooperatives were based primarily on the production of annual crops. And the average size of the associated arable land amounted to up to 7.000ha.

[63] Agricultural cooperatives: key to feeding world. Internet approach 20.06.2014. http://www.fao.org/fileadmin/templates/getinvolved/images/WFD2012_leaflet_en_low.pdf

Last in time, get bigger, generate income; Could be organized in any sector place, by diferent people and reasons. Cooperatives are owned by members, which have rights and responsibilities. Voting for decision making is democratic - governance with direct democracy. Members can also delegate authority to an individual or a committee, also they can elect, if needed, a board of directors for representative democracy. By voating members can solve any situation. Share of net income is equitable, positive and negative also. If net income is generated by empoyees it is profit, and if it is collected by members it is surplus. Surplus could be refunded as patronage. Members can hire empoyees. Startup financial assets are provided by members equity, buy-in or capital contribution. Even if some of them put more money then others, they still have one vote! Financing possibiities they choose mostly from: banks, funds and other credit options (investitors, individuals). Some of most famous American cooperatives lasted more than 50 years, from totaly diferent sectors.[64]

The direction in which the Republic of Serbia could have a serious growth and development would include a large number of small family subsistence producers, who could in joint action initially supply the community on the local level. Respecting the market and permaculture principles, knowledge, innovation, useof technology would help them to make the connection between manufacturer and customer. One of necessary steps to achieve food security is to support and invest in cooperatives, producer organizations and other rural institutions. This will alow producers to reduce costs, increase production, create jobs, make their goods, improve livehoods on local level, and this will also mean increasing food security in the world.[65]

The internet era, and technological advances allow constant revolutionary approaches to work. Based on the data from the Business Registers Agency, Ministry of Agriculture and SBS, it would be possible to make

---

[64] Some of those cop. collected more then 40 miion dollars, and have from 100 to 1000 members. www.americancoop/map.com Internet approach 20.06.2014.

[65] Agricultural cooperatives: key to feeding world, Internet approach 20.06.2014: http://www.fao.org/fileadmin/templates/getinvolved/images/WFD2012_leaflet_en_low.pdf

the internet platform where, small farmers from the surrounding rural areas would be mapped near each city . In addition it would be possible to see information about the planted crops, time of ripening, harvest and further placement.

The platform would include small manufacturers and a number of manufacturers joined in a cooperative. In addition the information on agricultural production of small manufacturers will easily and quickly be made available to any individal or a legal person. In this way, they could create and secure customers and the market. In addition to the primary activities of agriculture, small family farms could expand its activities in the direction of ecological and cultural tourism, so as to offer interested parties the workshops on agricultural activities.[66]

All the mentioned changes should implement permaculture ethics and principles.[67] Figure 1. shows elements of permaculture principles and ethics. The main idea is the connection of and care for: people, society and fair share. This is actually a real method to achive sustainibiity. Process of providing needs for people within ecological limits, requires cultural revolution. It is very important to keep in mind these principles mind in this historical context. Because of their universality, principles should be seen as slogans of checklist which shoud be considered in addition to support new ecologically correct systems. All the principles are applicable to our personal, economic, social and political fields – to be reorganized.

Speaking of principles, design and permacultural ethics, Holmgren points out that ethics are culturaly evolved mechanisms for more enlightened self-interest, more inclusive view of what constitutes »us«, and a longer-term understanding of good and bad outcomes (Holmgren, 2014, internet aproach 25.05.2014).

---

[66] Collecting medicinal herbs and mushrooms; Accommodation in environmentally constructed buildings, work actions, etc.

[67] Permaculture is relatively new discipline, started in late 70s. Permaculture is a creative design process that is based on ethics and design principles. It guides us to mimic the patterns and relationships we can find in nature and can be applied to all aspects of human habitation, from agriculture to ecological building, from appropriate technology to education and even economics.

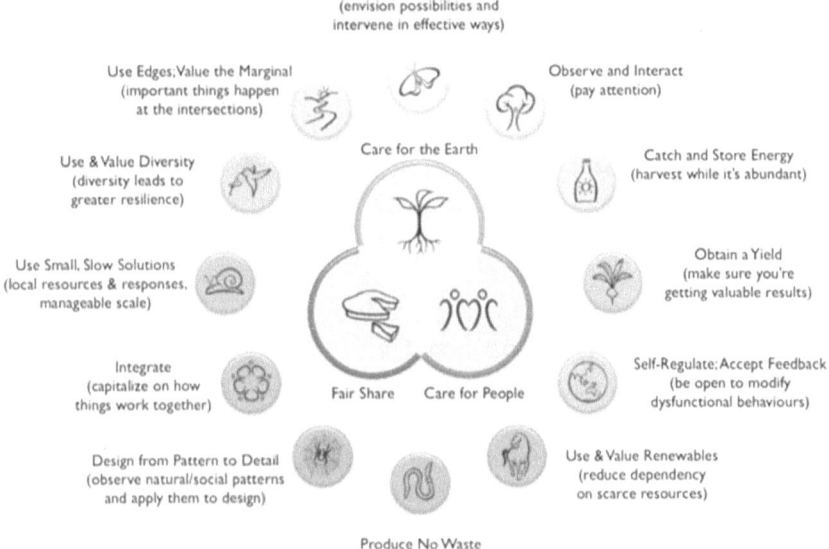

Figure 1. Permaculture principles

Source: Essence of Permaculture

CONCLUSION

The position of the farmers was the decades-long negative. Only individuals were able to boast good material well-being, but most of them were on the verge of poverty. The low level of literacy and education of the population in rural areas, migration from rural to urban areas in search for better living conditions and a lack of funding resulted in lagging of Serbian farmers compared to those in the European Union.

The development of industry at the expense of agriculture led to underestimation of the possibilities of this industry and its contribution to economic growth and development. In recent years in our country we cannotice slight changes in economic policy and national documents which subsidizes agro economy, especially its particular categories.

The common agricultural policy implemented by the EU in particular has highlighted the importance of agriculture for the environment, food safety and quality, working conditions and benefits of living in rural areas, ie. priority is given to non-economic measures of agriculture, with an emphasis on sustainable concept. New reforms related to ecologically clean agriculture and strengthening of rural development measures. And this can be achieved by respecting the ethics and principles of permaculture, along with the associatingin cooperatives.

In 2012 Serbia became a candidate for EU membership. It takes a lot of work to strengthen agricultural markets at the local, regional, national level, the harmonization of the common agricultural policy of the EU member states. More than 76% of the total arable land of the country is segmented in a number of small producers- *"These are households that have no realistic chance not only in agriculture, but "connected to agriculture". Application of the concept of integrated rural development, such as that which is practiced in the Western market economy, to enable efficient operation and small agricultural holdings based on the "family business", which involves dealing with different industries (tourism, trade services, trade, etc.). Within rural households." (Zakic, 2003).*

Of particular importance is the identification of opportunities, and timely response. The role and willingness of the state as a stimulator of the process of association of cooperatives is of utmost importance.

REFERENCES

1. Agricultural cooperatives: key to feeding world. Internet approach 20.06.2014. http://www.fao.org/fileadmin/templates/getinvolved/Figures/WFD2012_leaflet_en_low.pdf

2. Food and Agriculture Organization of the United Nations, http://www.fao.org/ fileadmin/templates/getinvolved/Figures/WFD2012_leaflet_en_low.pdf

3. http://holmgren.com.au/downloads/Essence_of_Pc_EN.pdf

4. Kocovic, M., Radovanovic, B., (2014), New incentives in agro industrial sector and their contributions to a balanced development, Deindustrialisation in Serbia- possibilities of revitalization of industrial sector, Institute of Economic sciences, Belgrade.

5. Lerman, Z., (2000): "Agriculture in transition economies: From common heritage to divergence".UK, Agricultural Economics.

6. Law on Organic Production 2010, Ministry of Agriculture, Forestry and Water Management, Republic of Serbia

7. Nikolic, M., (1994): "The scientific basis of the agricultural policy of Yugoslavia in free market conditions ", thematic collection, Institute of Agricultural Economics, Beograd,.

8. National Chamber of Commerce Serbia, www.pks.rs

9. Nikolic, M., Katic, B. (2006), Efects of transition on agrar sector in selected countries of CSE Europe, Economics of agrar. Belgrade.

10. "Organic farming in Serbia 2013", The National Association for the development of organic farming "Serbia Organica", January 2013 Belgrade

11. "Organic farming in Serbia 2014", The National Association for the development of organic farming, "Serbia Organica", January 2014 Belgrade

12. Pantic, O., Stevanovic, S., Milivojevic, S., (2013), "Waste Management Policy in Agriculture of the Republic of Serbia - Status and Prospects", Ecologica, Nau no-stru no društvo za zaštitu životne sredine, vol. 71, page 472

13. Radovic Markovic, Kocovic, et al., (2014), General Conditions For Development Of SMEs In Serbia, (FORTHCOMING).

14. Republic Institute for Statistics, www.stat.gov.rs

15. Stevanovi S., orovi M., (2009), "A comparative analysis of results of the transition processes in the agro-buisiness of Serbia and some CEE countries", Thematic collection: Agroculture and rural areas of Serbia, DAES, Beograd.

16. Swinnen,J.F.M., Mathijs,E. (1997): "Agricultural privatization, Land reform and Farm restructuring in CIE: A comparative analysis", Aldershot.

17. Zaki ,Z. (2003): "The new agricultural policy operational restructuring of family farms",Theme Collection: Institutional reforms and transition agribusiness in Serbia, Faculty of Economics, Beograd.

18. www.americancoop/map.com Internet approach 20.06.2014.

TRANSITION TOWARDS RENEWABLE ENERGY SUPPLY IN CROATIA

Neven Vidakovic[68]

INTRODUCTION

The main objective of this paper is to present a framework for Croatia to increase its use of renewable energy (RE). This process can also be called a transition towards renewable energy sources. However, this transition process has to be broken down into several different but strongly related parts, which all have a significant impact on the increase in the production of energy from renewable sources. In order to build an analysis framework, we have to consider both the macro and the microperspective on the problem.

From the macro perspective, there are current and expected market conditions regarding the economic situation in Croatia and how it will develop in the next few years. The current economic crisis presents a significant constraint concerning the process of increasing the use of renewable energy sources. Apart from the existing internal macroconstraints, there are expectations regarding the exogenous tasks imposed by the EU as presented in the Europe 2020plan. This plan makes clear demands for the use of renewable energies.

From the microperspective, there are issues regarding which sources of renewable energy to use (sun, wind, water) and through which projects the goals set can be achieved. A microframework is also important in terms of who will fund the investments and from which sources. There is also a need for a considerable amount of preparation in terms

---

[68]   Effectus University College for Law and Finance, Zagreb, Croatia, nvidakovic@vsfp.eu

of locations, investment plans and energy grid capacities. Therefore, any general goals and objectives need to have strongly developed microsupport and infrastructure.

The two perspectives on renewable energy in Croatia can also be presented from the viewpoint of the three main participants in RE in Croatia. Those three participants are theGovernment, the academic community and investors. The Government is in charge of the policies and laws pertaining to RE in Croatia. The main role of the Government in the process should be to facilitate the investors and create solid foundations for investments in RE. The second participant is the academic community in Croatia, which should be responsible for the research on the potential of RE and the possible environmental and economic impacts of RE on the Croatian economy. A special focus of the academic community should be the impact on the environment, but the main challenge lies in the interdisciplinary approach, which has to combine economics, ecology and engineering. The third and possibly the most important group of participants in the RE process is the investors, who are supposed to invest in RE projects in order to increase the RE production in Croatia. The investors need to have profitable projects and clear financing facilities.

All of the above participants have equal weight and importance. In this paper, we aim to investigate the current state of each of the aforementioned participants, how the participants can be brought together and how the targets set for the Croatian economy in terms of renewable energy sourcescan be achieved.

This paper is separated into the following parts. The second part provides a short macroeconomic overview to allowa full understanding of the harsh economic conditions that Croatia is facing. Part three presentsthe current state of energy consumption in Croatia and the long-term importance of increasing the use of renewable energy in Croatia. Parts four and five present the achievements of the academic community and government policies in terms of RE. Part six addresses the discrepancy between the academic research and the government policies. Part seven proposes several clear policies that can be implemented in order to stimulate investments in RE, and part eight contains the conclusions.

RECENT ECONOMIC CONDITIONS

The macro economy and the state of the fiscal policy in Croatia have considerably deteriorated during the recession. Consequently, for the general understanding of the Croatian economic environment, it is useful to present a brief overview of the impact of the crisis.

Croatia has been in recession for 5 years (2009–2013) and 2014[69] is expected to continue the trend. Overall, the GDP has decreased by 12% since the start of the crisis. The impact of the recession on investments has been greater. Using GDP data in terms of fixed 2005 prices, the gross investments as a percentage of the GDP were 31.5% in 2008 and 21.5% in 2013.[70] In terms of money, this is a 5 billion euro decrease per year. If we use 2008 as the base year and hold the investments constant as a percentage of the GDP, we can calculate the amount of money that was not invested in the time period 2009–2013 to be 21 billion euros. This number represents the value of investments lost due to the crisis. Therefore, the main long-term contributor to the crisis is the decrease in investments. It is clear that the investments have to be the main contributor to the economic growth that will end the recession.

A similar analysis can be performed with the total value of the GDP. The total GDP, in 2005 prices, in 2013 was on par with the 2006 GDP, so Croatia has achieved no economic real growth for seven years. Given these conditions, it is exceptionally challenging to promote clean energy since clean energy projects are investment-and capital-intensive.

The decreases in the GDP and the recession have also been accompanied by a decrease in employment. During the crisis, in the time period 2009–2014, Croatia has lost 200 000 jobs, which is 13% of the total employment or 4.5% of the total population. These numbers clearly indicate the depth of the crisis in Croatia, which is so prolonged that it can be called a full-blown depression.

---

[69]   The S&P rating agency estimates that Croatia's real GDP will also decrease by 0.5% in 2014.

[70]   Data taken from the Croatian Statistical Institute (www.dzs.hr) and calculated by the author.

This short macroeconomic introduction was important in order to present clearly theprincipalmacroeconomic constraint for any policy or development strategy. However, even given the prolonged recession and severe economic conditions, there are still economic tools that can be used through fiscal and monetary policy in order to increase the quantity of sources of renewable energy and in this paper we aim to propose several possible solutions.

ENERGY CONSUMPTION IN CROATIA

We will now briefly review the energy consumption and energy dependence to determine the potential of renewable energy in Croatia. The consumption of energy in Croatia has not had a clear constant over the last 25 years. Figure 1 shows that the energy consumption is unsurprisingly heavily dependent on the political and economic conditions.

The decrease in consumption during the period from 1990 to 1995 can be attributed to war, while the decrease in the period from 2010 to 2012 can be attributed to the deterioration of economic conditions due to recession. Industrial production has decreased by ca 15% since 2008[71] and this has decreased the energy demands.

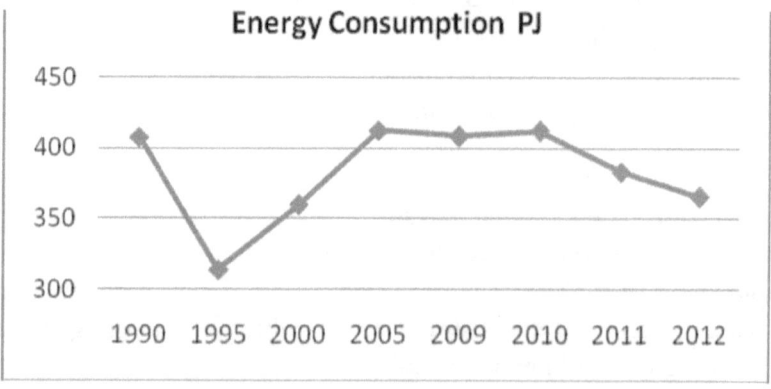

Figure 1. Energy consumption in Croatia (in peta joules)

Source: Energy in Croatia

---

[71]   Data taken from the CNB Bulletin.

From the perspective of this paper, it is necessary to verify the current state of renewable energy in Croatia and how RE affects the Croatian dependency on energy imports.

Figure 2 presents the importance of energy imports for Croatia in the time period 2001–2012. The variable import dependency was obtained by using the following formula: (energy imports – energy export) / (total inland consumption). As we can see, about half of the energy needs are produced in Croatia and the rest is imported.

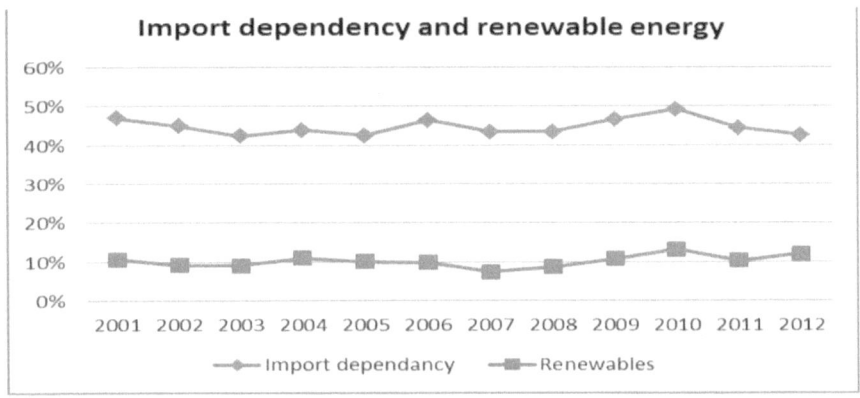

Figure 2. Energy dependency and renewable energy in Croatia

Source: Energy in Croatia

The second variable is renewables; this is the percentage of the renewable energy produced of the total inland consumption. What is clear from Figure 2 is that Croatia has a great need for energy imports and that it is energy-dependent, but at the same time very little energy is obtained from the RE sources. Therefore, there is clearly potential for investments in RE and for RE to be used to decrease the Croatian dependency on imported energy.

Following this basic overview of energy consumption in Croatia and the current level of RE in Croatian production, we will split our analysis into two fronts. First, we will present the efforts made in terms of research and the importance of RE and then we will analyze the government's actions to bring together the academic research and actual business projects.

RESEARCH ON THE RENEWABLE ENERGY POTENTIAL IN CROATIA

In order to understand fully the importance of the transition of Croatia towards RE, we can start with the study by Paši ko and Vlaši (2010), which projects that the potential of new jobs from RE sources could be 14500 new jobs created directly and another 58000 jobs created indirectly from RE investments. Together, theseamount to more than one-third of the total jobs lost during the recession. This analysis creates another dimension to RE energy, in which renewable energy is not just a source of energy, but a large opportunity to create new jobs.

We can separate the approach to the research on the potential of RE in Croatia into two separate segments. The first segment is the macro segment, which deals with broader issues of energy and the Croatian economy in general. The second approach to research focuses on one specific topic or issue.

An example of the macro approach to RE in Croatia can be found in the work by Vitalji (2006), who has an ambitious agenda. In this master's thesis, Vitalji investigates the potential of RE to decrease the total emission of CO_2. Through scenario tests, Vitalji investigates the CO_2 emission in Croatia. Another example of this broad kind of research is provided by Dui et al (2012), who investigate Croatia and the Kyoto Protocol.

However, for our research, a much more important approach is the micro approach, which focuses on very specific and focused problems dealing with renewable energy in Croatia.

The potential of RE has been investigated in terms of use on isolated islands as well. For example, Ba eli et al (2013) investigate what can be undertaken in terms of RE on Hvar, a remote island in the Adriatic Sea. The main conclusion of the paper is that RE should be the main source of energy on most Croatian islands. The use of RE can lead to the total energy independence of Croatian islands. Although this research focuses on Hvar, similar scenarios can be used on other islands.

Ridjan et al (2013) investigate the possibility to incorporate RE energy into transportation systems. The previous research was conducted on a geoFigureic area; this research is an example of target-specific research oriented towards what can be achieved when focusing directly on one sector of the economy.

While the previous two research examples investigate the possibility of RE in terms of supply, Pukšec et al (2013) examine the energy demand of the Croatian transportation sector. Other sector-oriented research relating to energy demands can be found in Pukšec et al (2013), who investigate the energy demand of households in Croatia, or Irsag, and Pukšec and Dui (2012), who explore the use of energy in tourism and the potential for energy savings in the tourism sector.

Pukšec and Dui (2011) provide an overview of the efforts made in the agriculture industry in terms of biogas and the potential of biogas in the Croatian farming industry. Croatian agriculture is experiencing a decline in terms of the share of GDP; agriculture declined from 5.38% of the GDP in 2000 to 3.97% of the GDP in 2013. This paper indicates the unexplored potential for Croatian agriculture. Pukšec and Dui 's (2011) paper also opens up the broader topic of the use of government subsidies for agriculture and how subsidies could be directed into other related areas and not just crops.

Even from this brief overview of the state of the research in Croatia, it is clear that the academic community has played its part in contributing to the implementation and the increase of RE in Croatia. However, the main problem remains on the side of the government and what it is contributing to RE.

GOVERNMENT STRATEGIES AND THE RELATION WITH RENEWABLE ENERGY

One of the aspects of joining the EU is the demands made by the EU for clear leadership and directions in all key areas. Consequently, the EU is trying to create long-terms targets and projections in order to bring the EU member countries together. The main objectives of the EU in terms of the time horizon can be found in the EU plan Europe 2020. This long-term plan has five main targets:

1. Employment: 75% of 20–64 yearolds to be employed
2. Research and development: 3% of the EU's GDP to be invested in research and development
3. Climate change and energy sustainability: greenhouse gas emissions 20% (or even 30%, if the conditions are right)lower than 1990, 20% of energy from renewables, a 20% increase in energy efficiency
4. Education: reducing the rates of early school leaving below 10%; at least 40% of 30–34yearolds completing tertiary-level education

Fighting poverty and social exclusion: at least 20 million fewer people in or at risk of poverty and social exclusion

Europe 2020 clearly states that in EU countries 20% of the energy should come from renewable sources. However, in reality, this calculation is not exactly 20% of the energy used in each country, but a complex calculation based on the starting position of each country and the per capita contribution. Therefore, each country has a different target and the total target for the EU should be 20%. The actual figure for Croatia has not yet been defined.[72]In order to achieve these aims, Croatia has produced three important strategies, which should, if implemented, make sure that Croatia achieves all of the above-stated targets. The three main strategies are:

- The Croatian Strategy for Education, Technologies and Science
- The Croatian Industrial Strategy 2014–2020
- The Croatian Strategy forEnergy Development

---

[72]   These data were taken from the Europe 2020 website (http://ec.europa.eu/ europe2020/ europe-2020-in-your-country/hrvatska/progress-towards-2020-targets/index_en.htm). As of May 1, 2020, the national energy target for Croatia is stated in thenational targets as undefined.

The Croatian Industrial Strategy 2014–2020 and the Croatian Strategy for Education, Technologies and Science were created and presented in 2013 and 2014, respectively, while the Croatian Strategy for Energy Development was presented in 2009.

Although the Strategy for Education, Technologies and Science is not directly connected to renewable sources of energy, it is important because of the sources of future labor for the renewable energy industry. The education strategy heavily emphasizes the importance of research and the connection of scientific research and scientific institutions with industry. From this strategy, it is clear there is a long-term objective to make the Croatian scientific community a source of new knowledge for the industry. For Croatia, for the transition towards increasing the use of renewable energy, such support from the academic community is important. In the previous chapter, we saw that in terms of research on renewable energy, the Croatian academic community has contributed its share.

The Croatian Industrial Strategy clearly states that there is a need for renewable sources of energy. This is not just due to the EU goal, but is a necessity for Croatia. Since Croatia is not able to satisfy all its energy needs from fossil fuels, there is a need to develop renewable sources of energy in order to increase Croatia's energy independence (page 61 of the Industrial Strategy). There are numerous mentions of renewable sources of energy in the Industrial Strategy; there is also a table presenting clear objectives for which EU funding (page 82of the Industrial Strategy) could be obtained for renewable energy projects. However, in the rest of the strategy, there are no other quantifiable data regarding how the renewable energy industry can help Croatia or what can be achieved in terms of employment or GDP growth if considerable investments are made in renewable sources of energy. There is also no mention of specific RE industry projects or investments.

On the other hand, the Croatian Energy Strategy places considerable emphasis on renewable sources of energy. Throughout the strategy, there are numerous references to how renewable energy could be used or the possible investments in RE projects, especially in water power plants. However, the Energy Strategy was developed mostly in 2008 and officially adopted in 2009, when the economic crisis had just started. The creators of the strategy did not take into consideration a prolonged recession and the effects of a recession on the Croatian economy. With the change of government in 2012, some energy projects were initiated, such as the water power plant Ombla. However, due to bureaucratic procedures and environmental concerns, most of those projects have been put on hold. Because of the change of government and unclear statusesfor energy projects, the Energy Strategy is of little impact or consequence at this point in time.

From this, we can see that the Croatian Government has achieved very little in terms of renewable energy. Because of the recession, the Energy Strategy needs to be completely redefined to include the new economic circumstances. The Industrial Strategy has to be augmented with clearer and more precise projects to involve RE in order to attract investors. The fact that Croatia has put major projects and investmentson hold, like the project Ombla, makes government-sponsored transition towards renewable energy sources highly unlikely.

DISCONTINUITY BETWEEN THE GOVERNMENT AND SCIENCE

The last two chapters have presented us with the main problem of RE in Croatia. On one side, there is the academic research, which has been thorough and focused on energy problems in Croatia. On the other side, there is the Government and its policies, which are clearly lagging.

The government documents are strategies thatmake little contribution in terms of the state of the real world and lack focused implementation. The implementation of any strategy and therefore the achievement of the Europe 2020 targets are also in question because of the time constraint. The Europe 2020 targets are targets that require several years of planning and implementation. At this point in time, in the year 2014 or the year 2015, a country should be well into the implementation stage of policies, not at the planning stage or, as presented in terms of the Energy Strategy in Croatia, practically at the beginning stages of implementation. Considering a time span of just six years before the Europe 2020 targets have to be reached, it is hard to believe that Croatia can, at least in terms of energy targets, move from the strategy creation stage towards target achievement.

However, the situation is not lost or incredibly complex. As this paper has presented, there is an existing body of research that can be implemented in order to move more quickly towards the Europe 2020 targets. Nevertheless, in order to benefit from the scientific research completely, investors need to see investment opportunities in renewable energy in Croatia. To achieve the targets, theGovernment has to move from the planning state into the fast implementation state and that cannot be achieved without clear and targeted government policies.

PROPOSALS FOR INCREASING RENEWABLE ENERGY PROJECTS

So far, this paper has presented the clear potential for RE energy in Croatia since Croatia is energy-dependent. It has also shown that there is a discrepancy between the state of the academic research, which is highly advanced, and the government strategies, which are either obsolete or undefined. The Government is still in the planning stages, while it should be in the implementation stages. The only way to move the Government from planning to action is to implement clear and targeted policies to foster the growth of RE investments in Croatia. This part of the paper will present several possible proposals to speed up the investments in RE in Croatia.

As presented in the Europe 2020 plan, renewable energy is a long-term strategic target for the EU and therefore for Croatia as well. If Croatia has a clear stance that renewable energy is an important product and project, then there has to be clear support for this policy direction from both the monetary and the fiscal side. Considering the short time span, it is important for Croatia to focus on the execution of the projects and not on cumbersome strategic planning.

To achieve afull transition to large-scale consumption of RE, there are several policies that could be implemented. The policies presented here are focused, targeted and easily executed policiesthat could be used in order to speed up the process of creation of new energy sources. The proposals here are concrete, matter-of-fact proposals and not abstract notions about the strategic planningneeded. We shall start with the monetary policy and banking industry.

The monetary policy in Croatia does not directly control banks' credit policy. However, the capital adequacy rules, which are proscribed by the Central Bank, can be used effectively to stir banks' decisions in order to increase or decrease certain credits in the banks' balance sheet. Currently, there are no distinctions in terms of capital adequacy when it comes to loans for RE. The Croatian Central Bank could introduce a new capital adequacy ponder for loans for RE projects. This new capital adequacy ponder should be 0 or 0.2 so that the banks have very few or no capital demands on RE projects.

In November 2013, the Croatian Central Bank proposed a decrease in regulation, which was conditioned on the increase in loans. However, the measure has had a limited result, as described by Vidakovi and Zbašnik (2014). A similar measure could be used in the case of renewable energy. There could also be a decrease in regulation for loans used for renewable energy projects. For example, loans given for renewable energy projects could be used as a deduction from the reserve requirement. This would significantly decrease the cost of funds for the banks, consequently decreasing the interest rates and making RE loans more attractive.

The Croatian Bank for Reconstruction and Development (HBOR) can also be used to fund loans for RE projects.HBOR operates lending projects for RE energy sources and the funds can be obtained directly from HBOR or from a commercial bank, but those projects are only available to corporations or local government, not to individuals. In addition, there are specifications regarding the project's purpose – wind or solar energy – or project scale – small business or households. For RE to be fully implemented as an investment opportunity, specialized projects are needed in order to stimulate lending for specific purposes and specific clients.

HBOR could also give loans to banks with the purpose of funding renewable energy projects and the Croatian National Bank should exclude this type of funding from the reserve requirement, making the cost of funds smaller for individual banks.

Currently, thebanking industry in Croatia does not have large-scale credit plans in order to fund RE. This is clearly indicated in terms of banks that are part of large international conglomerates. For example, Privredna banka Zagreb is a member of the Intesa Sanpaolo banking group and Privredna banka Zagreb does not have any special loans or credit facilities for RE projects. At the same time, Banka Koper, which is a member of the same banking group in Slovenia, has specialized loans for solar panel projects. The same banking group has different banking products in two different countries. This is a clear indication that the banks in Croatia do not view RE projects as worth funding. Therefore, a push from external sources, i.e. the Central Bank or the Government, is needed in order to increase the lending for RE.

The majority of funding for RE projects has to come from commercial banks, but as we have presented, there is an important role to be played by the Central Bank and HBOR. A combination of the proposed measure from the Central Bank with HBOR funding could be that push for the banks to start funding RE projects in Croatia.

Government policies can also contribute to increasing the investments in RE. In terms of the macro perspective, a new energy strategy is needed, which incorporates the existing economic conditions and proposes clear projects that can be implemented. The Energy Strategy from 2009 is a general document that does not have specific quantitative targets.

In terms of an economic policy for Croatia to increase the importance of RE in the Croatian economy, the basic approach is usually the simplest: a tax policy. The Croatian Government should foster RE investments through tax deductions, tax subsidies and lower tax rates. Furthermore, the household individual solar panel project, which was started by the Croatian Electrical Company (Hrvatska elektroprivreda), was abandoned. This project has to be reinstated. The starting of the subsidized solar panel project for households and then the abolishment of this project is a clear example of the lack of general direction and focus on the part ofthe Government.

Another clear government policy that can be used is government subsidies. By restructuring to whomthe subsidies are given, the Croatian Government could entice investments into RE. For example, moving subsidies from the shipyards and agriculture to RE could produce a considerable increase in the RE investments in Croatia; however, when and if this measure will be implemented remains to be seen.

Regarding the possibilities from implementing focused policies, a great suggestion was given by Pukšec and Dui (2011), who investigated the potential for methane production from farms. Directing subsidies from crops into the production of biogas plants can result in a more effective distribution of government subsidies. Redirecting subsidies towards another economic activity is just one of the possibilities whereby the Government can increase the RE energy in Croatia without increasingthe cost or the government expenditures.

CONCLUSION

The main objective of this paper was to define the involved parties and try to establish what each of the participants in the process of transition towards renewable energy has achieved so far.

There is a clear objective in terms of RE in Croatia. This objective was given exogenously to Croatia from the EU. However, there are several important constraints that Croatia is facing when it comes to the implementation of the EU plans.

One major constraint is the lack of a clear energy strategy. The last Energy Strategy was created in 2009 and it did not take into effect the prolonged economic recession that Croatia is experiencing. The existing Energy Strategy also does not have clear projects, participants and deadlines. Therefore, a new strategy is needed, one thattakes into consideration the current economic conditions.

Most work on moving Croatia closer to the objectives was undertaken by the academic community. From the academic perspective, the possibilities of RE in Croatia have been heavily researched, both on the supply side and on the demand side. Thus, there are opportunities to implement RE in Croatia. There is research clearly showing that RE could be a great source of new jobs. In spite of all this, the Government has done little to improve the RE and the use of RE in Croatia, since the Government is still in the stages of planning and creating strategies, not executing them. There are three main strategies that pertain to renewable energy, but that is all. In addition, the strategies themselves are not at the implementation stage, but at the discussion stage. The most important of them, the Energy Strategy, is obsolete, and given the existing economic conditions, it cannot be implemented.

The lack of government action has also discouraged private investors, who are not interested in investing in renewable energies. The best example of the difference between what the RE industry is doing and what the Government is doing was given at the Brown Forum in Zagreb in April 2014, by Mark Crandall, the founder of Continental Wind Partners. Continental Wind Partners, as a clean energy-producing company, is involved in wind projects in almost every country in the region (Poland, Romania, Serbia and Bulgaria[73]), except Croatia. This clearly points to the problem of the connection between the Government and the possible investors.

Because of the lack of government interest, investment facilities are also rare and not defined by the banks, since the banks do not have clear lines of credit for investors in renewable energy projects.

Considering the existing state of renewable energy in Croatia, it is clear that the path should be as follows. Academia has played its part; now theGovernment should abandon its lengthy strategies and focus on projects that will bring Croatia closer to the Europe 2020 plan. In addition, the monetary and fiscal policies should play their part by creating financial facilities for investors. Some proposals regarding those facilities were made in this paper as well.

---

[73]   http://www.continentalwind.com/overview

REFERENCES

1. Ba eli Medi , Z; osi , B; Dui , N, (2013) "Sustainability of remote communities: 100% renewable island of Hvar" Journal of Renewable and Sustainable Energy volume 5, issue 4;

2. CNB Bulletin (2014) Croatian Central Bank Bulletin number 202 http://www.hnb.hr/publikac/bilten/arhiv/bilten-02/hbilt202.pdf

3. Draft of the proposal for the industrial strategy of Republic of Croatia 2014.–2020 (2014) Ministry of Economy http://www.mingo.hr/default.aspx?id=4980

4. Dui , N; Jureti , F; Zeljko, M; Bogdan, Ž, (2005) "Croatia energy planning and Kyoto Protocol" Energy Policy 33-8, 1003-1010

5. Energy in Croatia 2012 (2014) Annual energy report, Ministry of Economy, Zagreb 257 pages

6. Irsag, B; Pukšec, T; Dui , N, (2012) "Long term energy demand projection and potential for energy savings of Croatian tourism-catering trade sector" Energy 48, 1; 398-405

7. Pukšec, T; Kraja i , G; Luli , Z; Mathiesen, B V; Dui , N, (2013) "Forecasting long-term energy demand of Croatian transport sector" Energy. 57 ; 169-176

8. Pukšec, T; Mathiesen, B V; Dui , N, (2013) "Potentials for energy savings and long term energy demand of Croatian households sector" Applied energy. 101 ; 15-25

9. Pukšec, Tomislav; Dui , Neven, (2011) "GeoFigureic distribution and economic potential of biogas from Croatian farming sector" Chemical Engineering Transactions 25; 899-904

10. Ridjan, I; Mathiesen, B V; Connolly, D; Duic, N, (2013) "The feasibility of synthetic fuels in renewable energy systems" Energy. 57; 76-84

11. Robert P, Sandra V (2010) "Green jobs in Croatia", UNDP Croatia 2010.

12. Strategy of Croatian energy development (2009) Narodne novine number 130, October 2009

13. Strategy of education, science and technology Ministry of Science, Education and Sport (2014) http://www.vlada.hr/hr/preuzimanja/strategije/strategija_obrazovanja_znanosti_i_tehnologije_radni_materijal_rujan_2013

14. Vidakovi N, Zbašnik D (2014) "New CNB measures to stimulate credit growth: problems and solutions" Ban ni Vestnik March 2014, pages 13-17

15. Vitalji, N. (2006) "Potential of renewable energy sources in reduction of CO_2 emissions", MSc thesis, FSB, Zagreb, 132 pp. http://powerlab.fsb.hr/neven/pdf/supervision_of_msc_thesis/21_02_2007_Vitaljic_magistarski_rad.pdf

IV. POLICIES AND MEASURES FOR THE PROMOTION SUSTAINABLE DEVELOPMENT AND GREEN ECONOMY IN THE WESTERN BALKANS

EUROPEAN UNION PUBLIC SPHERE AND GREEN ECONOMY – MEDIA AS A COMMUNICATION LINK

Radoslav Baltezarevic[74]

Vesna Baltezarevic[75]

INTRODUCTION

> *"It is time for the world to wake up, and smell the post-growth coffee" (Rupert, 2014, p.23)*

People have secure rights to public land as well as environmental assets, services, information and participation in decision-making processes. A green economy requires different ways of thinking and operating. Building green societies and green economies require well-informed populations. But, "the EU has not come up with any new ideas about how to run itself, despite the crises of the economy, climate change and biodiversity loss; its recent strategies, such as Europe 2020, are just old wine in new bottles" (Warleigh-Lack, 2014, p.3).

---

[74] Assistant Professor, Faculty of Business Economics and Entrepreneurship, Belgrade, Serbi, trilliongarden@yahoo.com

[75] Assistant Professor, Graduate School of Culture and Media, Megatrend University, Belgrade, Serbi, vesnabal@gmail.com

EU can green its polities, economies and societies only with close communication with European citizens. EU environmental policies have often failed to make the necessary impact on the ground which resulted with poor implementation and with the gap in taking green principles across the board (Jordan & Schout, 2006).

Good communication and close relationship with public is necessary for forming democratic at all EU levels. Warleigh-Lack is convinced that EU does less well against the criterion of participatory democracy and including the interests of those who cannot deliberate as future humans, other animals, the planet (Warleigh-Lack, 2014, p.9). Working on a green economy is a common good that will not be achieved by the pursuit of individual self-interest alone. There is a constant need to find ways of communicating this to people and motivate them to change. "A basic idea in ecologies is that our politics must never lose sight of the fact that we are animals, with bodies, embedded in nature" (Pearmain & Heatley, 2013, p.16)

"Government can help by providing greater opportunities for citizens to participate in environmental policymaking, and for making clear the ethical and normative questions at stake. It can provide more support for grassroots initiatives and create more opportunities for civic engagement" (Andrew, 2011, p.13). The fact is that on the EU level a democratic deficit exists as the addressee of political decisions is not identical with the sovereign demos, and a public deficit exists as the public sphere is nationally structured (Gerhards, 2000). Quality of public sphere always has an impact on the democratic quality. Any kind of deficits can make barriers to European political and social integration.

Mass media have the function to intermediate between the European public authorities and the citizens, in order to insure legitimacy and effectiveness of governance (Wimmel 2004, p. 8) and to support the European public sphere to develop with functioning democracy. The role of media in the modern world is extremely important. People in EU trust to "their" media and expect from them to be not only informed, but included in the communication process. Media "by disseminating commentaries, editorials, news analyses, and other interpretations of the news, tell their audiences how to react to what is going on around them." (Lasorsa, 1997, p.162).

EU PUBLIC SPHERE

The theory about public sphere started by Habermas with his best-known ideas about communicative action, in which actors, in society, seek to reach common understanding and to coordinate actions by reasoned argument, consensus, and cooperation rather than strategic action strictly in pursuit of their own goals (Habermas, 1984, p. 86).

Social dialogue is a key factor in identifying ways to improve the connection between people and their authorities. The dialogue includes the implementation of knowledge about the green economy and recording of risks and issues in relation to its implementation. "Democratic legitimacy resides primarily in reasoned public dialog, in citizens being heard by government, and feeling inside themselves that they have been heard", (Habermas1990).

Nowadays the life of EU citizens is affected in many ways by regulations made in the EU's institutional labyrinth. People have been overdosed with information, do not know how making the right selection among them. European Commission has a right, when concludes that "Communication is more than information" (European Commission 2005, p. 2). It means that people, as communicators, cannot be only the recipients of news and information. They have right to be included and to have an active role in creating progress which depends to all human beans. Public sphere is a communicative space which exists in such circumstances, "constructed by this communicative space and developing it" (Trenz 2002, p. 20).

As we have already pointed out, communication involves the inclusion of people during the communication process. In these endeavors, best members of government bodies are individuals who are characterized by emotional intelligence. Emotional intelligence is the ability to convince or motivate others to do something, the ability to build a relationship of friendship, to subdue one's own emotions as well as that of the other's, to accept 'feedback' sincerely and openly, to build coalitions, to observe and analyze their own and others' behavior. Only politicians, who can provide two-way communication channel with people, can improve communication to effective levels in the area of proper exercise of human rights.

The existence of a public sphere and its functionality are usually judged by the relative density of communicative activity (Koopmans & Erbe 2003). Neidhardt is considered that a public sphere consists of speakers, media, and an audience (Neidhardt, 1994). The skill of communicator/ speaker to establish a good communication relationship with others determines his/her position within the social group. However, communication is never simple or easily achieved when taking place in the society still undergoing transitional changes and one crisis accompany another in succession.

Audience is consisting of simple people. Modern man is confronted with constant changes and sometimes one is not able to adapt. The accelerated pace of life and new technology still cannot affect the human need to interact with other people, because man possesses constant urge to communicate. "Democratic politics are based on the notion that democratic legitimacy is contingent less on the method of aggregating preferences, but much rather on the quality of preceding debate, which needs to be characterized by four ideal conditions: freedom, rationality, equality, and publicity" (Eriksen, 2001, p.4f).

If EU policies listening to the people they will interact with them in the sense of "two-way" of communication channel and responding to their concerns with more empathy. Why citizens need more empathy? Each individual has an awareness of the self and his/her belonging to the specific type of people, as well as ability to identify its personality traits, skills and knowledge, share convictions, values and attitudes that are different in relation to any other group. A person builds its identity through preserving of the individual, while adapting to the collective behavior patterns. If faced with barriers surpassing his/her defensive mechanisms, the individual falls into depression and alienation. Since isolation and loneliness are not experienced as a natural condition, alienation from the collective leads to the weakening of the adaptive capacity. "Social communication, over time, has formed functional communicative spaces along the lines of national borders that work towards social cohesion and strengthening of collective identities" (Slaatta 2006, p. 16).

The relationship between EU-governance and its societal environment is not possible without communication-which is identified as the glue that holds the complex and multi-level institutional setting of EU-governance together (Kohler-Koch, 2000). Communication is important for achieving the projected goals and adaptation to the changes, because good communicators encourage adequate participation of the public and the achievement of goals. Good communication stimulates ideas and creativity. However, this can be achieved only in that public sphere in which the politicians are educated and applies communication skills that are necessary for establishing a two-way communication.

Man is, in every life role, faced with a number of communications challenges. Achieving good communication is an increasingly difficult task. Communication methods, as well as the position of man in a social setting, have been simultaneously changing with the development of human society and its technological advancement. There are numerous elements that account for the difficulties that exist in making the communication of Europe truly successful. The deficit is reflected in the ideas that power holders are not sufficiently accountable, nor their decisions are responsive to public preferences as a subject to their scrutiny (De Vreese, 2003). The right to information, freedom of expression and communication among citizens and power holders are at the heart of democracy in Europe. European citizens have the right to fair and full information about the green economy, as well as for all other topics and the right "to express their views and to have an opportunity for a dialogue with the decision-makers. After all, EU decisions have impacts on various areas of public life and accordingly merit close public scrutiny and involvement" (Kurpas, Meyer and Gialoglou, 2004, p.2).

Research made by the European Commission, has shown that 66% of Europeans consider that their voice does not count in the EU. Only 29% Europeans believe that their voice counts in the EU (European Commission, 2013).

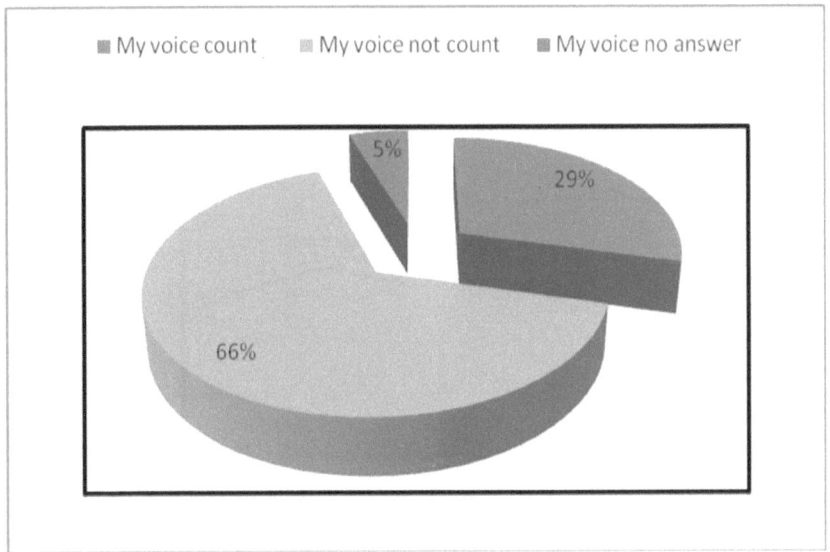

Figure 1. My voice counts in the European Union

Source: Authors

Alienation and increasing isolation is searching how to meet basic human needs in the time of transition. Accumulated effects of the global crisis resulting in restrictive human encounters and cause the communication deficit. Strong government performance makes people feel better about government–and ultimately more willing to cooperate with each other (Brehm & Rahn, 1997). People have confidence and trust when government is working well, but whatever government does. A trusting environment makes better possibility for government to act. It is a circle made up of government and citizens. No one can act independently. When the government cares about people and basically look after them people will increase trust in government.

Research made by the European Commission during 2013. has shown high percent of peoples' skepticism about government, more for the local than for EU.

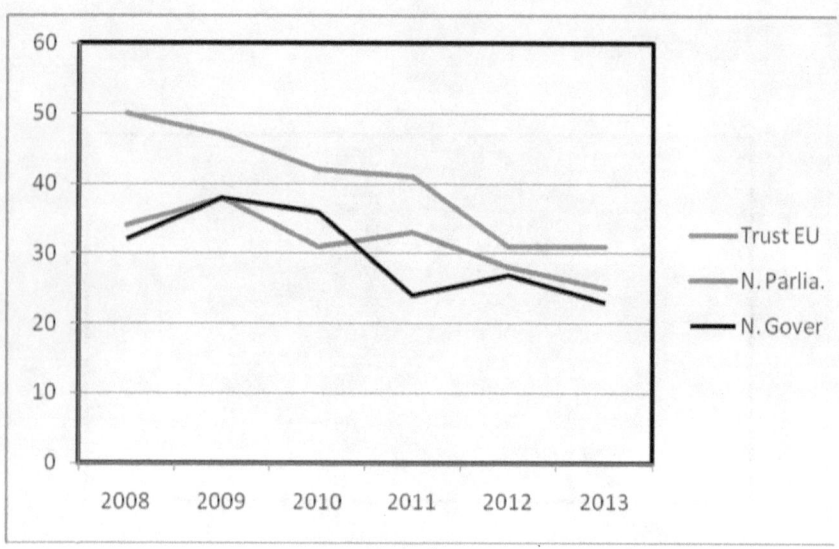

Figure 2. Trustin national governments and
parliaments, and in the European Union

Source: Authors

While trust in national political institutions (national governments
and national parliaments) continues to decrease trust in the European
Union is at a relatively higher level and remains unchanged (31%). The
proportions of Europeans who tend not to trust national governments
(72%) and national parliaments (69%) have increased, while the
number of respondents who do not trust the European Union has fallen
(58%, -2), (European Commission, 2013).

What can be done? People need more transparency, including in the
decision making process through open communication. What we have?
European public sphere as "a political public sphere which enables
citizens to take positions at the same time on the same topics of the
same relevance" (Habermas, 1995, p. 306).

There is a lack in the sense of belonging. How people can belong to the
European citizenship when European society is divided into spheres of
influence belonging to different interest groups (elites, experts, etc).
Power holders usually play their own game and forget that "public

debate is the single most important clue for the assessment of democratic quality" (Eriksen & Fossum 2000, p. 17).

Communication represents the process of creating and exchange of information within the network of people, with the purpose of finding the best communication modality within the single context. Governments can basically pose quality human resources in terms of their professional knowledge and expertise, while still experiencing the unsatisfactory levels of realization of strategic goals. Possible causes can include the insufficient communication potential of the power holders. This is a question about the links between elite and publics.

Good communication links can be established only if elite has a possibility to make adaptable communication, the ability to flexibly respond to the dynamics of changes in the environment and the ability to make a positive response to the requirements posed by the environment demands. This means that the most responsible for the promotion of European communication, European elite, should be able to provide fast and efficient use of all available data and information, as well as their distribution of the external and internal environment. Government must be able to manage all information, which is important for citizens, and achieve active participation in communication with all segments of the public sphere. Public opinion has become an important benchmark for political decisions and is often likely to be incorporated in policy making (De Vreese, 2004, p.3)

MEDIA AS A COMMUNICATION LINK

The media are one of the most important phenomena of mass society. The term "media" means all the ways and channels of information transfer (Wilkinson, 1997), or we can define media as "technical means that allows people to communicate and convey thoughts, regardless of their form and their ultimate goal" (Bal, 1997, p.1).

Man cannot live without interacting with other people. In the period of globalization, individuals and groups are becoming more focused on the 'contact' with the media that are transmitting information to them. But, media scene is increasingly serving the interests of the special interest groups that exert their influence on the media, and thereby elaborate methods for using media. Study of the Reuters Institute says that, if the trend continues, we will have media that no longer contain news (Reuters Institute, 2009).

Media has a significant impact on public opinion formation in cases where public knowledge is low, as it is about Green Economy. Over 90% of consumers receive information about food and biotechnology primarily through the popular press and television (Hoban & Kendall, 1993). Media scene worldwide, as well as in Europe shows an evident lack of quality. News often have the character of the tabloids, and the public is unable to find the necessary information in support of the democratic decision making process.

In Europe the Standard Eurobarometer 80 survey was conducted between 2 and 17 November 2013 in 34 countries or territories: the European Union's 28 Member States, the five candidate countries (the former Yugoslav Republic of Macedonia, Turkey, Iceland, Montenegro and Serbia), and in the Turkish Cypriot community in the part of the country that is not controlled by the government of the Republic of Cyprus. This report examines the media use by Europeans and their trust in the media.

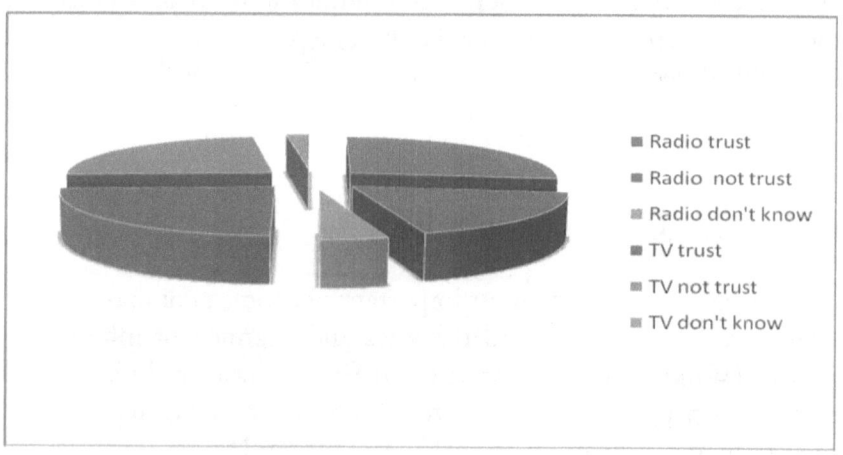

Figure 3. Europeans trust in mass media (Radio, & TV)

Source: Authors

Figure 3. shows that 54% Europeans trust the Radio, 37% don't trust and 9% don't have any opinion.

The regarding Television programs situation is: 48% trust, 48% don't trust and 4% don't have answers.

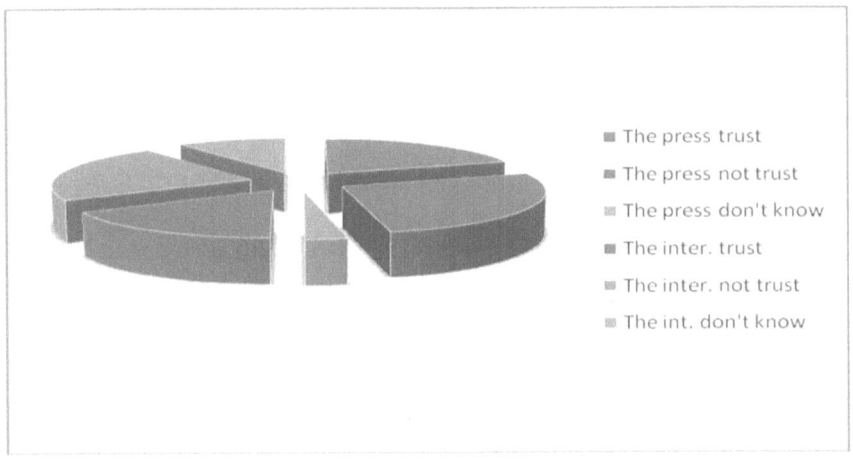

Figure 4. Europeans trust in mass media (The press & Internet)

Source: Authors

In the Figure 4 showns search results for public opinion concerning their trust in the press and Internet: 40% of Europeans trust the press, 54% don't trust and 6% do not know. The worst situation is with new mass media-Internet: 34% trust, 46% don't trust and 20% do not know.

The threat of withdrawal of advertising is generally sufficient to ensure that the media companies vigilantly filter the stories they present. In cases where a story manages to slip through, business organizations often combine forces to pressurize editors into reviewing the content in question. Investigative journalism is present in the negligible time slots on public and commercial channels. But, most people still form their opinions on the basis of mass media. As all media organizations are owned by companies with the same interests and have their content dictated by the advertisers and obtain their stories from the same sources, public is easily manipulated.

Modern man is accustomed to the fact of the media being an integral part of the daily life. The mass media have enabled information to become a global phenomenon and its distribution unconditioned by the local boundaries imposed by the geographical origin of the information. The term mass media indicate any means of communication, ie, the mass media are the extension of the human senses, namely: radio - an extension of the hearing, photography - an extension of the vision, and television as an extension of the sense of touch (Makluan, 1971, p. 386).

People have become a media addict and there is almost no one who, in some way, is not exposed to the influence of the media. It is believed that a modern individual receives the most of information through the media, which are the most powerful industry that produces and broadcasts information.

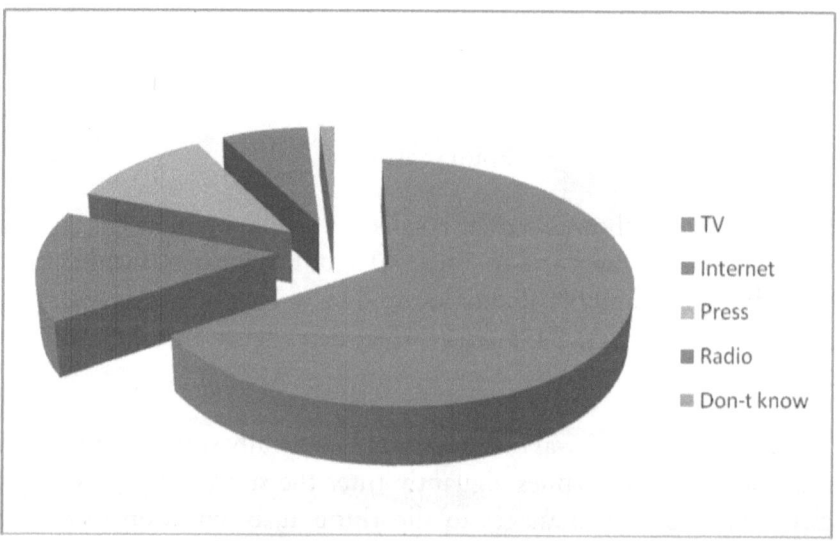

Figure 5. Europeans prefer television as a source of news

Source: Authors

Europeans are the most oriented to the television programs (62%), which represent a major source of information for them. The following on the list are: internet (14%), newspapers (11%) and radio (7%). (Europian Commission, 2013).

In the period of globalization, individuals and groups are becoming more focused on the 'contact' with the media that are transmitting information to them. The man, in the global space and time, is faced with a lack of time and opportunity to focus on personal pleasure and usually wait to take all the necessary information from the media.

If European governments want people to accept the economy changes, like green economy, it cannot be achieved if people are not involved in the dialogue, which should provide enough information for their decision. According the fact that European citizens viewed the media as the primary source of information, acceptance of green economy can be achieved only by the interaction of government, citizens and the media.

CONCLUSION

The information is distributed and exchanged through communication channels. Openness of the communicators in these activities enables the immediacy of the transmitting and receiving of messages. The ability of elite to listen to the public and to appropriately respond to their proposal communicating the message 'involve me in the process, because I have the best opinion about my life and my needs', demonstrates that the list of his/her competences includes the emotional intelligence.

The EU communication scene shows deep segmentation between elite and public. Most of people believe that the leadership of Europe is not paying much attention to what people think. The transition to a green economy will not be possible without well trained professionals able to tackle the challenges of globalization and to manage major socio-economic and environmental transformations. Nevertheless, it is important to determine the position of communication for application and improvement of the public scene. Therefore, we can freely say that the installation, maintenance and development of communication skills are the imperative of the modern relationship between European citizens and European authority.

Effective communication is a tool for coordination and control of individual socialization and group integration. The skill of communicator to establish a good communication relationship with others determines his/her position within the social group. The social interactions of millions of people around the Europe, along with the creation of their identities, social relationships and communities, can avoid alienation, increasing isolation and burden of searching for ways to meet basic human needs in times of transition. The global crisis accumulated effects in societies resulting in restrictive human encounters and the communication deficit.

The media's role is to support a new form of the global economic conquest of the world. The media is one of the most important phenomena of mass society. They are present in all areas of social life and are intertwined with politics, sports, education and entertainment, public and private life. In today's globalization, unfortunately, people are alienated from each other, overdosed with information, which they decreasingly share. Individuals and groups are becoming more focused on the 'contact' with the media that are transmitting information to them, while creating at the same time the attitudes of individuals and society. Increasing differentiation and segmentation of the media in communicating with 'its' audience has shaped new forms of mass communication, which is increasingly moving away from communication in the traditional sense.

How to guarantee the authenticity of data which transferred to EU citizens, if nobody has any reasonable arguments to refute the fact that the whole media system is orchestrated by a narrow world center, operated by the 'global company'.

European media scene shows an evident lack of quality. The media industry in Europe succumbed to the media conglomerate. The political pressure on regulators and public broadcasting is widespread. Media concentration is a common problem of modern EU media. As a result, viewers are unable to find the information they need for democratic decision making. Addressing the public through media, networks and any means of informal education are a fundamental aspect to develop public understanding and awareness in all the sectors of society, especially through multimedia communication strategies. Government has to encourage early dialogue on what a green economy would mean for the future of population.

REFERENCES

1. Bal F. (1997). Mo medija. (Media power) Beograd: Clio.

2. Brehm, J. & Wendy, R. (1997). "Individual Level Evidence for the Causes and Consequences of Social Capital", American Journal of Political Science, 41:888-1023.

3. de Vreese, C. H. (2003). Communicating Europe online. Available from: http://fpc.org.uk

4. Dobson, A. (2011) Sustainability Citizenship. Dorset, United Kingdom: Green House.

5. Eriksen, E. O. & Fossum, E. (2000): Post-national integration. In: Eriksen, Erik Oddvar /Fossum, Erik (eds.) (2000): Democracy in the European Union. Integration through deliberation? London/ New York: Routledge, 1-28.

6. Eriksen, E. O. (2001). 'Hvorfor deliberativt demokrati?' ARENA Working Paper 01/15. Oslo: ARENA.

7. European Commission (2005). 'Action Plan to Improve Communicating Europe by the Commission', SEC (2005) 985.

8. European Commission: Standard Eurobarometer 80/Autumn 2013 – TNS opinion & social PUBLIC OPINION IN THE EUROPEAN UNION, December 2013.

9. European Commission: Standard Eurobarometer 80 Autumn 2013. MEDIA USE IN THE EUROPEAN UNION REPORT, November 2013.

10. Gerhards, J. (2000). Europäisierung von Ökonomie und Politik und die Trägheit der Entstehung einer europäischen Öffentlichkeit. In: Bach, Maurizio (Hrsg.): Die Europäisierung nationaler Gesellschaften. Sonderheft 40 der Kölner Zeitschrift für Soziologie und Sozialpsychologie. Opladen, 277-305.

11. Habermas, J. (1984). Reason and the Rationalization of Society, Volume 1 of The Theory of Communicative Action, English translation by Thomas McCarthy. Boston: Beacon Press.

12. Habermas, J. (1990). Moral consciousness and communicative action. Cambridge, MA: The MIT Press.

13. Habermas, J. (1995). Comment on the paper by Dieter Grimm: ‚Does Europe need a constitution?', in: European Law Journal 1:3, 303-307.

14. Hoban, T.J., & Kendall, P.A. (1993). Consumer attitudes about food biotechnology. Raleigh, NC: North Carolina Cooperative Extension Service.

15. Jordan, A & Schout, A (2006). The Coordination of the European Union: Exploring the Capacities of Networked Governance Oxford: Oxford University Press.

16. Kohler-Koch, B. (2000). 'Framing: the Bottleneck of Constructing Legitimate Institutions', Journal of European Public Policy, 7(4): 513-31.

17. Koopmans, R. & Erbe, J. (2003). Towards a European Public Sphere? Vertical and Horizontal Dimensions of Europeanised Political Communication. Discussion Paper SP IV 2003-4003.

18. Kurpas, S., Meyer, Ch. & Gialoglou, K. (2004). "After the European Elections, Before the Constitution Referenda - Can the EU Communicate Better?" Centre for European Policy Studies, CEPS Policy Brief, No. 55. Available from: http://www.ceps.be.

19. Lasorsa, D. L. (1997). Media Agenda Setting and Press Performance: A Social System Approach for Building Theory. M. McCombs, D. L. Shaw and D. Weaver Eds. Communication and Democracy. Exploring the Intellectual Frontiers in Agenda-Setting Theory. Mahwah/London, Lawrence Erlbaum Associates: 155-167.

20. Lodge, J. (2005). 'Communicating Europe: from procedural transparency to grand forum', in her The 2004 Elections to the European Parliament. Macmillan, London.

21. Makluan, M. (1971). Poznavanje opštila – ovekovih produžetaka, Beograd: Prosveta.

22. Neidhardt, F. (1994), Die Rolle des Publikums. Anmerkungen zur Soziologie politischer Öffentlichkeit, in: Derlien, H.-U./ Gerhard, U./ Scharpf, F. W. (Eds.), Systemrationalität und Partialinteresse. Festschrift für Renate Mayntz. Baden-Baden, 315-328.

23. Pearmain A. & Heatley B. (2013). Smaller but Better? Post-growth Public Services, Dorset, United Kingdom: Green House.

24. Reuters Institute for the Study of Journalism (2009). 'What's Happening to Our News', Oxford Media Convention.

25. Rupert, (2014). Post-growth Common Sense: Political Communications For the Future. Dorset, United Kingdom: Green House.

26. Slaatta, T. (2006). 'Europeanisation and the News Media: Issues and Research Imperatives', Javnost 13(1): 5-24.

27. Trenz, H.-J. (2002), Zur Konstitution politischer Öffentlichkeit in der Europäischen Union. Zivilgesellschaftliche Subpolitik oder schaupolitische Inszenierung. Baden-Baden.

28. Warleigh A. L. (2014). Greening the European Union. Dorset, United Kingdom: Green House.

29. Wilkinson, P., (1997). The Media and Terrorism: A Reassessment, London: Frank Cass.

30. Wimmel, Andreas (2004) 'Transnationale Diskurse. Zur Analyse politischer Kommunikation in der europäischen Medienöffentlichkeit', Zeitschrift für Internationale Beziehungen 11(1), 7-25.

COMPLIANCE OF SERBIA WITH THE EU ENVIRONMENTAL STANDARDS WITH PARTICULAR FOCUS ON THE PROTECTION OF THE ENVIRONMENT THROUGH CRIMINAL LAW

Natasa Tanjevic[76]

Ana Opacic[77]

INTRODUCTION

Having in mind tremendous importance of regulating, improving and protecting the environment, international community has set respective legal standards that countries are obliged to implement into their national legislation. To this end, the European Union has made significant efforts to establish system of environmental preservation, development, improvement and protection. This refers particularly to establishment of the criminal justice system, taking into consideration that environmental crimes have become serious and growing problem in Europe and the entire world, which causes great harm to the environment and, consequently, endangers life and health of human beings.

The goal of the EU environmental policy is to promote sustainable development and preserve the environment for both present-day and future generations. In that respect, direct benefits of this policy are universal: better public health, preservation of natural resources,

---

[76] National Bank of Serbia; School of Business Economics and Entrepreneurship, Belgrade, Serbia, tanjevicn@gmail.com

[77] Assistant Professor, Faculty of Business Economics and Entrepreneurship, Belgrade, Serbia, ana.galjak@gmail.com

increase of economic competitiveness, higher level of employment and better quality of life.

On the other hand, the environment will definitely be one of the most important and, at the same time, one of the most challenging chapters in negotiations between our country and the European Union. This is due to a simple reason that one third of all EU laws regulates the environment.

The purpose of harmonizing the Serbian environmental regulations with the EU regulations is adjusting the national environmental laws in order to achieve complete compliance with the EU legislation. However, transfer of the EU regulations into the national legal system is only the first step in the process of harmonization with the EU standards. The most important is to ensure adequate implementation and enforcement of the adopted regulations, both at national and local level.

DEVELOPMENT OF THE EU ENVIRONMENTAL LAW

The European Union seeks to harmonize its environmental preservation and quality improvement requirements while integrating economic and environmental goals and promoting preventive measures (Jovasevic, 2009:4). Ever since 1967, regulations governing classification of packaging waste, hazardous substances marking and permitted noise levels start to emerge. However, even though foundations of the environmental protection were set in 1972 in the EU member states by the Environment Action Program, the environmental policy was built into the institutional structure of the Community by the 1987 Single European Act. The latter document introduces chapter titled "environment" (Articles 130s-t) thus ensuring explicit legal grounds for the Community's environmental policy. The document determines that environmental activities have to be based on the following principles: preventive action, environmental damage to be rectified at source and polluter pays principle (Cavoski, 2007:23).

Particularly important is the introduction of the integration principle, i.e. that the environmental requirements have to be integrated into other

Community polices. In that respect, Article 147 UEZ determines that the Community's environmental policy contributes to the following goals: preserving, protecting and improving the quality of the environment; protecting human health; prudent and rational utilization of natural resources and promoting measures at international level to deal with regional or worldwide environmental problems.

The role of this policy was further strengthened by the 1992 Maastricht Treaty that included in its main goals promotion of sustainable and non-inflationary growth respecting the environment (article 2). Thus, the precautionary principle was introduced in order to ensure high levels of environmental protection.

Provisions of the 1997 Treaty of Amsterdam explicitly define sustainable development as one of the Community's main goals. Article 2 defines that the Community's goal is to promote "balanced, harmonized and sustainable economic development "and "sustainable and non-inflationary growth", as well as "high level of employment and social protection, equality between women and men, high level of economic competitiveness and aligning economic impact, etc. In that respect, taking the environment into account in all policies is defined by Article 6 of the Treaty as "environmental protection requirements must be integrated into the definition and implementation of other Community policies" (Cavoski, 2007:24).

Unlike the previous treaties, which established only "preserving" the environment as the requirement, the Treaty of Lisbon defines, for the first time, not only protection but also "improvement of the quality of the environment" as the main environmental goal. According to the provisions of this Treaty, protection and improvement of the quality of the environment and sustainable development have to become main values not only within the EU but also in relations between the EU and the rest of the world (Article 3 of the Treaty). This is caused by understanding of the EU countries that certain matters, such as climate change and water pollution, affect everyone, without exceptions, and that it is necessary to strengthen both international cooperation and efficient measures at the national level in order to ensure efficient protection. The Treaty of Lisbon introduces as a novelty division of energy liability between the member states and the EU and emphasizes the need to decrease damage caused to the environment by inadequate use of energy sources (Article 194 of the Treaty).

Considered as a whole, a broad spectrum of the EU environmental directives and regulations is based on several main principles, traditionally divided into the principles of the environmental protection policy and the principles of the environmental protection enforcement. The previous group includes the principle of sustainable development and the principle of high level of protection and the latter includes the principle of subsidiarity, the principle of proportionality, the principle of integration, the precautionary principle, the principle of preventive action, the principle of environmental damage to be rectified at source and the polluter pays principle (Dudas, 2013).

ENVIRONMENTAL PROTECTION CHALLENGES OF THE EU ACCESSION PROCESS

Complete implementation of one of the most complex EU legislative fields implies significant number of challenges for countries in the European integration process (Damjanovic, 2011:21). Some of the most important are:

1. Financial;
2. Administrative;
3. Energy;
4. Political.

The financial challenge encompasses total costs of harmonization with demanding standards of the EU environmental protection laws. According to the 1997 estimates of the European Commission, the total costs for the then eight candidate countries from Central and Eastern Europe amounted from 80 to 110 billion Euros. Countries that became members of the EU in 2004 faced great difficulties in attracting structural and cohesion funds in majority of cases, while flaws in preparation, application submission and implementation, in some cases, called for Commission to request financial corrections. After joining the EU in 2007, Romania and Bulgaria started allocating net contributions to the EU budget on the basis of slow mobilization of the EU non-refundable funds (grants). This was caused by inadequate financial planning and poor non-refundable funding program which consequently led to less than 10 % of the available funds being withdrawn during the first three years of the EU membership (National Environmental Approximation Strategy, 2011:23).

According to the National Environmental Approximation Strategy (Official Gazette of the Republic of Serbia, no. 80/11), it is estimated that total costs of fulfilling all EU environmental requirements will amount for the Republic of Serbia to approximately 10.6 billion Euros (until 2030), majority of which will be allocated to the following sectors: water (5.6 billion Euros), waste (2.8 billion Euros) and industrial pollution (1.3 billion Euros). Operational costs which cannot be financed from international sources of finance, but from the national budget, private sector or compensations are significant part of the total costs. It is estimated that additional budget funding will reach its peak of approximately 360 million Euros during 2018, and then it should steadily decrease by 2025, when the reimbursement of total costs might be achieved.

However, direct economic benefits of environmental harmonization should surpass the costs by nearly 2.4 times by 2030. This is exactly why we need sustainable and long-lasting environmental finance system, which will be enforced by strong administration at all levels (Mestrovic, 2013).

Administrative challenge refers to capability of administration to harmonize and enforce environmental laws. In the previous years, this has been one of the most important challenges faced by countries seeking EU membership. Insufficient number of qualified civil servants, vague institutional division of jurisdiction for particularly complex tasks, etc. are the most common issues noted by the European Commission as well. It especially has to be taken into account that, in our case, this challenge might be faced by local and provincial administration, which will be in charge of a large number of tasks related to enforcement of environmental laws (Damjanovic, 2011:22). Insufficient capacity of state bodies, i.e. insufficient number of civil servants included in this process, are at the same time consequence of the fact that current educational institutions are not prepared to a sufficient extent to train adequate number of environmental experts. The aforementioned facts emphasize the need that environmental education and sustainable development should be ensured at all educational levels (Open Society Foundation, Centre for Applied European Studies, 2009:32).

This challenge was faced by almost all countries that joined the EU in the previous years. Examples are Slovakia, Slovenia, Hungary, etc. In fact, insufficiently developed administrative structure has surfaced as one of the main problems in the pre-accession process. For example, departments for "legislative harmonization" existed in all relevant sectors in Slovakia, from the very beginning of the process, as well as constant lack of capacity to prepare harmonization process impact and costs analysis (Todic, 2011:312).

Apart from the aforementioned, one of the most serious challenges faced by the countries is gradual transformation and harmonization of energy sector with the environmental protection requirements. The situation is particularly difficult in such countries as ours which based their development in the twentieth century on the energy-intensive industries, such as chemical industry, steel industry, mining, etc. Furthermore, lignite is considered as the biggest source of electricity generation in Serbia with about two thirds of electricity produced by its burning, and this source of energy is known to be especially unfavorable in terms of environmental protection (Trbovic, Crnobrnja, 2009).

The political challenge refers primarily to political will to overcome all the aforementioned challenges in the best possible way. This is possible only if protecting and improving the environment are one of the main priorities of the government and if all capacities are engaged: institutional, administrative, financial, etc. Finally, political will is essential since the process of europeisation of Serbia implies not only adoption of the EU standards, but also adoption and consistent enforcement of the European development principles, where political will plays major role in terms of ensuring that all adopted laws, principles and standards are continuously enforced in practice.

In relation to all the aforementioned, it is obvious that negotiations with regard to the Chapter 27, the one encompassing the environmental protection, will not be simple at all. On the contrary, experiences of the countries after the last enlargement of the EU show that negotiations involving this chapter were the most difficult ones because of the volume of regulations, financial resources, lack of administrative capacities, number of environmental protection issues, infrastructure, etc.

Finally, it has to be taken into account that this chapter also includes some of politically sensitive aspects (such as, cross-border pollution, foreign trade, etc.).

HARMONIZATION WITH THE EU ENVIRONMENTAL REGULATIONS – MEASURES UNDERTAKEN AT THE NATIONAL LEVEL

Countries seeking EU membership, including the Republic of Serbia, must harmonize their laws and regulations on protecting and improving the environment with the existing legislation of the member states. The goal of this harmonization process is to achieve "complete harmonization of the national environmental legislation (and corresponding administrative system) in order to reach complete (one hundred percent) compliance with the EU legislation. And not just formally, but in reality as well." (Guide to the Approximation of the European Union Environmental Legislation, 1997). At the same time, one of the most demanding chapters in the negotiations with the EU is precisely the one referring to the environmental protection, simply because one third of the entire EU legislation refers to the environment.

Harmonization of national regulations with *acquis communautaire* is performed based on the Article 107 of the 2006 Constitution of the Republic of Serbia, Article 72 of the Stabilization and Association Agreement and Chapter III of the Transient Agreement. Accordingly, Serbia has undertaken the commitment to gradually, in the period of six years, harmonize both its current and future laws and regulations with the EU regulations, and to ensure adequate enforcement of both present and future laws.

Right to a healthy environment, as one of the fundamental human rights and liberties, is defined by the Constitution of the Republic of Serbia. Article 97 of the Constitution determines that the Republic of Serbia regulates and ensures sustainable development, system of protection and improvement of the environment, protection and enhancement of plants and animals, etc. These provisions are further elaborated in over 30 environmental protection laws and over one hundred corresponding subordinate regulations in force in our country. Reform of the environmental laws and regulations started with adoption of the Law on Environmental Protection in 2004 (Official Gazette of the Republic of Serbia no.135/04), and the Law on Environmental Impact Assessment (Official Gazette of the Republic of Serbia no.135/04), Law on Strategic Environmental Impact Assessment (Official Gazette of the Republic of Serbia no.135/04) and the Law on Integrated Pollution Prevention and Control (Official Gazette of the Republic of Serbia no.135/04).

The Serbian government has so far adopted several strategic documents referring to different matters with environmental impact – Sustainable Development Strategy with Action Plan, National Economic Development Strategy of the Republic of Serbia 2006 - 2012, Energy Sector Development Strategy until 2015, Cleaner Production Strategy, and others.[78]

Additionally, the Serbian government adopted on 23rd of March 2010 the National Environmental Protection Program. This Program is based on the previously adopted Law on Environmental Protection and represents the most important strategic document in this field. Planning and management of the environmental protection over a ten-year period is based on that document.

---

[78]   The government strategic documents available at http://www.srbija.gov.rs/vesti/ dokumenti_sekcija.php?id=45678;

Lastly, on 20th December 2011, the already mentioned National Environmental Approximation Strategy was adopted. Its goals are dual: dealing with complexity of all challenges referring to implementation of the EU environmental regulations in the Republic of Serbia and ensuring solid grounds for accession negotiations in terms of Article 27. As it is stated in the Strategy itself, its goal is to encompass "all challenges that the approximation process will place before the national legislation (including dealing with the flaws of the current legal procedures in the Republic of Serbia), volume of changes to organization and activities of the environmental institutions, as well as the approach for overcoming financial difficulties which occur as a consequence of "common procedures or common practices" until complete harmonization with the EU legislation".

The European Council decided to begin accession negotiations with Serbia on 28th of June 2013. The European Commission has begun, based on these decisions, to draft the negotiation framework and in parallel the screening process.

In terms of environmental protection, the main priorities of the environmental policy include:

1. Development and strengthening of strategic, regulatory and financial monitoring mechanisms in order to ensure sustainable development including raising environmental awareness.
2. Support for climate change adjustment, mitigation of consequences and risk prevention.
3. Ensuring sustainable environment through efficient management of natural resources and reducing pollution.[79]

REGIONAL ENVIRONMENTAL COOPERATION

Regional environmental cooperation is condition for success/failure of development of environmental protection system in each country (Mihajlov, 2009:59). At the same time, a treaty regulating regional

---

[79]   http://euintegracije.skgo.org/sr/news/details/37

environmental cooperation would also be beneficial for integration of the Western Balkan in the EU.

However, as enforcement of ratified international environmental treaties in the countries of the region is very poor and as some of important international treaties have not yet been ratified by all countries in the region, potential for this cooperation is insufficiently utilized. Additionally, there are lot of challenges, including relations and interests in the region. Unfortunately, poor flow of information in the region is also one of the issues. Due to all the above mentioned, environment is still not a priority in the region even though Stabilization and Association Agreement foresees regional environmental cooperation.

Notwithstanding, there is room for improvement in terms of sharing information, experiences and good practices, cross-border cooperation, education, etc. Therefore, environmental protection should be recognized as an important topic for the decision-makers at the highest level, as green economy, spatial planning and climate change are some of the sectors requiring regional cooperation.

EUROPEAN ENVIRONMENTAL CRIMINAL LAW

Environmental crimes are serious and increasing problem in Europe and in the world, which cause great harm to the environment and, at the same time, endanger life and health of human beings.

Protection of the environment through criminal sanctions commenced in 1998 when the Council of Europe adopted the Convention on the Protection of the Environment through Criminal Law (CETS No:172). The main goals of the Convention are: enforcing common penalty policy for environmental crimes, protecting life and health of human beings, fauna and flora and other natural resources by all possible means, including criminal law measures, defining violation of environmental protection principles as criminal offences punishable by criminal sanctions, strengthening international cooperation in order to more efficiently prosecute and penalize perpetrators of environmental crimes, etc.

Majority of the EU environmental regulations is laid down in form of directives and the main related issue is introduction of directives into national laws and their subsequent implementation (Cavoski, 2007:26). Even though environmental directives are numerous, the concept of the European environmental criminal law is firmly established by adoption of the Directive 2008/99/EC on the Protection of the Environment through Criminal Law. The Directive obliges member states to develop a system of criminal sanctions in their respective national legislation addressing serious violation of provisions of the Community environmental regulations. Its provisions should ensure that common regulations addressing criminal offences, criminal responsibility and criminal sanctions create conditions for utilization of effective research methods and assistance within and between member states in order to achieve more efficient environmental protection (Astakolska, Srbinoska-Doncevski, 2009:281).

Based on the provisions of the Article 3 of the Directive, member states shall ensure that certain conduct constitutes a criminal offence, when unlawful and committed intentionally or with at least serious negligence. To that end, the Directive contains list of environmental crimes that, if perpetrated or if their perpetration was assisted or encouraged intentionally or out of gross negligence, as such have to be defined by national laws of the member states (Article 3 of the Directive).

These are, among others, the following illegal acts: the discharge, emission or introduction of a quantity of materials or ionizing radiation into air, soil or water, which causes or is likely to cause death or serious injury to any person or substantial damage to the quality of air, the quality of soil or the quality of water, or to animals or plants; trading in specimens of protected wild fauna or flora species or parts or derivatives thereof, except for cases where the conduct concerns a negligible quantity of such specimens and has a negligible impact on the conservation status of the species; the production, importation, exportation, placing on the market or use of ozone-depleting substances; any conduct which causes the significant deterioration of a habitat within a protected site; the killing, destruction, possession or taking of specimens of protected wild fauna or flora species, except for cases where the conduct concerns a negligible quantity of such specimens and has a negligible impact on the conservation status of the species; the operation of a plant in which a dangerous activity is carried out or in which dangerous substances or preparations are stored or used and which, outside the plant, causes or is likely to cause death or serious injury to any person or substantial damage to the quality of air, the quality of soil or the quality of water, or to animals or plants, etc.

Lastly, the Directive particularly highlights the need for introduction and implementation of the efficient criminal justice system in order to discourage legal entities to act in a way that causes harm to the environment, air, including stratosphere, soil, water, fauna and flora and preservation of species.

APPLICATION OF THE EUROPEAN STANDARDS IN THE FIGHT AGAINST ENVIRONMENTAL CRIMES IN THE REPUBLIC OF SERBIA

In our country, protection of the environment through criminal law is primarily achieved through provisions of the Criminal Code. The 2005 Criminal Code (Official Gazette of the Republic of Serbia no. 85/05) systemizes, for the first time, environmental crimes in the separate chapter, which justifiably sets the environmental protection as primary and independent type of group object protected under it. Additionally, the Law on the Liability of Legal Entities for Criminal Offences was adopted in 2008 (Official Gazette of the Republic of Serbia no. 97/08), which lays down criminal liability of legal entities and whose adoption is highly important for combating environmental crimes, due to the fact that the largest polluters of the environment are precisely legal entities (Tanjevic, 2013). Completing the criminal justice framework continued in 2009 and 2010 by adoption of numerous so called sectoral laws which additionally regulate economic offences and misdemeanors and address different aspects of environmental regulation, improvement and protection. [80]

---

[80]   E.g., Law on Non-Ionizing Radiation Protection, Law on Ionizing Radiation Protection and Nuclear Safety, Law on Packaging and Packaging Waste, Law

However, even though significant progress in harmonization with standards and requirements of the EU has been achieved, the European trends in this field are still not being promoted and represented to the sufficient extent in the national legislation nor applied in case law.

This is confirmed by the fact that participation of the environmental crimes in total crimes is quite low. In fact, according to the data of the Statistical Office of the Republic of Serbia, in 2012 (the last available data) the total number of filed charges was 92879 out of which only 1841 for environmental crimes.[81] Additionally, and in other observed years, participation of the charges filed for environmental crimes in the total number of filed charges is negligible.

Table 1. Adult offenders, 2006-2012[82]

Filed charges	2006	2007	2008	2009	2010	2011	2012
Total	105701	98702	101723	100026	74279	88207	92879
Environmental crimes	2009	1831	1895	2081	1568	1789	1841

Compared to the number of filed charges, the number of convictions is even smaller and in some cases negligible. In the last observed year, out of total number of filed charges, 430 persons were convicted.

---

on Waste Management, Law on Air Protection, Law on Environmental Noise Protection.

[81]   See Eco-Bulletin of the Statistical Office, no. 571, available at http://webrzs.stat. gov.rs/WebSite/repository/documents/00/01/23/65/SB_571_EKOBILTEN. pdf, accessed on 3rd of April 2014.

[82]   See report of the Statistical Office no. 203 from 19th of July 2012, available at   http://webrzs.stat.gov.rs/WebSite/repository/documents/00/00/73/95/ sk12122011.pdf

Table 2. Convicted legal adults for environmental crimes
as per type of crime and criminal sanctions, 2012[83]

Criminal offence	Total	Imprisonment	Pecuniary sanctions	Probation	Community service	Judicial warning
	430	52	99	257	15	6
Killing and cruelty to animals	23	1	10	11		1
Forest deterioration	36	2	10	24	-	-
Forest products theft	297	41	65	175	11	4
Illegal hunting	27	3	6	17	1	-
Illegal fishing	33	2	5	22	3	1
Environmental degradation	6	1	1	4		
Other	8	2	2	4	-	-

In terms of structure of the environmental crimes, the data show that public prosecutors in practice prosecute crimes that were previously considered economic crimes (forest products theft, illegal hunting and fishing), while prosecuting "real" environmental crimes, such as primarily environmental pollution, is mostly nonexistent (Tanjevic, Opacic, 2012). Big issue is court expertise, being on one side very expensive and complex and on the other requiring adequate expert knowledge.

On the other hand, even though very strict penalties, both of imprisonment and pecuniary, are prescribed and enforced for environmental crimes in comparative legislation, judiciary penalty policy in our country is very mild, as probation prevails in the structure of penalties. That is confirmed by the fact that out of total number of persons convicted for environmental crimes in 2012 (430), as high as

---

[83]   http://webrzs.stat.gov.rs/WebSite/repository/documents/00/01/23/65/ SB_571_EKOBILTEN.pdf, accessed on 3rd of April 2014.

257 were sentenced to probation. This is, at the same time, consequence of the fact that petty crimes come before courts, as the most serious environmental crimes are difficult to detect and prove.

CONCLUSION

The high level of environmental protection is one of the main goals defined by the Treaty on European Union, together with the principles of sustainable development and integration of environmental protection into all EU policies. Even though the European Commission has estimated that the Republic of Serbia made significant progress in terms of harmonizing its environmental protection laws, horizontal legislation, waste management, protection of nature, chemicals management with the EU *acquis communautaire,* the European trends have not yet been promoted and represented to the sufficient extent in the national laws nor applied in case law. This especially refers to the criminal justice system. Participation of the environmental crimes in total crimes is negligible, forest products thefts, illegal hunting and forest deterioration prevail in the structure of reported crimes, while general environmental crime, environmental pollution, is practically not applied in practice at all. Furthermore, in terms of penalty structure in the previous years, a general trend of mild judiciary penalty policy is noticed. This is why further efforts should be focused on higher level of implementation of laws, as well as professional training of judges, prosecutors, court experts and generally all parties involved in the fight against this type of crime. Special attention should be paid to preventive measures which include, among others, raising environmental awareness.

On the other hand, this is one of the most important fields and, at the same time, one of the most demanding chapters in negotiations between our country and the European Union. This is caused by a simple reason that one third of all EU laws refers to the environment. Consequently, the Serbian government should set as one of its main priorities allocation of its budgetary resources to environment as it faces lack of human resources and financial support while accelerating law adoption process and making higher investments in environmental protection. Significant challenge will represent ensuring capacities for introduction of integrated monitoring/tracking of *de facto* situation in the field of environment and methodology for acquiring comparable data on pollution factors and impact on all areas.

Therefore, harmonization with the EU legislation encompassed by this Chapter requires significant investments, as well as strong and well equipped administration at both state and local levels, which is essential for its enforcement and execution.

In further EU accession process and harmonization of environmental regulations, it is certain that Serbia will face numerous challenges and therefore experiences from the previous EU enlargement process will be useful. However, the most important factor on that journey is political will, i.e. ensuring consistent enforcement of all regulations that will be harmonized with the EU legislation. This will contribute to efforts to improve environment in Serbia and consequently achieve better quality of life for all citizens of our country.

REFERENCES

1. Aštakolska, T., Srbinovska-Don evski, A. (2009) Protection of the Environment through Criminal Law with Particluar Emphasis on the Crimes Committed by Legal Entities, Collection of papers: Ecology and Law, Faculty of Law, University of Nis, Nis.

2. Convention on the Protection of the Environment through Criminal Law CETS No:172.

3. avoški, A. (2007) Bases of the EU Environmental Law, Faculty of Law, Union University, Official Gazette, Belgrade.

4. Damjanovi , D. (2011) Challenges of the European Integration Process in terms of Environmental Protection and Sustainable Development of Local Communities, Paglo Centre, Belgrade.

5. Dudaš, A. (2013) Principles of the Environmental Protection Policy in the EU Law, Collection of papers of the Faculty of Law, Novi Sad, vol. 47, no. 3.

6. Jovaševi , D. (2009) System of Environmental Crimes in Serbia, Case Law, no.4

7. Open Society Foundation, Centre for Applied European Studies, (2009) Protection of the Environment: Condition for Sustainable Development: Belgrade.

8. Mihajlov, A. (2009) Municipalities and Cities in Serbia in Environmental Integration Process on their Journey to the EU, European Standards in Serbia, Centre for Democracy, Belgrade.

9. Mitrovi , S. (2013) Challenges of the EU Accession Process in terms of Environmental Protection at Local Level in Serbia, SEIO

10. Tanjevi , N. (2013) Protection of the Environment trough Criminal Law and Fight against Environmental Crimes in Serbia, Almanac, Academy of Criminalistic and Police Studies, Belgrade.

11. Tanjevi , N., Opa i , A. (2012) Protection of the Environment through Criminal law of the Republic of Serbia and Incentives for the European Integration Process, Ecology and Law, Faculty of Law, Union University, Institute of Comparative Law, Belgrade.

12. Todi , D. (2011) Guide to the EU policies – Environment, European Movement in Serbia, Loznica.

13. Trbovi , A., Crnobrnja (2009) Effects of the EU Integration Process of Serbia, Faculty of Economy, Finances and Administration, Singidunum University, Belgrade.

ENVIRONMENTAL REGULATIONS AND ECONOMIC GROWTH[84]

Djuro Djuric[85]

Bozo Draskovic[86]

INTRODUCTION

Since the beginning of the process of harmonization of national legislation with the EU law, Republic of Serbia has made a significant progress. According to the Report on the implementation of the National Programme for Integration of Serbia in the European Union (NPI)[87], Serbian Government adopted more than 200 draft laws since July 2008, whereby the National Assemblyadopted about 200 laws, which makes more than 90% of regulations prescribed in the NPI or adopted more than 800 regulations of total 1017.

Until 1st March 2012 the harmonization of national legislation with the European Union was not a formal obligation for the Republic of Serbia.

---

[84] Thispaper is partof research projectsunder codes47009(European integrationandsocio-economic changes inthe economyof Serbia towardsEU) and179015(Challenges and prospects of structuralchanges in Serbia: Strategic Directions forEconomic Developmentandharmonizationwith EU requirements), fundedby the Ministry ofEducationand Scienceof the Republic ofSerbia.

[85] Research Associate, Institute of Economic Sciences, Belgrade, Serbia, djuro. djuric@ien.bg.ac.rs.

[86] PhD, Full Professor, Institute of Economic Sciences, Belgrade, Serbia, bozo. draskovic@ien.bg.ac.rs.

[87] Izveštaj o sprovo enju tre eg i izmenjenog i dopunjenog Nacionalnog programa za integraciju Republike Srbije u Evropsku unije, za prvo tromese je 2012.godine, Kancelarija za evropske integracije, www.seio.gov.rs, 10.04.2014.

On that date, the European Council endorsed the recommendation of the Council of Ministers and the opinion of the European Commission, and granted Serbia candidate status for EU membership. However, Serbia already began to unilaterally implement key documents for EU for the accession in 2008. Thus, on 10th September 2008, the National Assembly of the Republic of Serbia ratified the Stabilization and Association Agreement between the European Communities and their Member States and the Republic of Serbia[88] and the Interim Agreementon Trade and trade-related matters[89]. Both documents are applicable in Serbia as of 30thJanuary 2009. The EU, in turn, delayed the implementation of the Interim Agreement till the adoption of a positive conclusion of the Council of Ministerson Serbia's cooperation with the ICTYin The Hague. Therefore, the EUapplies this Agreementas of 7thDecember 2009.

Harmonization of national legislation with the *acquis communautaire* is conducted on the basis of Art. 107 of the Constitution of the Republic of Serbia from 2006 and the Art.72 of the Stabilization and Association Agreement and Chapter III of the Interim Agreement. Thus, Serbia has undertaken to gradually, over a period of six years, align current and future laws and regulations with the EU regulations, and to ensure the proper application of both the current and future legislation[90]. A successful process of harmonization of regulations depends on many factors, but primarily on the political will, legal proceedings, administrative capacity, and finally, on funds.

---

[88] Law on ratification of teh Stabilization and Association Agreement between European Communities and their member states and Republic of Serbia, "Official GazetteRS" N°83/2008.

[89] Law on ratification of the InterimAgreementon Trade andtrade-related matters between European Communities and Republic of Serbia, "Official GazetteRS" N°83/2008.

[90] Todori , V., Jovanovi , N.(2011), Mind the gap: *Studija o implementaciji evropskog zakonodavstva u Srbiji*, Centar za novu politiku, p.15.

THE LEGALFRAMEWORK FOR ENVIRONMENTAL PROTECTIONIN THE REPUBLIC OFSERBIA

EU policy in the field of environmental protection aims to promote sustainable development and protect the environment for present and future generations. It is based on the integration of environmental policy with other EU policies, preventive action, the "polluter pays" and "consumer pay" principles, the elimination of environmental damage at source and shared responsibility. *Acquis communautaire* in the field of environmental protection includes over 200 major legal acts covering horizontal issues, water and air quality, waste management, nature protection, industrial pollution and risk management, chemical substances and noise. Ensuring compliance with the EU *acquis* requires significant investment, but also brings significant benefits. A strong and well-equipped administration at national and local level is essential for the implementation and enforcement of the EU *acquis* in the field of environmental protection.

Stabilization and Association Agreement establishes cooperation aimed to strengthen administrative structures and procedures in order to ensure strategic planning of environmental issues and coordination between the relevant decision makers and focuses on the harmonization of Serbian legislation with the EU *acquis*. The Serbian Constitution provides for every citizen the right to a healthy environment and timely and full information about its condition[91]. Republic and autonomousprovinces are responsible for environmental protection and the Serbian constitution defines the power sofmanagement on protection of the environment at the national, provincialand local government level. The legal framework for the protection of the environmentis the Law on Environmental Protection adopted in 2004, amended in 2009[92].

On 23rd March 2010 the Government of the Republic of Serbia adopted the National Environmental Strategy[93]. This document is based on the

---

[91]   Constitution of the Republicof Serbia, Art. 74. "Official GazetteRS" N°98/2006.

[92]   Law on environmental protection, "Official GazetteRS" N°135/2004, 36/2009 (36/2009 - dr. zakon, 72/2009 - dr. zakon, 43/2011 - odluka US.

[93]   Ministry of natural resources, mining and space planning of the Republic of

previously adopted Law on Environmental Protection and it is the most important policy document in this area. Planning and management of environmental protection over a period of ten years is based on this document. The goal of the national program is the development of modern environmental policy in the Republic of Serbia. Achieving this objective is provided through the Action Plan, which is a legal and institutional framework for the withdrawal of funds from the EU-funded projects, as well as from funds intended for the candidate countries [8]. National Program defines priorities in improving environmental quality and in general the quality of life of the population in Serbia. Also on 20th December 2011 the National Strategy for the approximation of the environment was presented[9]. This strategy is based on three documents: the National Program on the Integration of Serbia in the EU [10], the National Program for the Environment[94]and the National Strategy for Sustainable Development[95].

For harmonization of regulations, both formal and functional, and its application in practice Serbia needs about 10 billion euros or 1400 euros per capita by the year 2030[96]. The strategy provides for the application of three basic policies: harmonization with EU standards, optimization of use of grants and implementation according to the EU requirements.

According to the EU[97], Serbia has made great progress in the field of environmental protection, especially in the area of waste management,

---

Serbia, http://www.ekoplan.gov.rs/src/15-Ostala-dokumenta-127-document. htm, 15.04.2014.

[94]   Djuri , Dj., Ivanovi , V., Balaban M.(2011), *"Regional policy funds: How prepared is Serbia to access European Union regional policy funds?"*, in: *Serbia and the European Union: economic lessons from the new member states*, University of Coimbra, Portugal, p. 303.

[95]   Ministry of natural resources, mining and space planning of the Republic of Serbia, http://www.ekoplan.gov.rs/src/15-Ostala-dokumenta-127-document. htm, 15.04.2014.

[96]   European Integration Office, www.seio.gov.rs, 10.04. 2014.

[97]   Ministry of natural resources, mining and space planning of the Republic of Serbia, http://www.ekoplan.gov.rs/src/15-Ostala-dokumenta-127-document. htm, 15.04.2014.

nature protection and management of chemicals, while significant investments need to be made in the waste water management. Thus, the most investment of 5.6 billion euros is needed in the water sector, in the waste sector 2.8 billion and in the sector of industrial pollution 1.3 billion. In addition to the above, part of the funds in the amount of 962 million went to operating expenses to be borne by the budget[98]. According to the adopted regulations, the new plant will have to be built in line with EU standards, and the old will be renovated in accordance with the new requirements. For this, there is a corresponding transition period.

In 2007 the Ministry of Environment, Mining and Spatial Planning was established as aninstitutional and administrative authority on environment protection[99], and in 2010 it received the authority in the field of mining and waste processing industries. It also formed the Agency for Environmental Protection and Planning for the development of a national information system for environmental protection and Chemicals Agency. However, formal coordination, information and shared decision-making between the administrative authorities in the effective implementation of the EU *acquis*is still weak. The responsibility for the protection and management of water resources is divided between the Ministry of Agriculture, Ministry of Health and the Ministry of Infrastructure. In addition, the Agency for Environmental Protection needs to strengthen human resources. At the local level, environmental protection is not sufficient and requires strengthening and further decentralization. The Law on Environmental Protection from 2004[100]envisaged basic functions, duties and powers of inspectors at the national, provincial and local levels.These duties are in addition to the above, furnished by the Law on Environmental Impact Assessment[101]and the Law on

---

[98]   Ministry of natural resources, mining and space planning of the Republic of Serbia, http://www.ekoplan.gov.rs/DNA/docs/strategija_rs.pdf, 15.04.2014.

[99]   European Integration Office, www.seio.gov.rs, 10.04. 2014.

[100]   Commission staff working paper, Serbia 2011 progress report, accompanying Communication from the Commission to the European Parliament and the Council, Commission Opinion on Serbia's application for membership of the European Union, Brussels, *ec.europa.eu*, 10.05.2014.

[101]   Commission staff working paper, Serbia 2011 progress report, accompanying Communication from the Commission to the European Parliament and the

integrated prevention and control of pollution of the environment[102]. These regulations give broad powers to environment inspectors. Thus, they may ban, confiscate and order actions to meet legal obligations. However, inspectors are faced with significant limitations, because no court order can access the sites without notice or take samples[103].

Ministry of Environmental Protection implemented the minimum criteria for environmental inspection ssince 2007. This provides the first assessment of the effectiveness of environmental inspection and penalties. However, a more thorough happlication inpractice and strengthened cooperation between different inspectorates are needed, as well as the delineation of their responsibilities and cooperation with police and prosecutors[104].

Horizontal legislation of the Republic of Serbiais largely in line with European standards[105]and Government Regulations applied on a nationalist of environmental indicators[106], but it is necessary to further harmonize the legislate on with regard to cross-border aspects of environmental impact assessments. Also, it is necessary for Serbia to join the amendments to the Espoo Convention[107]and to implement the Directive on environmental liability[108]. This is the first and the second amendment, relating to the notification of the environment and access to justice.

Council, Commission Opinion on Serbia's application for membership of the European Union, Brussels, *ec.europa.eu*,10.05. 2014.

[102] Law on environmental protection, "Official GazetteRS" N°135/2004, 36/2009, 36/2009 - dr. zakon, 72/2009 - dr. zakon, 43/2011 - odluka US.

[103] Law on Assessment of Influence on Environment, "Official GazetteRS" N°135/2004, 36/2009.

[104] Law on integrated prevention and control of polution of environment, "Official GazetteRS" N°135/2004.

[105] Commission staff working paper, Serbia 2011 progress report, ec.europa.eu, 10.05. 2014.

[106] Ateljevi , V., Sreti , Z., Mitrovi , S., Plavši , P.(2011), Izazovi evropskih integracija u oblastima zaštite životne sredine i održivog razvoja lokalnih zajednica, PALGO Centar, p. 59.

[107] Commission staff working paper, Serbia 2011 progress report, ec.europa.eu, 10.05. 2014.

[108] Regulation on national list of indicators of environment protection, "Official

In terms of air quality, the Republic of Serbia has made progress in the harmonization of legislation, so that it is almost completely harmonized with the Framework Directive on air quality[109], but it remains to include provisions relating to arsenic, cadmium, mercury, nickel and polycyclic aromatic hydrocarbons in the air as well as to harmonize regulations with the National Directive on emission ceilings[110]and with the standards in terms of fuel.Air qualities are monitored in large urban areas and in the cities of Belgrade, Novi Sad and Bor and plans for air quality are prepared. This became possible since the Agency for Environmental Protection established a network of automatic monitoring through municipal and other authorities.

In addition, national legislation is in line with key EU policies on waste management and hazardous waste management and applies the principles of prevention, reuse, recycle and re- obtain. In addition, legislation has been harmonized and applied when it comes to packaging and packaging waste in special cases, as well as the separation of waste. It remains to be seen how the application will work in practice, particularly in rural areas and landfills[111].

Whenit comes to managing waste and sewage waste from the manufacturing industry, it is not sufficiently aligned with EU legislation and in particular the expected adoption of the provisions of EU Framework Directiveon Waste[112].

GazetteRS" N°37/2011.

[109] Convention on Environmental Impact Assessment in a Transboundary Context (Espoo, 1991), www.unece.org/espoo-convention.html, 03.04.2014.

[110] EUDirective 2004/35/CE of 21st April 2004 on environmental liability with regard to the prevention and remedying of environmental damage, Official Journal of the European Union, N° L 143/56, 30.4.2004.

[111] Framework Directive 96/62/EC of 27 September 1996 on ambient air quality assessment and management, OfficialJournal of the European Union, N° L 296/55, 21.11.1996.

[112] Directive 2001/81/EC of 23 October 2001 on national emission ceilings for certain atmospheric pollutants, OfficialJournal of the European Union, N° L 309/22, 27.11.2001.

In terms of the quality of drinking water, the legislation of the Republic of Serbia is significantly aligned with the EU acquis, but it is necessary to adopt the standards of the Water Framework Directive[113], particularly when it comes to cost recovery for water suppliers, the introduction of water basin separation and the competent bodies. Also, it is necessary to harmonize regulations with the EU regulations on the protection of groundwater pollution and deterioration, monitoring of groundwater and EU directives on nitrates and treatment of urbanwaste water[114].

Significant progress has been reported in the area of nature protection. It comprises the introduction of the provisions of the Birds Directive and the Habitats Directive, as well as the effective implementati on of the biodiversity of the Republic of Serbia and the Action Plan 2010-2017[115]. Further, it implies application of the regulation on compensation for damage caused by unlawfulactions against explicitly protected wild life.

Serbia aligned its legislation and began to implement the EU Directive on Integrated Pollution Prevention and Control Directive[116]and the control of major hazardous accidents- Seveso II[117,] which was a progress in the area of industrial pollution control and risk management. Also, the Lawon Environmental Protection enabled the application of so called "voluntary instruments", such as the ISO14001 standards, eco-management and the audit scheme, and national eco-labels, cleaner production, management, and technical standards[118].

---

[113]   EU Commission report on Serbia, 2010, *ec.europa.eu*, 10.05. 2014.

[114]   Directive 2008/98/EC of 19 November 2008 on waste and repealing certain Directives, OfficialJournal of the European Union, N° L 312/3, 22.11.2008.

[115]   Directive 2000/60/EC of 23 October 2000 establishing a framework for Community action in the field of water policy, OfficialJournal of the European Union, N° L 327/1, 22.12.2000.

[116]   Council Directive 91/676/EEC of 12 December 1991 concerning the protection of waters against pollution caused by nitrates from agricultural sources, OfficialJournal of the European Union, N° L 375/1, 31.12.1991.

[117]   Ministry of natural resources, mining and space planning of the Republic of Serbia, www.ekoplan.gov.rs, 15.04.2014.

[118]   Law on integrated prevention and control of polution of environment, "Official GazetteRS" N°135/2004.

When it comes to chemicals, the regulations on chemicals and biocidesare harmonized with the EU acquis, in particular with the REACH Regulation[119], the Regulation on classification, labeling and packaging of substances and mixtures[120]and the Directive on the release of biocide products on the market[121]. In addition, Serbia has ratified the Rotterdam Convention on consent procedure on the prior informed procedure for certain hazardous chemicals[122]and pesticidesin international trade and the Stockholm Convention on Persistent OrganicPollutants[123].

In regard to the protection and monitoring of soil condition our legislation lags behind EU standards. When it comes to noise, our Law on noise protection in the environment[124]is in compliance with

---

[119] Council Directive 96/82/EC of 9 December 1996 on control of major accident hazards involving dangerous substances, OfficialJournal of the European Union, N° L 10/13, 14.1.1997.

[120] Institut za standardizaciju Srbije, www.iss.rs, 15.04.2012.

[121] Regulation (EC) No 1907/2006 of 18 December 2006 concerning the Registration, Evaluation, Authorization and Restriction of Chemicals (REACH), establishing a European Chemicals Agency, amending Directive 1999/45/EC and repealing CouncilRegulation (EEC) No 793/93 and Commission Regulation (EC) No 1488/94 as well as Council Directive76/769/EEC and Commission Directives 91/155/EEC, 93/67/EEC, 93/105/EC and 2000/21/EC, OfficialJournal of the European Union, N° L 136/3, 29.5.2007.

[122] Regulation (EC) No 1272/2008 of 16 December 2008 on classification, labelling and packaging of substances and mixtures, amending and repealing Directives 67/548/EEC and 1999/45/EC, and amending Regulation (EC) No 1907/2006, OfficialJournal of the European Union, N° L 353/1, 31.12.2008.

[123] Directive 98/8/EC of 16 February 1998 concerning the placing of biocidal products on the market, OfficialJournal of the European Union, N° L 123/1, 24.4.2008.

[124] Law on ratification of Rotterdam Convention on procedure of authorizationupon previous notification for certain dangerous chemicals and pesticides in the international trade, "Official GazetteRS", International conventions, N°38/2009. Law on chemicals, "Official GazetteRS" N°36/2009 and Law on biocide products, "Official GazetteRS" N°36/2009.

the EU Directive on the Protection from the noise[125]. Also, there has been progress in the area of civil protection, in particular through integrated emergency management, adoption of the Law on emergency situations[126] and the establishment of the Department of Emergency Management within the Ministry of Interior.

Serbia has ratified the Kyoto Protocol and UN Framework Convention on climate changes[127] and the Government adopted the National Strategy on Clean Development[128] and submitted national report with an assessment of the effects of greenhouse gases and the projections for 2012 and 2013[129].

In terms of legislation related to climate change, the process of harmonization with the EU *acquis* is at an early stage, and the area has covered only some sector laws. Serbia is a signatory to Article 5 of the Montreal Protocol on substances that deplete the Ozone Layer[130].

REVENUES FROMNATURAL RESOURCE USE

Of all the natural goods and resources for which fees or rent is charged, only the aspect that relates to the exploitation of mineral resources is

[125]   Convention on persistent organic pollutants, chm.pops.int/Countries/StatusofRatifications/, 12.jul 2012.

[126]   Law on protection of noise in the environment, "Official GazetteRS" N°36/2009 i 88/2010.

[127]   Directive 2002/49/EC of 25 June 2002 relating to the assessment and management of environmental noise, OfficialJournal of the European Union, N° L 189/12, 18.7.2002.

[128]   Law on emergency situation activity, "Official GazetteRS" N°111/2009, 92/2011.

[129]   Kyoto Protocol to the United Nations Framework Convention on Climate Change, of 11th December 1997, http://unfccc.int/essential_background/kyoto_protocol/items/1678.php, 14.05.2014.

[130]   United Nations Framework Convention on climate change, of 9th of May 1992, http://unfccc.int/essential_background/convention/status_of_ratification/items/2631.php, Serbia is a non-Annex-1 Party to the United Nations Framework Convention on Climate Change UNFCCC.

presented here[131]. Natural values, natural resources and natural capital are shared resources that are located in the state property. Using these values is subjected to a special form of rents that are within the legal framework defined as compensation. The most important natural resources, when excluding charges for the use of land, for which a fee is charged, are: mineral resources, coal, oil shale, hydrocarbons - oil and gas, radioactive raw materials and metallic materials, secondary raw material and non-metallic materials. In Serbia, the amount of fees or natural rent for the use of these resources is low. Crude oil and gas account for only 3 % of the total revenues of companies that exploit them. Natural rent for coal and oil shale is only 1%. The level of fees and natural rents has no incentive character, which would ensure sustainable exploitation of the resources listed.

The share of total income from fees in the sum of all budgets (Republic, autonomous provinces and local governments) in the period 2008-2010 has a steady increase from 2.2% in 2008 to 2.4% in 2009 and 2.6% in 2010. When observing the budget of the Republic, the increase in the share of fees had a significant growth from 0.9% in 2008 to 1.6% in 2010 which shows a relative increase of nearly 78%. The largest structural contribution of this growth has given rise to "environmental fees" that in the same period in the central budget recorded a growth of 0.2% share in 2008 to 0.7% in 2010. In the period 2008 – 2010 the environmental taxes total revenue budget increased from 0.3% share to 0.6% of the total revenues in the budget. The share of total income from fees in the total budget of the state institutions in Serbia ranged from 4.6% in 2008 to a fall to 4.4% in 2009 and then they rose to 4.7% in 2010.

In relation to the total GDP, total environmental taxes, in the broad and narrow sense, had the following participation per year. Total fees charged which include fees for planning and construction land use accounted to GDP in the year 2008 which was 2.12%, in 2009 2.09% and in 2010 2.26%. Environmental taxes in the strict sense in relation to GDP had the following participation: in 2008 of 0.13%, in 2009

---

[131]   National Strategy on integration of the Republic of Serbia in the mechanism of Clean development of Kyoto Protocol for sectors of waste management, agriculture and forests, http://www.ekoplan.gov.rs/, 10.05.1014.

increased to 0.21%, recording a further increase in the amount of 0.29% in 2010.

Environmental taxes in a broader sense, which exclude compensation for furnishing and the use of land, and include environmental taxes in the strict sense, along with the charges for water, agriculture and forestry fees, travel and spa fees, road tolls, fees for mineral and mineral resources, in relation to the GDP had a share of 1.03% in 2008 and growth at 1.15% in 2009, while in 2010 they amounted to 1.25%.

Table 1. The total amount offeesand participationinrelation to GDP
The valuesexpressedin millions ofEUR

The valuesexpressedin millions ofEUR

Year	GDP	TotalFees	% of to GDP	Ecological compensation in the strict sense	% to GDP	Ecological compensation in broad terms	% to GDP
2008	32.668,2	691	2,12	44	0,13	335	1,03
2009	28.956,6	608	2,09	60	0,21	332	1,15
2010	28.066,1	635	2,26	82	0,29	352	1,25

Data source: National Bureau of Statistics, Ministry of Finance of Serbia.

Note: For the calculation of the value of the RSD denominated in EUR the exchange rate for 1 euro = 88.60 RSD for the year 2008 wasused, for the year 2009 =95.89 RSD, for 2010 = 105.50 RSD.

In the table presented total fees include environmental taxes in the strict sense and fees charged for the use of construction equipment and land. Environmental fees are fees in the strict sense and include all kinds of fees for the use of natural resources and values, as well as fees that are paid for environmental pollution.

THE FUNDFORENVIRONMENTAL PROTECTION

In Serbia in the period from 2006 up to and concluding the year 2012 a specialized Fund for environmental protection was established and operated as a separate unit. The Fund's collected income from the following sources:

1. Consideration for the supply of wild flora and fauna, fees for registration to EMAS system, compensation for environmental pollution and compensation for environmental pollution in areas of special state concern;
2. Purpose Fund budget of the Republic of Serbia earned from fees in accordance with the law;
3. Funds generated on the basis of international bilateral and multilateral cooperation on programs, projects and other activities in the field of environmental protection and renewable energy;
4. Funds from the cash management of the Fund;
5. Contributions, donations, gifts and grants;
6. Interest, or annuity loans;
7. Fee for the provision of professional services (the height of the fees prescribed by the board of directors of the Fund), with the prior approval of the Ministry of Environmental Protection and the funds are paid into a special account of the public revenue and are used for the operation of the Fund;
8. Other sources in accordance with the law.

In the past three years, most of the revenues of the fund have been generated from the fees for tradein wild flora and fauna, and they are all based on the Regulation on control of use and trade of wild flora and fauna adopted in 2005. Revenues are collected from various recompenses, such as fees based on the principle of "polluterpays", on the basis of the Regulationon the types of pollutant swhich specifies criteria for calculating compensation for environmental pollution and bonds, amount and method of calculation and payment offees. This regulation was also adopted in 2005. When it comes to special funds from the budget and resources of the international financial assistance, this form of financing is carried out in accordance with Article 89 of the Law on Environmental Protection.

Table 2. Achieved revenues of 2006, 2007, 2008, 2009 and 2010

The values expressed in RSD

Fees	Actual 2006	Actual2007	Actual2008	Actual2009	Actual2010
Fee for wild flora and fauna	38,700,000.00	50,288,547.50	48,061,819.86	61.850.380,00	72.421.465,45
Fee for owners of motor vehicles	363,100,000.00	411,872,411,60	445,056,986,65	657.114.609,00	809.516.074,43
Fee for SO2, NO2, particulate matter produced or disposed of waste	481,600,000.00	503,233,844,54	549,133,635.40	1.635.299.571,00	2.541.947.230,26
Fee for substances that deplete the ozone layer	5,300,000.00	6,850,648.01	3,682,321.24	7.787,987.00	4.570.299,90
Fees for the use of fishing areas					29.265.264,95
The fee for products that after use become special waste streams					1.334.484.362,31
Total	888,700,000.00	972,245,491.65	1,045,934,763.15	2.362.052.547,00	4.792.204.697,30
Returned to Budget				800.166.949,27	
Total	888,700,000.00	972,245,491.65	1,045,934,763.15	1.561.885.597,73	4.792.204.697,30

Data source: http://www.sepf.gov.rs

Inthe presentedtableis adatastructure ofthe source andfoundationto raise money forthe FundforEnvironmental Protection. Also, according to the above mentioned data, it can be concludedthat the incomeof the fundin nominal andreal termsincreased from about888millionin 2006 to4.7billionin 2010.

ELEMENTS OF CASE STUDIES

In the Republic of Serbia 522120 hectares of land, forests, pastures, ponds, wetlands covering 463areas, or 5.91% of the territory of Serbia are under the regime of environmental protection. Protected areas are managed by different entities, non-governmental organizations across the private companies to public companies owned by the state. For example, only "Srbijašume" manages 96 protected areas that encompass 216,804.88 hectares comprising 41.52% of the total protected area in Serbia.

Is 2007 the Government of the Republic of Serbia adopted the National Sustainable Development Strategy which sets out national priorities for environmental protection in relation to economic development. The strategyis focused on the objectives of raising the level of protection, conservation and enhancement of biodiversity, the increase of areas under strict protection up to a level of 10% of the territory of the republic, expanding the network of protected areas and the establishment of ecological corridors. The Regional Development Plan of the Republic of Serbia for the period from 2010 to 2020 provides the increase of the total area under the regime of special environmental protection to 12% of the territory of the Republic. The management of protected areas is defined as an activity of public interest.

The right of protected areas with in the defined rules is assigned by the Government of Republic of Serbia .Inchoosing the manager defacto there is no discrimination from the perspective of property forms, or forms of property rights on which the manager is constituted. Territorial complexes or areas that are put under the regime of protection and are given under the management have different forms of ownership (private, cooperativeorstate). The entity that manages certain protected areas usually has noproperty rights in protected areas. From the standpoint of property rights, the property of different persons (legal or natural) remains unchanged, but some restrictions are set to the owners on the use of those assets. An example of this is to limit the exploitation of resources, the use of fertilizers, the discharge of waste material, mode of construction land, etc.

In the regime of protected areas in Serbia the following forms are classified: national parks, strict nature reserves, natural monuments, protected habitats, landscapes of exceptional quality and nature parks.

National parks are areas with a large number of diverse ecosystems of national significance with special landscape features and cultural heritage of the region where people can live in harmony with nature. National parks are intended to preserve the existing natural values, geological resources and biodiversity. It is possible to perform scientific, educational, spiritual, aesthetic, cultural, tourism, health and recreational purposes in them, as well as other activities in accordance with the rules and principles of conservation and protection of nature.

Strict Nature Reserve, the area with the unmodified natural features that include representative natural ecosystems that represent an area of unchanged nature, genetic stock and maintained ecological balance. Implementing scientific research is allowed, provided thatthe natural features, phenomena, values and processes are not disturbed.

Special Nature Reserves are areas where the unaltered or slightly altered state of nature is present, which is important because of the uniqueness, rarity or representativeness. They are also the habitat of endangered wild fauna and flora. These areas are usually not or sparsely populated areas in which people live in harmony with nature. These areas are intended for the preservation of existing natural features, genetic, ecological balance, monitoring of natural phenomena and processes. The areas are permitted for scientific research, visits of tourists are controlled in order to preserve the traditional, inherited natural resources. Special nature reserves according to what the natural resources contain can be in a form of a forest, zoological, geological, hydro geological, hydrological, botanical.

Monuments of nature are less unchanged or partially changed natural areas or units, objects or phenomena that are clearly physically distinct, identifiable and unique. They are representatives of geomorphologic, geological, hydrological, botanical or other features. Monuments of nature may be areas in which human activity caused or created some of the botanical values that can be used in scientific, cultural, educational, aesthetic and tourism purposes. The following natural resources or assets can be proclaimed as natural monuments: geological, geomorphologic, caves, hydrological and botanic.

Protected habitats are areas that include one or more types of habitats that are important for the preservation of single or multiple populations of wild species and their communities.

Landscape protected areas are areas that have a distinctive and special appearance with significant natural biological - ecological, aesthetic, cultural and historical values. A key feature of these areas is that they are created as a result of the interaction of nature and natural resources on one hand and the traditional way of human activity on the other. Area of exceptional importance may be a natural area of exceptional importance and cultural landscape of exceptional quality. These areas are areas that have a significant biological, ecological and aesthetic values, where traditional ways of the local population have not significantly eroded nature and natural ecosystems.

The cultural landscapes of exceptional quality are areas that have significant features, benefits, and cultural and historical values that have developed over time due to the interaction of nature and natural resources of the area and the traditional way of life of the population that lived or live in these areas.

The following table presents data on the types of protected areas, their number, surface and also on the largest comparative individual manager of these goods, "Srbijašume".

Table 3. Protected areas in Serbia in 2011

N°	Types of protected areas in Serbia	Serbia		PE "Srbijašume"	
		N°	Area (ha)	N°	Area (ha)
1.	National Parks	5	158.986,36		
2.	Nature Parks	12	215.760,57	3	197.261,00
3.	Regional Nature Parks	4	361,86	1	296,64
4.	Area of exceptional importance	12	33.406,80	3	4.348,96
5.	Landscapes of special natural beauty	4	12.105,63	3	11.265,00
6.	Forest Park	1	19,65	1	19,65
7.	Strict Nature Reserve	42	2.207,28	35	561,89
8.	General Nature Reserve	4	60,49	4	60,49
9.	Special Nature Reserves	17	87.410,14	2	123,50
10.	Monuments of nature	327	7.681,00	36	2.222,44
11.	Memorial natural monuments	19	2.394,67	5	442,95
12.	Premises in the vicinity of immovable cultural property	16	1.725,55	4	202,36
13.	Strictly protected species	1681			
14.	Protected species	821			
	Total 1-12	463	522.120,00	96	216.804,88

Data source: Table constituted on the basis of data obtained from a decision to designate protected areas "Srbijašume" data and data of the Institute for Nature Protection of Serbia.

From a total of 463 protected areas with an area of 522 thousand hectares, 5 national parks are covering an area of approximately 159 thousand hectares or 30.45% of the total protected area. Total 12 nature parks accounted for 41.32% of the total surface of protected areas. Some 17 special nature reserves are in the third place, occupying 16.74% of the territory of the total protected area in Serbia. Other 429 protected areas occupy only 11.49% of the total surface of protected areas. The largest single control of protected areas is in the public company which manages "Srbija šume" which manages 41.52% of the total protected area.

Empirical research carried out in early 2012 included the residents of villages located on the edge of a special nature reserve "Zasavica". Some 103 subjects of different ages and sex were surveyed by the method of interview. The study focused on the attitudes of the population regarding the natural resources that are in SNR "Zasavica". A short aspect of the study is presented here.

When asked to define key natural values that are found in the reserve respondents expressed the following value structure:

- Respondents definednaturalvalues andraritiesthat are in "Zasavica", asthe mostvaluedunspoiled nature(15.64% of respondents), followedbyrarespecieswith14.66%, which takes aneco-tourism as a developmentbusiness opportunity, and thenfollowed bythe valueof clean air(11.73% of the respondents), the water supply(8.47%), healthy food (6.51%) and arrangement of space (3.58%).
- Rarespecies were valued relativelymodestly as a specificity of Zasavica, for example beaver with 10.75%, "mangulica" pork with 9.45%, aprairie oxwith2.93%.
- Inresponseto the question whether they have sufferedany damage causedbyorrelated tothe reserveonly14.56%of respondentsstated that they had suffereddamage, while85.44% of respondentsexpressedthe view that they did not sufferany damage.

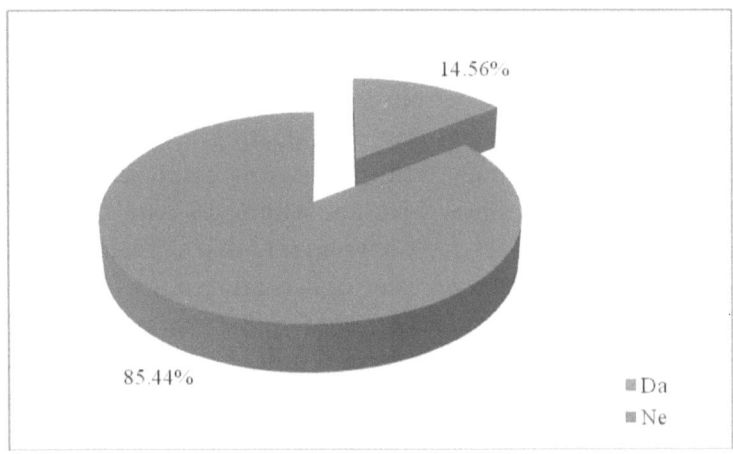

Graphic 1. Does the population suffer any damage
from the national reserve. Blue – yes, red – no.

Whenit comes to theattitude of the respondentsinrelation topossible changes of the statusof protectedareas in terms ofits converse on intofarmland the respondentsexpressedtheir views as follows (blues-yes, red-no).

Only 8.7% of all respondents expressed theview that thepurposeof "Zasavica" should be changedfromthe Special Nature Reserveinto an agricultural land. On the contrary, 91.3% of the respondents expressedthe viewthat the purpose ofa nature reserve should not be changed.

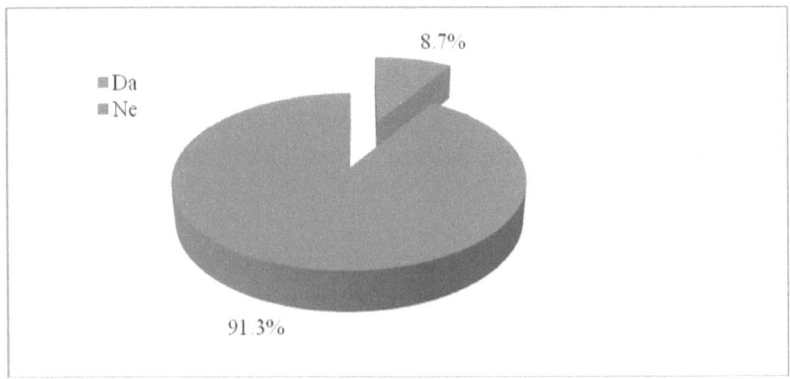

Graphic 2. Changes of the statusof the national
reserve. Blue – yes, red – no.

The view of the respondents regarding their assessment of how much the special nature reserve is worth, expressed in money, were characteristic. Out of 103 interviewed persons only one person had no position regarding the value. The problem of evaluating SNR "Zasavica" and expressing values in money were particularly important during the interview. Most respondents were not willing to state the monetary value of "Zasavica". In fact, 65% of them said that the value "cannot be expressed in money," the total value of natural resources is beyond the scope of monetary expression. "Zasavica" value expressed in money is defined greater than 2-4 million or $ 5 million or more by the 11.7% of respondents. The value in the range of up to 500 euros and up to 1.5 million euros was defined by the 10.7% of respondents.

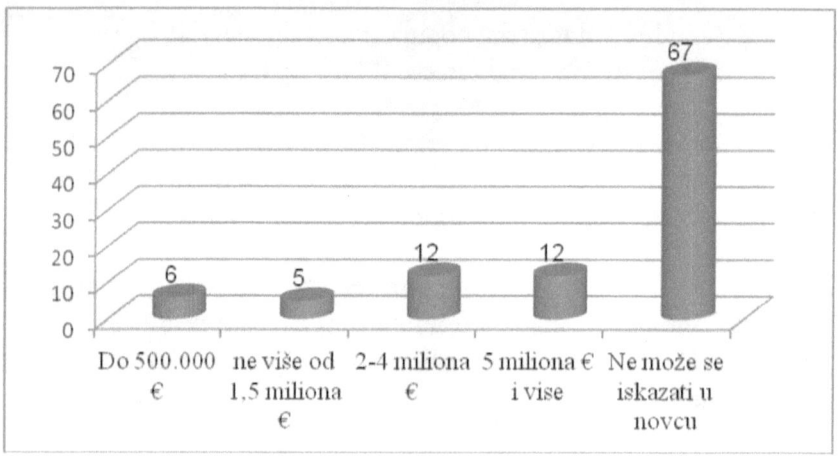

Graphic 3. Assessment of value of the special nature reserve "Zasavica". 1. Up to 500.000 euros, 2. not more than 1,5 Million euros, 3. 2-4 Million euros, 4.5 or more Milion euros, 5.can not be expressed in money.

In contrast to theapproachof a neutralevaluation ofthe value ofnature reserves, on thequestion of how muchthey would be willingto pay, andfor which pricethey would be willingto buy thereserve, most respondents expressedthe monetaryvalueof the reserve.

Out of103respondents96of themdefined thescaleof monetaryvalues, while7 ofthemdid not have aposition on thevalue.The dominantresponseof the respondentswasthat thereservewas worthover 5million euros.

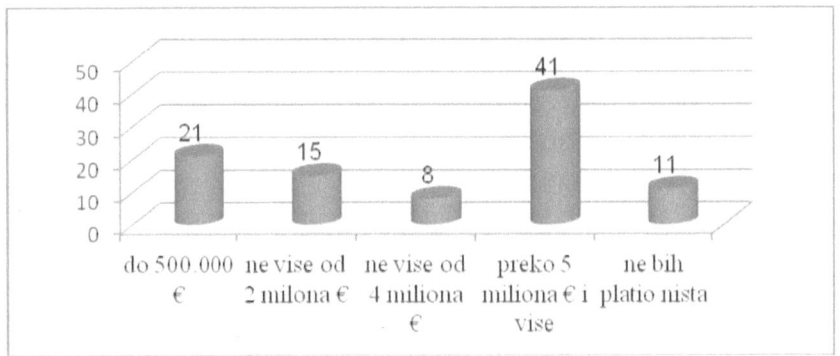

Graphic 4. Assessment of value of the special nature reserve "Zasavica". 1. Up to 500.000 euros, 2. not more than 2 Million euros, 3. not more than 4 Million euros, 4. over 5 Milion euros and more, 5. nothing.

Unlike theinteresting neutral valuationin whichfor most respondents the value of "Zasavica" cannot beexpressedin money, when the respondents wereplaced inthe position ofa potential buyerof the complex, theirapproach tonatural resourcevaluationchanges. The maximum monetary value of "Zasavica" of over 5million is attributed by the39.8% of the respondents, the value of up to 500.000 euros isvalued by 20.4%of the respondents, not more than 2million euros by 14.6%and notmore than 4million Euro by78% of the respondents. A relatively highpercentage ofrespondentsexpressed the view thatthey would bewilling to pay "nothing" for "Zasavica" and that attitude wasexpressed by 10.7% of the respondents.

CONCLUSION

According to the European Commission, the Republic of Serbia has made a significant progress in aligning its legislation with the EU *acquis communautaire* in the field of environmental protection, horizontal legislation, as well as in the field of waste management, nature protection and dealing with chemicals. However, further alignment is necessary in terms of water quality and climate change. In addition to the legal framework, there are necessary administrative capacities. However, more coordinated work and sustained efforts are needed with the aim of harmonization and effective implementation of the EU *acquis*. In relation to that, a substantial investment and strengthening the administrative capacity are needed in order to implement the legislation and to achieve the medium-term compliance on key issues including the climate change. Full compliance with the *acquis* is only possible in the long term and would require a higher level of investment.

Funding adjustments and raising awareness of its benefits are considered as the main obstacles. For example, in the field of environmental protection by the year 2030 the approximation of standards is expected, so it is necessary to invest about 10.5 billion euros, but the future income will be approximately 15 billion euros, which means a profit of around 5 billion euros. There are of course political constraints in the implementation of regulations. There is also the question of the feasibility of compliance. Time frame alignment is defined through negotiations with the EU, and it is possible and feasible. In preparation for the start of the negotiations, the starting position of Serbia is relatively good. The Serbian government also anticipated the costs of the compliance of regulations. However, the question of funding and assessment of political gain remains. A period of political stability, especially the stable executive power in the Republic of Serbia is also required.

REFERENCES

1. Ateljevi , V., Sreti , Z., Mitrovi , S., Plavši , P. (2011), Izazovi evropskih integracija u oblastima zaštite životne sredine i održivog razvoja lokalnih zajednica, PALGO Centar.

2. Commission staff working paper, Serbia 2011 progress report, ec.europa.eu, 10.05. 2014.

3. Commission staff working paper, Serbia 2011 progress report, accompanying Communication from the Commission to the

European Parliament and the Council, Commission Opinion
on Serbia's application for membership of the European Union,
Brussels, ec.europa.eu,10.05. 2014.

4. Constitution of the Republic of Serbia, "Official Gazette RS"
    N°98/2006.

5. Convention on Environmental Impact Assessment in a
    Transboundary Context (Espoo, 1991), www.unece.org/espoo-
    convention.html, 03.04.2014.

6. Convention on persistent organic pollutants, chm.pops.int/
    Countries/StatusofRatifications, 12. jul 2012.

7. Council Directive 91/676/EEC of 12 December 1991 concerning
    the protection of waters against pollution caused by nitrates from
    agricultural sources, Official Journal of the European Union, N° L
    375/1, 31.12.1991.

8. Council Directive 96/82/EC of 9 December 1996 on control of
    major accident hazards involving dangerous substances, Official
    Journal of the European Union, N° L 10/13, 14.1.1997.

9. Djuri , Dj., Ivanovi , V., Balaban M. (2011), "Regional policy funds:
    How prepared is Serbia to access European Union regional policy
    funds?", in: Serbia and the European Union: economic lessons from
    the new member states, University of Coimbra, Portugal.

10. Draškovi , B. (2012), Ekološki aspekti ekonomske politike, Institut
    ekonomskih nauka Beograd, p.28-41.

11. EU Commission report on Serbia, 2010, ec.europa.eu, 10.05. 2014.

12. European Integration Office, www.seio.gov.rs, 10.04. 2014.

13. EU Directive 98/8/EC of 16 February 1998 concerning the placing
    of biocidal products on the market, Official Journal of the European
    Union, N° L 123/1, 24.4.2008.

14. EU Directive 2004/35/CE of 21st April 2004 on environmental liability with regard to the prevention and remedying of environmental damage, Official Journal of the European Union, N° L 143/56, 30.4.2004.

15. EU Directive 2000/60/EC of 23 October 2000 establishing a framework for Community action in the field of water policy, Official Journal of the European Union, N° L 327/1, 22.12.2000.

16. EU Directive 2001/81/EC of 23 October 2001 on national emission ceilings for certain atmospheric pollutants, Official Journal of the European Union, N° L 309/22, 27.11.2001.

17. EU Directive 2002/49/EC of 25 June 2002 relating to the assessment and management of environmental noise, Official Journal of the European Union, N° L 189/12, 18.7.2002.

18. EU Directive 2008/98/EC of 19 November 2008 on waste and repealing certain Directives, Official Journal of the European Union, N° L 312/3, 22.11.2008.

19. Framework Directive 96/62/EC of 27 September 1996 on ambient air quality assessment and management, Official Journal of the European Union, N° L 296/55, 21.11.1996.

20. Institut za standardizaciju Srbije, www.iss.rs, 15.04.2012.

21. Izveštaj o sprovo enju tre eg i izmenjenog i dopunjenog Nacionalnog programa za integraciju Republike Srbije u Evropsku unije, za prvo tromese je 2012. godine, Kancelarija za evropske integracije, www. seio.gov.rs, 10.04.2014.

22. Kyoto Protocol to the United Nations Framework Convention on Climate Change, of 11th December 1997, http://unfccc.int/ essential_background/kyoto_protocol/items/1678.php, 14.05.2014.

23. Law on Assessment of Influence on Environment, "Official Gazette RS" N°135/2004, 36/2009.

24. Law on chemicals, "Official Gazette RS" N°36/2009 and Law on biocide products, "Official Gazette RS" N°36/2009.

25. Law on emergency situation activity, "Official Gazette RS" N°111/2009, 92/2011.

26. Law on environmental protection, "Official Gazette RS" N°135/2004, 36/2009 (36/2009 - dr. zakon, 72/2009 - dr. zakon, 43/2011 - odluka US.

27. Law on integrated prevention and control of polution of environment, "Official Gazette RS" N°135/2004.

28. Law on protection of noise in the environment, "Official Gazette RS" N°36/2009 i 88/2010.

29. Law on ratification of the Interim Agreement on Trade and trade-related matters between European Communities and Republic of Serbia, "Official Gazette RS" N°83/2008.

30. Law on ratification of Rotterdam Convention on procedure of authorizationupon previous notification for certain dangerous chemicals and pesticides in the international trade, "Official Gazette RS", International conventions, N°38/2009.

31. Law on ratification of the Stabilization and Association Agreement between European Communities and their member states and Republic of Serbia, "Official Gazette RS" N°83/2008.

32. Ministry of natural resources, mining and space planning of the Republic of Serbia, http://www.ekoplan.gov.rs/src/15-Ostala-dokumenta-127-document.htm, 15.04.2014.

33. Ministry of natural resources, mining and space planning of the Republic of Serbia, http://www.ekoplan.gov.rs/DNA/docs/strategija_rs.pdf, 15.04.2014.

34. Ministry of natural resources, mining and space planning of the Republic of Serbia, www.ekoplan.gov.rs, 15.04.2014.

35. Montreal Protocol on Substances that Deplete the Ozone Layer of 16 September 1987, www.unep.org, 15.04.2014.

36. National Strategy on integration of the Republic of Serbia in the mechanism of Clean development of Kyoto Protocol for sectors of waste management, agriculture and forests, http://www.ekoplan. gov.rs/, 10.05.1014.

37. Regulation (EC) No 1272/2008 of 16 December 2008 on classification, labelling and packaging of substances and mixtures, amending and repealing Directives 67/548/EEC and 1999/45/EC, and amending Regulation (EC) No 1907/2006, Official Journal of the European Union, N° L 353/1, 31.12.2008.

38. Regulation (EC) No 1907/2006 of 18 December 2006 concerning the Registration, Evaluation, Authorization and Restriction of Chemicals (REACH), establishing a European Chemicals Agency, amending Directive 1999/45/EC and repealing Council Regulation (EEC) No 793/93 and Commission Regulation (EC) No 1488/94 as well as Council Directive 76/769/EEC and Commission Directives 91/155/EEC, 93/67/EEC, 93/105/EC and 2000/21/EC, Official Journal of the European Union, N° L 136/3, 29.5.2007.

39. Regulation on national list of indicators of environment protection, "Official Gazette RS" N°37/2011.

40. Todori , V., Jovanovi (2011), N., Mind the gap: Studija o implementaciji evropskog zakonodavstva u Srbiji, Centar za novu politiku.

41. United Nations Framework Convention on climate change, of 9th of May 1992, http://unfccc.int/essential_background/convention/ status_of_ratification/items/2631.php, Serbia is a non-Annex-1 Party to the United Nations Framework Convention on Climate Change UNFCCC.

SUSTAINABLE ENERGY POLICY FOR THE FUTURE

Zorana Nikitović[132]

Dragan Skobalj[133]

INTRODUCTION

The energy security and stability of any country - Serbia, the EU and wider - have become the key issue of every economic, trade and social system. These issues are also linked to the concept of sustainable development. The connection of the energy sector with the competitiveness of the economy leads to a willingness to forego the relevance of the battle for creating legal, institutional, technical, economic and social presumptions for a successful and sustainable battle for climate changes (Djereg, 2008) due to economic 'progress'. The energy system of each country should in the future be based on the following: energy efficiency, as well as introducing renewable energy sources in production, transmission, distribution and consumption – in other words, satisfying energy needs. This is an exceptionally demanding task for Serbia, but also for all new EU members, which should meet all the demands of the numerous directives linked with this area. Thus it is important that each country creates a sustainable energy policy for the future, which defers to all limitations but at the same time secures a sustainable development of energy as well as the entire socio-economic system, which is also the aim of this study.

ENERGY AND ITS SIGNIFICANCE

---

[132] Assistant Professor, Faculty of Business Economics and Entrepreneurship, Belgrade, Serbia, zorana.nikitovic@vspep.edu.rs

[133] International University of Brcko, Bosnia and Hercegovina

Along with water and food, energy is one of the fundamental needs of man and it is a key for every contemporary production. Without it, there is no development or any improving of the quality of life on this planet, which also gives it a global significance. In fact, it can be said that war is waged over it, and thus, the world is very interested in creating a rational use of energy (Djuricic, 2013).

Energy sources are classified into non-renewable energy sources (hereinafter: NRES) and renewable energy sources (RES) (Table 1).

Table 1. Types of energy sources (Djuricic, 2013)

NON-RENEWABLE (NRES)	RENEWABLE (RES)

1. FOSSIL fuels
  - Petroleum
  - Gas and
  - Coal
2. NUCLEAR ENERGY
	- HYDROENERGY
	- WIND ENERGY
	- SOLAR ENERGY
	- GEOTHERMAL
	  ENERGY and
	- BIOMASS

In world proportions, the reserves of fossil fuels are limited while energy use is permanently growing. NRES are quickly and surely disappearing, and along with this we also have the occurrence of global warming.

RES has become the priority of the development of the EU and the developed world, as well as the majority of the developing countries. Thus, Germany has set as its aim the securing of more than 50% of the total energy needs from RES by the year 2050. Serbia possesses solid RES energy potential, which is assessed to make up about 28% of the total primary energy (Table 2).

However, Serbia adheres to the share of energy costs in a unit of GNP, which is from 2.5 to 3 times larger than in the EU-15 countries.The reasons for this are the following: a decrease of industrial production, low price of energy, a difference in the price of energy and energy sources, etc.

Table 2. The assessed structures of renewable energy sources in Serbia

TYPE OF RES	MToe/year/	Participation /%/
BIOMASS	2.7	63
HYDROENERGY	0.6	14
GEOTHERMAL ENERGY	0.2	4,5
WIND ENERGY	0.2	4,5
SOLAR ENERGY	0.6	14
TOTAL	4.3	100

Source:Energy Development Strategy of
theRepublic of Serbia up to year 2015.

Most European experts consider that the universal approach in energy use can be shown in the following formula:

$$ES_{(2020)} = 3E + (3 \times 20)$$

whereupon:

ES-energy saving-

- 3E – efficiency, economy and ecology.
- 3 x 20 tasks of EU15 countries by 2020.
- 20% increased RES use.
- 20% increased energy efficiency and
- 20% reducing of gas emissions with a greenhouse effect.

An example of a possible potential for increasing energy efficiency in Serbia by 20% is the following: 1. Production of primary energy: about 14 Mten, 2. Production of electrical energy: about 35000 GWh (about 2,22 Mten), 3. Consumption of final energy: 7,5 Mten, 4. Increase of energy efficiency by 20% making up an amount of primary energy: 2,8

Mten, and 5. Equivalent to electrical energy of 0,84 Mten or energy produced in TE 1.5 - 2.0 GW (Source: Agency for the Energy System of the Republic of Serbia, www.aers.org.rs).

Within this, 10% of share of bio fuels is planned within the total use of petrol and diesel fuel.

ENERGY NEEDS AND THE AVAILABLE ENERGY RESOURCES OF SERBIA

Serbia belongs to the group of developing European countries and its gross domestic product is 40% less than the EU average (Figure 1). This is also in direct correlation with the energy consumption in Serbia, half of which is taken up by buildings (60% of this on heating), on transportation (27%) and only 23% of the total use is industrial (http://www.efikasnost.com/wp-content/uploads/2011/12/potrosnja-energije.jpg, 28.09.2012). From this we can see the possible tendency of activities in the aim of achieving greater energy efficiency, as the best way to attain successful energy management.

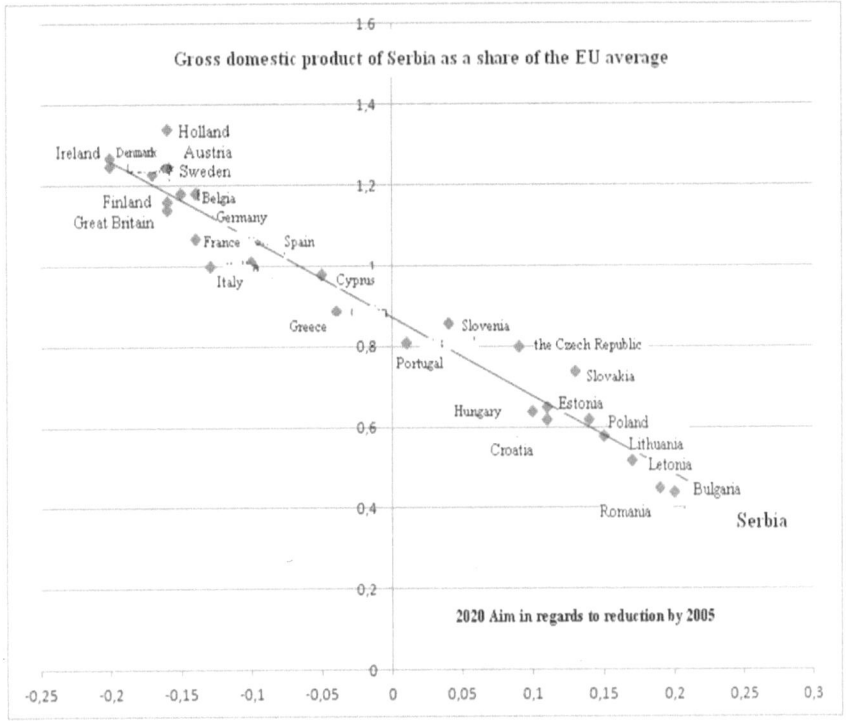

Figure 1. Gross domestic product of Serbia
as a share of the EU average.

Source: http://webrzs.stat.gov.rs/WebSite/userFiles/file/Energetika/
bilans/Bilans%20elekrticne%20energije,%202010.pdf

According to the official data of the authorized Ministry, petroleum products
(30%) and electrical energy (27%) have the greatest share (Figure 2) in the
total use of energy in Serbia in 2010.

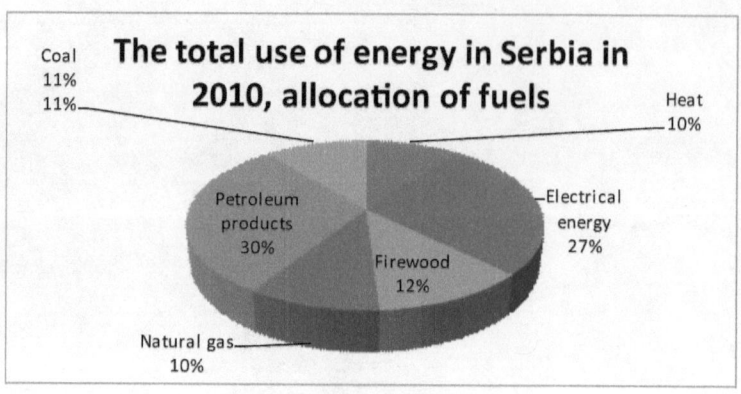

Figure 2. The total use of energy in Serbia in 2010, allocation of fuels.

Source: The energy balance sheet of the Republic
of Serbia for 2012, CRES 2010, IRG 2008.

Figure 3 shows the production of electrical energy by sources in
the period from 2007 to 2010, which indicates that power plants
continue to dominate, followed by large hydropower plants.

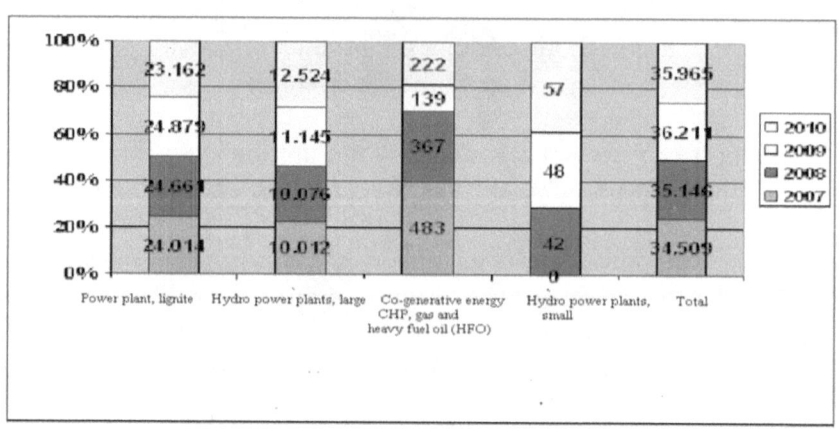

Figure 3. The production of electrical energy by
sources in the period from 2007 to 2010.

Source: http://www.efikasnost.com/wp-content/
uploads/2011/12/potrosnja-energije.jpg, 25.09.2012.

Serbia has significant sources of renewable energy (Table 3), but does not use them sufficiently (Table 4), which indicates the significant reserves linked with rational energy use. The Energy Development Strategy of Serbia until 2015 specifies that the share ofnew renewable sources(without large hydro power plants) in total primary energy use should be increased from zero to 1.1% in 2015, while the share in the total final energy use should be increased to 1.5 – 2% in the period from 2006-2015.

Table 3. The allocation of specific renewable energy sources.

Source of renewable energy	Annual potential	Appropriate saving in energy (PJ)
Biomass	100,4 PJ	100,4
Hydro energy, of which 856 are hydropower plants <10 M	5200 GWh/year 1800 GWh/year	16,7 (only small hydro power plants)
Geothermal energy	8,3 PJ	8,3
Wind energy (requires testing and detailed studies in the future)	7,9 PJ	7,9
Solar energy	26,7 PJ	26,7
Total		160

Source: Program of applying the Energy Development Strategy for 2007-2012, Sector for renewable energy sources.

Table 4. Allocation of energy from renewable sources in total primary energy use, according to the Energy Development Strategy, in a setting of dynamic economic development.

	2006	2009	2012	2015
Total primary energy consumption (in PJ)	615	647	715	753
Energy share from renewable sources (without large hydropower plants) in %	0.8	1.1	1.05	1.1

Source: Energy Development Strategy of the Republic of Serbia to 2015.

The energy needs of Serbiawithout Kosovo and Metohija were in 2011 estimated to be 16.2 million tons of equivalent petrol (mtoe) which is greater by 0.7 mtoe than in 2010. The import dependency in 2010 was 33.6%, and somewhat less in 2011.

Of the shown sources of primary energy, coal has the greatest share in the domestic production. The consumption of the total final energy in Serbia in 2010 was 8.9 mtoe, and it was estimated to be 9.3 mtoe in 2011. The following had the greatest allocation in the use of final energy in Serbia in 2010: households (35%), industry (28%), traffic (24%), other (12%) and agriculture (1%).

The structure of electrical energy use in the period 2005-2011 /GWh/ is shown in Table 5, and it can be seen that the total use of this energy source in that period increased by 7.6%. The most increased use of high voltage power supply was 26%, the low voltage power users which are not households and medium voltage supply, which indicates an increased activity of industry. By working more efficiently, electricity power plants have also reduced the use of energy in the process of production.

Table 5. The structure of electrical energy production in the period 2005-2011/GWh/.

Category of use	2005.	2006.	2007.	2008.	2009.	2010.	2011.	2011/ 2005(%)
Households	14.407	14.276	14.145	14.313	14.412	14.645	14.666	101.8
Others on low voltage power (0.4 kV)	4.957	5.195	5.379	5.614	5.567	5.534	5.640	113.8
Total on low voltage power (0.4 kV)	19.364	19.471	19.524	19.927	19.979	20.179	20.305	104.9
Buyers using low voltage power (10.20 and 35 kV)	4.967	5.125	5.247	5.345	5.127	5.317	5.553	111.8
Buyers using high voltage power (110 kV)	2.183	2.337	2.430	2.570	2.216	2.555	2.751	126.0
Delivered to end customers	26.514	26.933	27.201	27.842	27.322	28.051	28.609	107.9
Usage by power plants and hydropower plants for personal needs	521	662	447	431	492	436	476	91.4
Total usage	27.035	27.595	27.648	28.273	27.814	28.487	29.085	107.6

Source: The energy balance sheet of the Republic of Serbia for 2012, CRES 2010, IRG 2008.

The production, import and processing of crude oil in Serbia is carried out entirely by the NIS-Gaspromnjeft company and in 2011 the total use of raw oil and half-products in Serbia was around 2.5 million tons. The company NIS Naftagas in Serbia and Angola produce crude oil. In 2011 around 1.03 million tons (43.1%) were produced in Serbia, in Angola around 80,000 tons, and around 1.36 million tons (56.9%) was secured from import, mostly from Russia (energy balance sheet of the Republic of Serbia for 2012).

The structure of the production of petroleum products consists of the following manufactures: 1. diesel with 31%, 2. motor gasoline with 19%, 3. heating oil with 16%, 4. liquefied petroleum gas (LPG) with 4% and 5. other derivatives with 30%. Petroleum products, as the end products, are also secured by export, except for refining (2.33 million tons). In 2011, around 1.59 million tons of petroleum products were imported (almost 70% more than in 2010), primarily Euro diesel (EN 590) and TNG, as well as smaller amounts of unleaded petrol.

In the 2005-2011 period, there was an increase of TNG use by over 20%, as well as a total decrease of petrol use by around 5%, along with a simultaneous increase of the use of unleaded petrol on the account of leaded petrol. Also, there was an increase of the use of diesel fuel by about 3%, along with an increase of the use of Euro diesel by 50%, while the use of D2 diesel was reduced by nearly 35%.

In the structure of petroleum products use, motor fuels participated with 72%, oils with 16%, and other products with 12%.

The forecast is that the drivers of heating demand and their impact on heating demand in the period up to 2020 will occur like in Table 6.

Table 6. Drivers of heating demand and their impact
on heating demand in the period up to 2020.

Driver	Impact on heating demand
External temperature	Reducing of specific heating demand in a long-term period
Population	Reducing the overall heating demand due to less need
Efficiency of conversion	Reduction of specific heating demand
Available income	Long-term sustainable increase could lead to an increase of the overall heating demand. The medium-term impact is negligible in both directions. The elasticity of demand at the current levels is low.
Number, age and education level of the household members	Uncertain
Individual preferences	Uncertain

Source: The energy balance sheet of the Republic
of Serbia for 2012, CRES 2010, IRG 2008.

Heating apartments represents a great possibility to save energy in Serbia. According to official statistical data, the allocation of fuels in the production of district heating (hereinafter: DH) in Serbia in 2007 amounted to the following: 1. Natural gas – 65%, 2. Liquid fuel -25% and 3. Lignite -11%. Individual family houses are mostly heated by solid fuels (wood and coal), but due to the low price of electrical energy, many apartments use electricity in their homes. In the recent years, there has been an increasing gasification of central Serbia as well. According to official statistics, 35% of the total natural gas was used for heating plants and households in 2011, while the remaining 65% was used for industries and others. Apartments are mostly insufficiently thermally isolated so the annual costs of heating an average 60 m² apartment is 10,920 kWh (Figure 4), which is a result of the current state of affairs in Serbia and is sure to experience significant changes in the following period, as transitional Serbia imports over one third of its annual needs for primary energy. Thus in 2009, 34% was imported, and importing 37% of the needed energy on an annual level was planned in 2011.

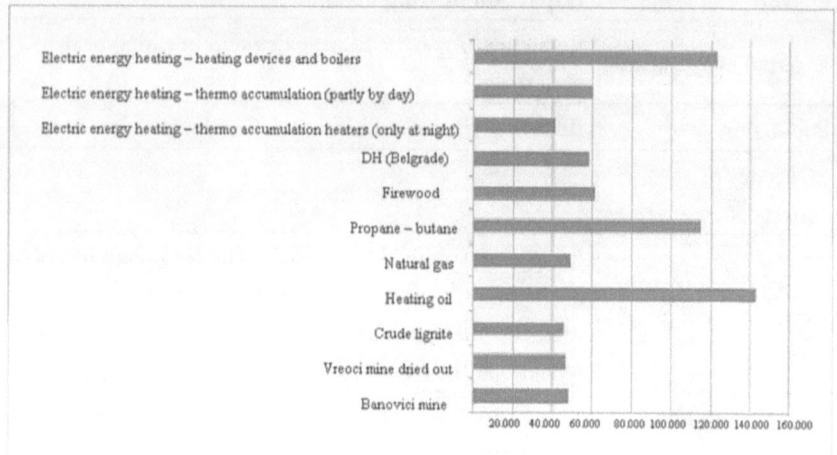

Figure 4. Annual costs of heating an average 60 m² apartment with 10,920 kWh.

Source: The energy balance sheet of the Republic of Serbia for 2012, CRES 2010, IRG 2008.

A SUSTAINABLE ENERGY POLICY FOR THE FUTURE

Developed countries have extensively planned their energy system future with well thought-out energy policies. The EU supports a joint energy policy directed towards reducing use, a larger integration of the European energy market, technological progress and securing greater energy safety. The current efforts of the EU are directed towards the adopting and carrying out of the package for an integrated European infrastructure in the aim of establishing a joint energy policy.

On October 25, 2005, Serbia signed a contract on founding an Energy Community, which came into effect on July 1, 2006. The basic tasks of the Energy Community are the following: to create a stable regulatory and market framework in South-Eastern Europe (SEE) and the EU in the aim of attracting investments in the sector of electrical energy and natural gas in order to enable a stable supply of energy which is needed for economic development and social stability; creating a unique legal framework for trading with electrical energy and gas in the SEE and EU; promoting the security of supply in the SEE region; improving the state of the environment; increasing energy efficiency and the use of renewable energy sources in the region; and developing a competitive energy market. By obtaining the status of an EU member candidate, Serbia attained the possibility to participate in meetings of EU countries as an observer, thus obtaining a referential setting in the energy area.

As part of the one-year presiding status of Serbia over the Energy Community in 2013, the 11th meeting of the Ministerial Council of the Energy Community was held in Belgrade on October 24, 2013. On that occasion, adopted were, among others, lists of projects of interest for the Energy Community – a total of 35 projects, 13 among them from Serbia, from the area of electrical energy production and electrical and gas infrastructure (http://www.mfa.gov.rs/sr/index.php/spoljna-politika/eu/saradnja-republike-srbije-i-evropske-unije-u-sektorskim-politikama/11378-2013-07-15-09-13-27?lang=lat).

The Serbian Energy Development Strategy is defined by the energy balance sheet of certain sectors (Table 7). This is the foundation for creating and realizing a sustainable Serbian energy policy, in the aim of:

- Increasing security of energy supplies and their more efficient use,
- Increasing competitiveness,
- Reducing the negative impact on the environment and
- Encouraging responsible behavior towards energy.

Planning the development of activities within the energy sector is based on the guidelines of the energy policy (http://www.eps.rs/Lat/Article.aspx?lista=Sitemap&id=97) and planning the development of energy in the Republic of Serbia based on the Law on Energy. The energy policy is more closely analyzed and carried out by the Energy Development Strategy of the Republic of Serbia (http://www.eps.rs/Lat/Article.aspx?lista=Sitemap&id=97), and the Program of carrying out the Strategy and the energy balance sheet of the Republic of Serbia (Figure 5).

Table 7. The energy balance sheet of the sector.

SECTOR BALANCE SHEET (Dynamic economic development): Needs = production + net import/export.					
	2003	2006	2009	2012	2015
OIL SECTOR (Mten)					
Final use	2.71	2.88	3.05	3.24	3.44
Energy transformations	0.24	0.12	0.12	0.12	0.12
Non-energy use	0.52	0.55	0.58	0.61	0.64
Losses/ personal use	0.30	0.31	0.32	0.33	0.34
Total needs	3.77	3.86	4.07	4.30	4.54
Domestic production	0.68	0.75	0.95	1.00	1.00
Oil import	3.09	3.11	3.12	3.30	3.54
NATURAL GAS SECTOR (Mm^3)					
Final use	1877	2124	2371	2630	2939
Energy transformations	50	200	200	200 *	308 *
Non-energy use	321	395	469	555	667
Losses/personal use	74	86	98	111	125
Total needs	2322	2805	3138	3495 *	4039 *
Domestic production	333	395	444	495	495
Import of natural gas	1989	2410	2694	3000	3444
COAL SECTOR (Mten)					
Final use	0.91	0.98	1.04	1.11	1.17
For energy transformations	5.91	6.42	6.48	7.75	7.75
For energy transf. (M t lignite)	32.75	35.94	36.38	43.46	43.46
Losses	0.14	0.14	0.14	0.14	0.14
Total needs	6.96	7.51	7.65	8.99	9.05
Domestic production	6.63	7.11	7.20	8.48	8.48
Import of coal	0.33	0.40	0.45	0.51	0.57
Domestic production (M t lignite)	35.66	38.04	38.16	44.07	43.74

Production from PEU (M t brown coal)	0.48	0.62	0.81	1.34	1.50
ELECTRICAL ENERGY SECTOR (GWh)					
Overall use	30584	32023	33726	35568	37453
Mandatory deliveries	1287	1600	1600	1600	1600
Total needs	31781	33623	35326	37168	39047
Domestic production	30871	33810	34990	39820	39850
Net: import(-)/export(+)	-1000	187	-336	2652	803

* Additional gas consumption for an optional priority-A priority of emergency investments, new energy sources with gas technologies, for a joint production of electrical and heat energy. Source:http://www.eps.rs/Lat/Article.aspx?lista=Sitemap&id=97

Figure 5. Components of the energy policy of the Republic of Serbia.

Source: The Energy Development Strategy of the Republic of Serbia up to 2015.

ENERGY MANAGEMENT – A NECESSITY OF MODERN DAY SERBIA

All the above mentioned clearly points to the fact that energy management and sustainable energy development must be approached systematically and from a scientific standpoint. Thus, there should be a focus on the available unused energy potentials of Serbia, which are the following:

- the remaining lignite reserves in the open pits (for the replacement capacities of 1000-1500 MW),
- around 30% of the hydro potential for high-powered hydropower plants,
- increasing energy efficiency,
- adopting spatial and economic development plans,
- bringing municipality regulations,
- deciding on investments in the municipal infrastructure,
- disposing with certain stimulus mechanisms,
- setting conditions and issuing various licenses for building facilities and
- initiating actions and informing.

The potential for increasing energy efficiency can be seen in the chain of energy transformations: 1. Exploitation of energy resources – mining, 2. Transformation into electrical and/or heat energy (co-generation), 3. Transmitting and distributing electrical and heat energy, 4. Final use (all branches of industry, communal systems, households, residential and public buildings, agriculture and all traffic categories). The estimate is that the greatest increase of electrical energy can be achieved in the following: 1. in industry – a reduction of 0.25 ten/1000$, to around 0.15 ten/1000$, 2. communal activities – introducing co-generation systems, 3. Increasing the of degree of efficacy from 58% to 85% of fuel use, 4. Introducing gas cycles into small heating plants of new 350 – 580 MWe (only in Belgrade), 5. For households and public buildings: – reducing specific heating use from 150-170 kWh/m² year to the European average of 100-120 kWh/m² year.

Reducing the use of electrical energy is especially relevant for households, as the total final energy in Serbia is – 3500 kWh/head, of which some 50% - 1750 kWh/head is used by households. In Belgrade, the average energy use is around 2300 kWh/head, while the European average in households is around 1700 kWh/head (but for a higher standard).

There is a great reserve regarding traffic as it is estimated that in Belgrade in 2005 around 8.7 lit/100km was spent, in comparison with 6.5 lit/100km in 2005 in Europe. In Belgrade, the specific use of final energy in traffic is 0.187 ten/$GDP, or 1.14 ten/vehicle, and in the EU it is around 0.050 ten/$GDP, or 0.8 ten/vehicle.

A municipality system of energy management is an excellent tool for realizing the aforementioned aims of a municipality's energy policy as its concept and program essentially depends on its aims. Figure 6 shows a possible model of energy management.

CONCLUSION

The development of the energy system and rational energy management are of a priority for the development of every country, including Serbia.

The energy policy of Serbia is not and must not be a static document. It must adapt to each and every reaction of a quirky environment. In that aim, the priorities are the following activities:

- creating a government strategy and a policy for increasing energy efficiency;
- innovating a program for realizing the Energy Development Strategy;
- priority choice – separating the national (state) priorities and aims of a particular interest to the industry and individuals;
- bringing measures and strategies for the technological modernization of energy plants;
- introducing compulsory monitoring and measuring of material and energy flows in industry;
- establishing an optimal coordinating of activities of the authorized Ministries in the aim of creating conditions for an optimal development of the energy system of Serbia;
- start applying the adopted laws, by-laws and regulations;
- secure in industry and communal activities a monitoring of material and energy flows as a basis for further activity;
- tightening inspections and control over the work of energy plants;

- introducing the payment of heating energy according to costs;
- founding of qualified and up to date equipped attested laboratories;

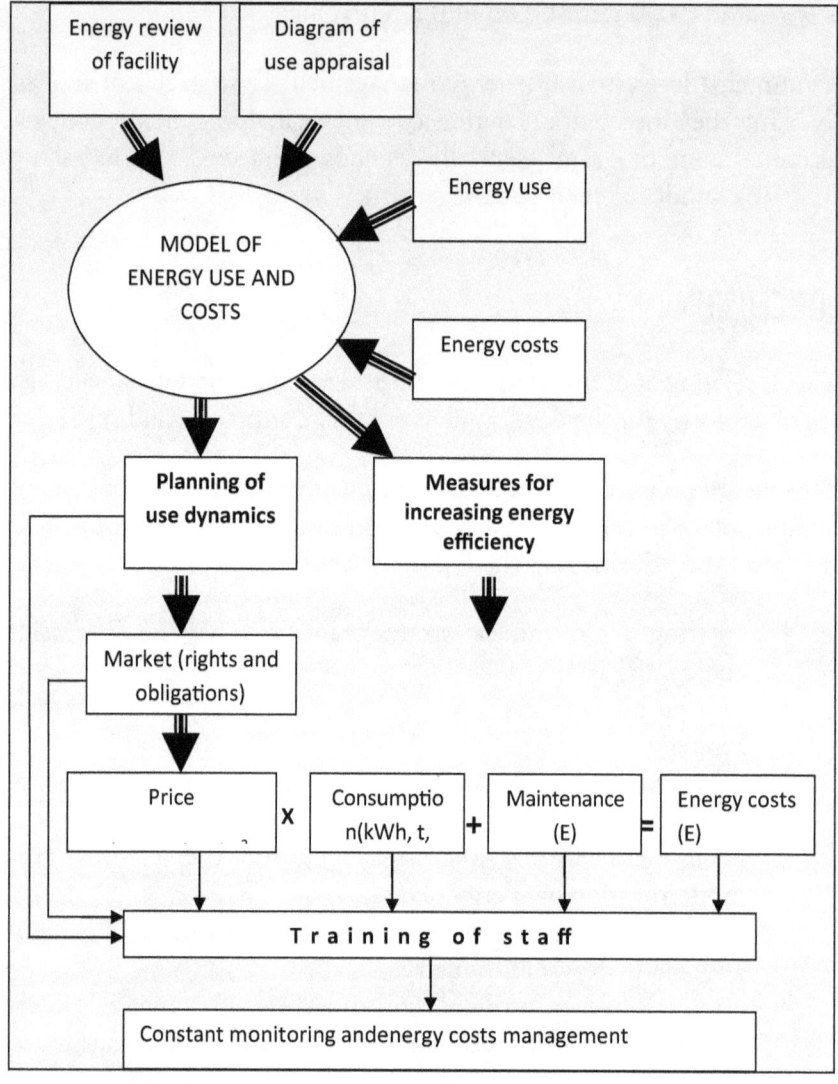

Figure 6. A possible model of energy management.

Source: Djuri i R.M., 2013.

- Creating an optimal economic, legal and financial environment for individuals and companies which carry out activities for increasing energy efficiency;
- Creating an optimal economic, legal and financial environment for individuals and companies who carry out activities for using local fuel, waste fuels, waste heat and RES;
- Larger financing of scientific and research projects in the area of energy efficiency, technological development and use of RES;
- Developing training for energy efficiency on all levels of education as well as in lifelong learning;
- Intensifying the activities on implementing EN 16001 – the system of energy management and ISO 50001, as international systems of managing energy with a proven access for developing a plan for energy management and solving critical aspects of energy efficiency, including the use of energy, measuring, reporting, developing and public supply practice, as well as other variables which can be measured and monitored;
- Strengthening the capacities of the local authorities for planning, preparation, realization and monitoring of projects, as well as capacities for accessing donor funds in the aim of achieving a larger degree of energy efficiency;
- Tools should be prepared and activities carried out for raising the capacities of units of local authorities for applying energy efficiency measurements;
- During the engaging of energy managers, experts who are not employed in local authorities but have the needed knowledge and experience should also be engaged.

REFERENCES

1. Agencija za energetiku Republike Srbije, www.aers.org.rs

2. Brindle B. and Eldridge M., (2007), The Twin Pillars of Sustainable Energy: Synergies between Energy Efficiency and Renewable Energy Technology and Policy, American Council for an Energy Efficient Economy.

3. Djuri i R.M., Škobalj., D., Djuri i M.M.,(2013), Energy as a factor of Serbian Industry, CESNA B, Beograd.

4. Ekonomski položaj industrijskih grana i projekcije rasta 2011-2020 u Republici Srbiji (The economic position of industrial branches and growth projections 2011-2020 in the Republic of Serbia).

5. Markovi D., (2012), Energetski menadžment u opštinama (Energy management in municipalities), Prezentacija iz Procesne i energetske efikasnosti školske 2011/12, Fakultet za menadžment, Beograd.

6. Obnovljivi izvori energije u Srbiji - preporuke, potencijali i kriterijumi (Renewable energy sources in Serbia – recommendations and criteria), Urednica Nataša ereg, Centar za ekologiju i održivi razvoj, Subotica, 2008.

7. Oka S., (2009), Problemi racionalnog koriš enja energije i pove anja energetske efikasnosti u Srbiji (The problems of rational energy use and increase of energy efficiency in Serbia), Okrugli sto: Energetika Srbije – gde smo i kuda idemo? Akademija inženjerskih nauka Srbije, Beograd, 29 oktobar 2009.

8. Postkrizni model ekonomskog rasta i razvoja Srbije 2011-2020 (The post-crisis model of economic growth and development), Ekonomski institut i Ekonomski fakultet, 2010.

9. Program primene Strategije razvoja energije u Srbiji za 2007-2012 (The Program of applying the Energy Development Strategy for 2007-2012), Ministarstvo energetike, sektor o obnovljivim izvorima energije; Beograd, 2007.

10. Prvi akcioni plan za energetsku efikasnost Republike Srbije u periodu od 2010 do 2012 (The First Action Plan for energy efficiency of the Republic of Serbia in the 2010-2012 period), Vlada Republike Srbije.

11. Republi ki zavod za razvoj i Ekonomski institut, 2010 Energetski bilans Republike Srbije za 2012.

12. Savi LJ. (2009), Srpska industrijalizacija za dvadeset prvi vek (Serbian industrialization for the 21st century), Industrija, Beograd.

13. Strategija razvoja energetike Republike Srbije do 2015 godine (The Energy Development Strategy of the Republic of Serbia up to 2015), Vlada Republike Srbije, Beograd, 2007.

14. http://webrzs.stat.gov.rs/WebSite/userFiles/file/Energetika/bilans/Bilans%20elekrticne%20energije,%202010.pdf, 28.09.2012.

15. http://www.efikasnost.com/wp-content/uploads/2011/12/potrosnja-energije.jpg, 28.09.2012.

16. http://www.efikasnost.com/wp-content/uploads/2011/12/potrosnja-energije.jpg, 28.09.2012.

17. http://www.mfa.gov.rs/sr/index.php/spoljna-politika/eu/saradnja-republike-srbije-i-evropske-unije-u-sektorskim-politikama/11378-2013-07-15-09-13-27?lang=lat

18. http://www.eps.rs/Lat/Article.aspx?lista=Sitemap&id=97

19. http://www.eea.europa.eu/publications/european-union-greenhouse-gas-inventory-2011

20. http://www.iea.org/stats/balancetable.asp?COUNTRY_CODE=RS

21. http://www.efikasnost.com/w-content/uploads/2011/12/potrosnja-energije.jpg, 25.09.2012.

ABOUT THE EDITORS

Acad.Mirjana Radovic-Markovic,Ph.D is a full professor of Entrepreneurship .She is a Fellow (Academician) of the Academia Europaea ,London (UK) ,European Academy of of Arts and Science (EASA), World Academy of Art and Science (United States), The Euro Mediterranean Academy of Arts and Sciences ,Athens (Greece),the Royal Society of the Arts in the UK (the RSA) ,London (UK) and Bulgarian Academy of Science and Arts (BASA).She has employed at Faculty of Business economics and Entrepreneurship and Institute of Economic Sciences,Belgrade.Serbia.She has written thirty books and more than hundred peers' journal articles. Professor 's book Women and Entrepreneurship: Female Durability, Persistence and Intuition at Work; Gower Publishing, Ltd., 2013.became best-seller book in 2014. in United States.In line with this, she expects to repeat the success of her previous book with this new one.

Zorana Nikitovic,Ph.D is an assistant professor.She was born in Valjevo,Republic of Serbia. Undergraduate and Master studies she completed at the University of Belgrade, Faculty of Organizational Sciences in Belgrade. Postgraduate studies she completed at Faculty of Tourism and Hospitality in Ohrid, and the PhD thesis she defended at the University of Business Engineering and Management, Faculty of Economy, Banja Luka,Republic of Srpska. The areas of her professional interest are marketing, management and entrepreneurship.

Dragica Jovancevic,Ph.D is an assistant professor.She was born in Cacak,Republic of Serbia. Undergraduate studies she completed at the Faculty of Economics, Belgrade (foreign trade). Postgraduate studies she completed at The University "St. Cyril and Methodius", Bitola,FYR Macedonia and the PhD thesis she defended at the Faculty of Economy, Banja Luka,Republic of Srpska. The areas of her professional interest are finance and marketing.

www.ingramcontent.com/pod-product-compliance
Lightning Source LLC
Chambersburg PA
CBHW020727180526
45163CB00001B/137